Essential Spanish

Edited by
Enrique Montes and Suzanne McQuade

Content in this program has been modified and enhanced from *Starting Out in Spanish*, published in 2008.

Published in the United States by Living Language, an imprint of Random House, Inc.

www.livinglanguage.com

Editor: Suzanne McQuade
Production Editor: Carolyn Roth
Production Manager: Tom Marshall
Interior Design: Sophie Chin
Illustrations: Sophie Chin

First Edition

Library of Congress Cataloging-in-Publication Data

Essential Spanish / edited by Enrique Montes and Suzanne McQuade. -- 1st ed.
    p. cm.
 ISBN 978-0-307-97162-3
1. Spanish language--Textbooks for foreign speakers--English. 2. Spanish language--Grammar. 3. Spanish language--Spoken Spanish. I. Montes, Enrique. II. McQuade, Suzanne.
 PC4129.E5E88 2011
 468.2'421--dc23

                    2011021880

PRINTED IN THE UNITED STATES OF AMERICA

10 9 8 7 6

Acknowledgments

Thanks to the Living Language team: Amanda D'Acierno, Christopher Warnasch, Suzanne McQuade, Laura Riggio, Erin Quirk, Amanda Munoz, Fabrizio LaRocca, Siobhan O'Hare, Sophie Chin, Sue Daulton, Alison Skrabek, Carolyn Roth, Ciara Robinson, and Tom Marshall.

How to Use This Course **6**

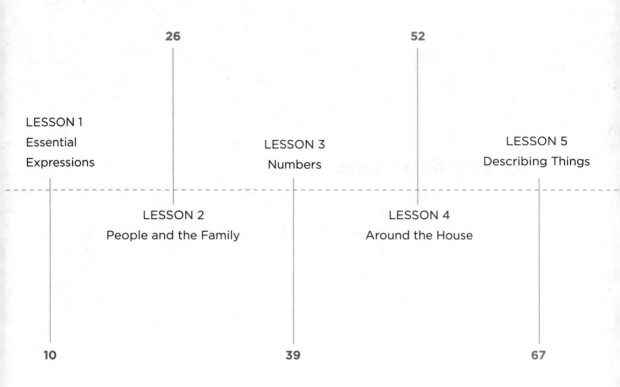
C O U R S E

OUTLINE

How to Use This Course

¡Buenos días!

Welcome to *Living Language Essential Spanish*! Ready to learn how to speak, read, and write Spanish?

Before we begin, let's go over what you'll see in this course. It's very easy to use, but this section will help you get started.

PHONETICS

The first five lessons of this course contain phonetics (in other words, [OH-lah] in addition to **hola**) to help you get started with Spanish pronunciation. However, please keep in mind that phonetics are not exact—they are just a general approximation of sounds—and thus you should rely most on the audio, *not* the phonetics, to further your pronunciation skills.

For a guide to our phonetics system, see the Pronunciation Guide at the end of the course.

LESSONS

There are 10 lessons in this course. Each lesson is divided into three parts and has the following components:

- **Welcome** at the beginning, outlining what you will cover in each of the three parts of the lesson.

PART 1
- **Vocabulary Builder 1** listing the key words and phrases for that lesson.

- **Vocabulary Practice 1** to practice what you learned in Vocabulary Builder 1.

- **Grammar Builder 1** to guide you through the structure of the Spanish language (how to form sentences, questions, and so on).

PART 2
- **Vocabulary Builder 2** listing more key words and phrases.

- **Vocabulary Practice 2** to practice what you learned in Vocabulary Builder 2.

- **Grammar Builder 2** for more information on language structure.

- **Work Out 1** for a comprehensive practice of what you've learned so far.

PART 3
- **Bring It All Together** to put what you've learned in a conversational context through a dialogue, monologue, description, or other similar text.

- **Work Out 2** for another helpful practice exercise.

- **Drive It Home** to ingrain an important point of Spanish structure for the long term.

- **Parting Words** outlining what you learned in the lesson.

TAKE IT FURTHER
- **Take It Further** sections scattered throughout the lesson to provide extra information about the new vocabulary you just saw, expand on some grammar points, or introduce additional words and phrases.

WORD RECALL

Word Recall sections appear in between lessons. They review important vocabulary and grammar from previous lessons, including the one you just finished. These sections will reinforce what you've learned so far in the course and help you retain the information for the long term.

QUIZZES

This course contains two quizzes: **Quiz 1** is halfway through the course (after Lesson 5), and **Quiz 2** appears after the last lesson (Lesson 10). The quizzes are self-graded so it's easy for you to test your progress and see if you should go back and review.

REVIEW DIALOGUES

There are five **Review Dialogues** at the end of the course, after Quiz 2. These everyday dialogues review what you learned in Lessons 1–10, introduce some new vocabulary and structures, and allow you to become more familiar with conversational Spanish. Each dialogue is followed by comprehension questions that serve as the course's final review.

PROGRESS BAR

You will see a **Progress Bar** on almost every page that has course material. It indicates your current position in the course and lets you know how much progress you're making. Each line in the bar represents a lesson, with the final line representing the Review Dialogues.

AUDIO

Look for this symbol ▶ to help guide you through the audio as you're reading the book. It will tell you which track to listen to for each section that has audio. When you see the symbol, select the indicated track and start listening! If you don't see the symbol, then there isn't any audio for that section. You'll also see ⏸, which will tell you where that track ends.

The audio can be used on its own—in other words, without the book—when you're on the go. Whether in your car or at the gym, you can listen to the audio to brush up on your pronunciation, review what you've learned in the book, or even use it as a stand-alone course.

PRONUNCIATION GUIDE, GRAMMAR SUMMARY, GLOSSARY

At the back of this book you will find a **Pronunciation Guide**, **Grammar Summary**, and **Glossary**. The Pronunciation Guide provides information on Spanish pronunciation and the phonetics system used in this course. The Grammar Summary contains a helpful, brief overview of key points in the Spanish grammar system. The Glossary (Spanish-English and English-Spanish) includes all of the essential words from the ten lessons, as well as additional key vocabulary.

FREE ONLINE TOOLS

Go to **www.livinglanguage.com/languagelab** to access your free online tools. The tools are organized around lessons in this course, with audiovisual flash cards, as well as interactive games and quizzes for each lesson. These tools will help you to review and practice the vocabulary and grammar that you've seen in the lessons, as well as provide some extra words and phrases related to the lesson's topic.

Lesson 1: Essential Expressions

Lección uno: Expresiones esenciales

lehk-see-OHN OO-noh:
ehks-preh-see-OH-nehs eh-sehn-see-AH-lehs

¡Bienvenidos! [ibyen-beh-NEE-dohs!] *Welcome!* By the end of this lesson, you'll be able to:

☐ Greet someone and ask how he or she is doing

☐ Address someone formally and informally

☐ Ask someone for his or her name

☐ Make introductions

☐ Use what you've learned when meeting people for the first time

Let's get started with some basic vocabulary. **¿Listos?** [¿LEES-tohs?] *Ready?*

Remember to look for this symbol ⊙ to help guide you through the audio as you're reading the book. It will tell you which track to listen to for each section that has audio. When you see the symbol, select the indicated track and start listening! If you don't see the symbol, then there isn't any audio for that section. You'll also see ⑪, which will tell you where that track ends. However, remember that there will sometimes be additional audio-related instructions, or even different audio-only exercises, that aren't printed in the book. Also keep in mind that the audio can be used on its own when you're on the go!

Vocabulary Builder 1

▶ 1B Vocabulary Builder 1 (CD 1, Track 2)

Hello.	Hola.	OH-lah.*
Good morning.	Buenos días.	BWEH-nohs DEE-ahs.
Good afternoon.	Buenas tardes.	BWEH-nahs TAHR-dehs.
Good evening./Good night.	Buenas noches.	BWEH-nahs NOH-chehs.
How are you? (informal)	¿Cómo estás tú?	¿KOH-moh ehs-TAHS TOO?
How are you? (formal)	¿Cómo está usted?	¿KOH-moh ehs-TAH oos-TEHD?
What's happening?	¿Qué tal?	¿keh TAHL?
I'm fine.	Estoy bien.	ehs-TOY BYEHN.
Thanks.	Gracias.	GRAH-syahs.
You're welcome.	De nada.	deh NAH-dah.
Please.	Por favor.	pohr fah-BOHR.
Good-bye.	Adiós.	ah-DYOHS.
I'll see you later.	Hasta luego.	AHS-tah LWEH-goh.

*You'll see phonetics in the first five lessons of *Essential Spanish* to help you get started. For a guide to the phonetics system used here, see the **Pronunciation Guide** at the end of the course.

Vocabulary Practice 1

Now let's practice what you've learned!

Fill in the right-hand column with the Spanish translations of the English phrases to the left. Always feel free to use a dictionary or the glossary if you need to.

Hello. _Hola_

Good morning. _Buenos Dias._

Good afternoon. _Buenas Tardes_

Good evening./Good night. _Buenas noches_

How are you? (informal) _Como estas tu?_

How are you? (formal) _Como esta usted_

What's happening? _Que tal?_

I'm fine. _estoy bien_

Thanks. _Gracias_

You're welcome. _De nada_

Please. _Por Favor_

Good-bye. _Adios_

I'll see you later. _Hasta luego_

Grammar Builder 1
▶ 1C Grammar Builder 1 (CD 1, Track 3)

Okay, let's stop there. You learned how to greet a person:

in the morning	**Buenos días.**
in the afternoon	**Buenas tardes.**
in the evening	**Buenas noches.**
any time of the day	**Hola.**

You also learned how to say *good-bye*:

Adiós.	**Hasta luego.**

You also learned how to ask how a person is feeling:

¿Qué tal?	**¿Cómo estás tú?**

Another similar expression is ¿Cómo está usted? In Spanish there is a formal and an informal way of referring to the person that you're talking to. Tú [TOO] is used to refer to a person in an informal way. Use tú when talking to your friends, members of your family, or people who are younger than you. Use the more respectful usted [oos-TEHD] when talking to someone who is older or who you don't know very   . well. ¿Cómo estás (tú)? is the question you would ask when speaking to a friend or someone who's younger than you. Use the expression ¿Cómo está (usted)? when talking to an adult or someone you don't know very well. And speaking of people that you don't know very well, let's learn some new courtesy expressions.

To summarize:

INFORMAL	FORMAL
tú (you)	usted (you)
¿Cómo estás (tú)? (How are you?)	¿Cómo está usted? (How are you?)
¿Qué tal?	

Take It Further

In these sections, we'll expand on what you've seen so far.

We might break down some of the new phrases or sentences that you've seen, look more closely at additional words that were introduced, or expand on some of the grammar points. You'll also get a basic introduction to words and constructions that will be covered more in detail later on in Essential Spanish, or even in Levels 2 or 3.

For example, let's break down some of the phrases you saw in Vocabulary Builder 1, starting with ¿Cómo estás (tú)? and ¿Cómo está usted?.

¿Cómo estás (tú)? (How are you?)	¿Cómo está usted? (How are you?)

Cómo is a question word meaning *how* or *what*, **estás** and **está** are forms of the verb **estar** [ehs-TAHR] which means *to be*, and **tú** and **usted** you already know. Individually, these words will turn up again a lot in Spanish, so it is good to start to become familiar with them. For now, though, it's fine to just memorize these phrases as set expressions and worry about how each individual part of the sentence works down the line as you move forward in this course.

Vocabulary Builder 2

▶ 1D Vocabulary Builder 2 (CD 1, Track 4)

What's your name? (informal)	¿Cómo te llamas?	¿KOH-moh teh YAH-mahs?
What's your name? (formal)	¿Cómo se llama usted?	¿KOH-moh seh YAH-mah oos-TEHD?
My name is …	Me llamo …	meh YAH-moh …
It's a pleasure.	Mucho gusto.	MOO-choh GOOS-toh.
Pleased to meet you.	Encantado./Encantada.	ehn-kahn-TAH-doh/dah.
Let me introduce you to …	Te presento a …	teh preh-SEHN-toh ah …
Welcome.	Bienvenido./ Bienvenida.	byehn-beh-NEE-doh/dah.
I'm sorry.	Lo siento.	loh SYEHN-toh.
Excuse me. (informal)	Perdón./Disculpa.	pehr-DOHN./dees-KOOL-pah.
Excuse me. (formal)	Perdón./Disculpe.	pehr-DOHN./dees-KOOL-peh.
Do you speak English? (informal)	¿Hablas inglés?	¿AH-blahs een-GLEHS?

| Do you speak English? (formal) | ¿Habla usted inglés? | ¿AH-blah oos-TEHD een-GLEHS? |
| May I please … ? | ¿Me permite … ? | ¿meh pehr-MEE-teh … ? |

✎ Vocabulary Practice 2

Just like in Vocabulary Practice 1, fill in the column to the right with the correct Spanish translations.

What's your name? (informal) Como te llama

What's your name? (formal) Como se llama usted

My name is … Me llama

It's a pleasure. Mucho gusto

Pleased to meet you. encartada lo

Let me introduce you to … te presento a

Welcome. bievenido la

I'm sorry. Lo siento

Excuse me. (informal) perdon / disculpa

Excuse me. (formal) perdon / disculpe

Do you speak English? (informal) Hablas ingles?

Do you speak English? (formal) Habla usted ingles

May I please … ? Me permite

Grammar Builder 2

▶ 1E Grammar Builder 2 (CD 1, Track 5)

Let's pause. First you learned greetings and different ways to say *good-bye*. Now you've just learned how to introduce yourself and how to introduce others. Notice that two of the questions have two different forms depending on whether you're asking someone formally or informally.

Again, you should use the more formal question **¿Cómo se llama usted?** [¿KOH-moh seh YAH-mah oos-TEHD?] or **¿Habla usted inglés?** [¿AH-blah oos-TEHD een-GLEHS?] when talking to someone who is older or of higher rank (a professor, your boss, or your doctor), or in a more formal environment. Use **¿Cómo te llamas?** [¿KOH-moh teh YAH-mahs?] or **¿Hablas inglés?** [¿AH-blahs een-GLEHS?] when talking to a younger person or at an informal party or gathering. You probably noticed that there are two ways of saying *welcome* in Spanish. Use **bienvenido** [byehn-beh-NEE-doh] when talking to a man and **bienvenida** [byehn-beh-NEE-dah] when talking to a woman.

You probably also noticed two different ways of saying *pleased to meet you*. The masculine form is **encantado** [ehn-kahn-TAH-doh], and the feminine form is **encantada** [ehn-kahn-TAH-dah]. The reason for this is that Spanish adjectives change according to the gender (masculine or feminine) and number (singular or plural) of the noun they modify. We'll talk more about gender in the next lesson.

⏸

To summarize:

FORMAL		
What's your name?	**¿Cómo se llama usted?**	¿KOH-moh seh YAH-mah oos-TEHD?
Do you speak English?	**¿Habla usted inglés?**	¿AH-blah oos-TEHD een-GLEHS?

INFORMAL		
What's your name?	**¿Cómo te llamas?**	¿KOH-moh teh YAH-mahs?
Do you speak English?	**¿Hablas inglés?**	¿AH-blahs een-GLEHS?

And don't forget gender differences:

Welcome. (speaking to a man)	**Bienvenido.**	byehn-beh-NEE-doh.
Welcome. (speaking to a woman)	**Bienvenida.**	byehn-beh-NEE-dah.
It's a pleasure to meet you. (if you are a man)	**Encantado.**	ehn-kahn-TAH-doh.
It's a pleasure to meet you. (if you are a woman)	**Encantada.**	ehn-kahn-TAH-dah.

✎ Work Out 1

Okay, let's put everything you've learned so far together in a short comprehension exercise. Fill in the blank with the appropriate Spanish word. Use the English translations as a guide. Be sure to try to complete the exercise before you listen to the audio; the full Spanish phrases are read on the CD. When you're ready to hear the answers, hit play on the CD. You'll hear the English first, and then the Spanish, and then you should repeat the Spanish for practice.

▶ 1F Work Out 1 (CD 1, Track 6)

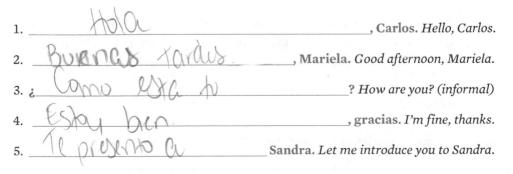

1. _____Hola_____, **Carlos.** *Hello, Carlos.*

2. ___Buenas tardes_____, **Mariela.** *Good afternoon, Mariela.*

3. ¿___Como esta tu_____? *How are you? (informal)*

4. ___Estoy bien_____, **gracias.** *I'm fine, thanks.*

5. ___Te presento a_____ **Sandra.** *Let me introduce you to Sandra.*

6. _Mucho gusto_, Sandra. *It's a pleasure, Sandra.*
7. _Encantada_. *Pleased to meet you.*
8. _Hasta luego_, Carlos. *See you later, Carlos.*
9. _Adiós_, Mariela. *Good-bye, Mariela.*

ANSWER KEY
1. Hola, Carlos. 2. Buenas tardes, Mariela. 3. ¿Cómo estás? 4. Estoy bien, gracias. 5. Te presento a Sandra. 6. Mucho gusto, Sandra. 7. Encantada. 8. Hasta luego, Carlos. 9. Adiós, Mariela.

Take It Further

You may have noticed the unique punctuation in Spanish: every question begins with an upside-down question mark.

¿Qué tal?
¿keh tahl?
What's happening?

This is also the case with exclamation points:

¡Hola!
¡OH-lah!
Hello!

But note that if you add someone's name or another independent clause before the question or exclamation, the upside-down punctuation mark will still appear with the question/statement instead of around the entire phrase:

Perdón, ¿habla inglés?
pehr-DOHN, ¿AH-blah een-GLEHS?
Excuse me, do you speak English? (formal)

Marco, ¿qué tal?

MAHR-koh, ¿keh tahl?

Marco, what's happening?

¿Qué tal, Marco?

¿keh tahl, MAHR-koh?

What's happening, Marco?

Marco, ¡hola!

MAHR-koh, ¡OH-lah!

Marco, hello!

¡Hola, Marco!

¡OH-lah, MAHR-koh!

Hello Marco!

Bring It All Together

▶ 1G Bring It All Together (CD 1, Track 7)

Now let's bring it all together, and add a little bit more vocabulary and structure.

Hello, Felipe!
¡Hola, Felipe!
¡OH-lah feh-LEE-peh!

Welcome to the party, Josefina.
Bienvenida a la fiesta, Josefina.
byehn-beh-NEE-dah ah lah FYEHS-tah, hoh-seh-FEE-nah.

How is everything going?
¿Cómo va todo?
¿KOH-moh bah TOH-doh?

Everything's going well, and you?
Todo va bien, ¿y tú?
¿TOH-doh bah BYEHN, ee TOO?

Everything is okay, thanks.
Más o menos, gracias.
MAHS oh MEH-nohs, grah-syahs.

Let me introduce you to my friend Joaquín.
Te presento a mi amigo Joaquín.
teh preh-SEHN-toh ah mee ah-MEE-goh hwah-KEEN.

Excuse me, what's your name?
Perdón, ¿cómo te llamas?
pehr-DOHN, ¿KOH-moh teh YAH-mahs?

My name's Joaquín.
Me llamo Joaquín.
meh YAH-moh hwah-KEEN.

It's a pleasure.
Es un placer.
ehs oon plah-SEHR.

May I use the phone?
¿Me permites usar el teléfono?
¿meh pehr-MEE-tehs oo-SAHR ehl teh-LEH-foh-noh?

Of course!

¡Claro que sí!

iklah-roh keh SEE!

⏸

Take It Further

▶ 1H Take It Further (CD 1, Track 8)

You probably figured out that the word **todo** [TOH-doh] means *everything* and **todo va bien** [TOH-doh bah BYEHN] means *everything's going well.* The verb *to go* is **ir** [eer] in Spanish. You'll see more about that verb in a later lesson. There are some other new expressions that you may have noticed. You probably noticed **más o menos**, which means *more or less, so-so,* or *just okay.* Another new expression is **es un placer**, meaning *it's a pleasure.* Finally, you may use any Spanish verb, such as **usar** [oo-SAHR] (*to use*) or **ir** (*to go*), after the expression **¿Me permite ... ?** (formal) or **¿Me permites ... ?** (informal) whenever you want to ask for permission to do something. You'll learn more about these and other useful verbs later.

⏸

✎ Work Out 2

▶ 1l Work Out 2 (CD 1, Track 9)

A. Now let's practice some of what you've learned. Translate the following phrases from Spanish to English.

1. Perdón. _____ excuse me _____

2. Me llamo … _____ my name is _____

3. ¿Cómo te llamas? _____ whats your name (?) _____

4. Buenas noches. _____ good night _____

5. Hola. _____ Hello _____

6. Buenas tardes. _____ good afternoon _____

7. ¿Cómo está usted? _____ how are you (F) _____

8. Bienvenido. _____ Welcome _____

B. Now translate the following phrases from English to Spanish.

1. *Good morning.* _____ buenas dias _____

2. *I'm fine.* _____ stoy bien _____

3. *You're welcome.* _____ de nada _____

4. *I'll see you later.* _____ hasta luego _____

5. *It's a pleasure.* _____ es un placer / mucho gusto _____

6. *What's your name? (formal)* _____ como se llama usted _____

7. *I'm sorry.* _____ lo siento _____

⑪

✎ Drive It Home

Ask the person indicated in each line how he or she is doing.

1. *Your elderly neighbor* _Como esta usted_

2. *A stranger on the street* _Como esta usted_

3. *The principal of your school* _Como esta usted_

4. *Your sister* _Como estas tu_

5. *Your best friend* _Como estas tu_

6. *Your husband or wife* _Como estas tu_

Parting Words

¡Felicitaciones! [ifeh-lee-see-tah-see-OH-nehs!] *Congratulations!* You've finished your first lesson: **la primera lección** [lah pree-MEH-rah lehk-SYOHN]. You've just learned the basic vocabulary you need to socialize and get by in Spanish. You should now be able to:

☐ Greet someone and ask how he or she is doing

☐ Address someone formally and informally

☐ Ask someone for his or her name

☐ Make introductions

☐ Use what you've learned when meeting people for the first time

Don't forget to practice and reinforce what you've learned by visiting **www.livinglanguage.com/ languagelab** for flashcards, games, and quizzes for Lesson 1!

Take It Further

▶ 1J Take It Further (CD 1, Track 10)

You may of course want to extend your vocabulary a bit. To say that you're learning Spanish, say **Estoy aprendiendo español** [ehs-TOY ah-prehn-DYEHN-doh ehs-pah-NYOHL]. You may also want to say that at this point you speak only a little (**Hablo un poco de español** [AH-bloh oon POH-koh deh ehs-pah-NYOHL]). When you're learning a new language, you may have to ask the other person to speak more slowly (**Hable más despacio, por favor** [AH-bleh mahs dehs-PAH-syoh, pohr fah-BOHR]). There are times that you'll have to ask someone to repeat something for you (**Repita, por favor** [reh-PEE-tah, pohr fah-BOHR]), and you may even have to ask, *Can you help me?* (**¿Puede ayudarme?** [¿PWEH-deh ay-yoo-DAHR-meh?]).

⏸

A few verbs used in the phrases above that you'll see in later lessons:

estar	to be
hablar	to speak
poder	to be able to
ayudar	to help
repetir	to repeat

Don't worry about why they look different here than they do in the phrases above; you'll learn more about how to conjugate verbs in a later lesson.

Word Recall

Answer the following questions with the correct Spanish word or expression.

1. *You want to greet someone in the afternoon, what do you say?*

   buenas tardes

2. *What is your response if someone says to you Gracias?*

   de nada

3. *You want to introduce someone to a good friend, what do you say?*

   Te presento a

4. *What do you say if you want to welcome someone to your house or party?*

   Bienvienido/a

5. *What would you say if you want to tell someone your name?*

   Me llamo es

6. *What do you say if you want to greet someone late in the evening?*

   Buenas noches

ANSWER KEY
1. **Buenas tardes**; 2. **De nada**; 3. **Te presento a** … ; 4. **Bienvenido/a**; 5. **Me llamo** … ; 6. **Buenas noches**

Lesson 2: People and the Family

Lección dos: La gente y la familia

lehk-SYOHN DOHS: lah HEHN-teh ee lah fah-MEE-lyah

Hola y bienvenidos a la lección dos. [OH-lah ee byehn-beh-NEE-dohs ah lah lehk-SYOHN DOHS] *Hello and welcome to Lesson 2.* By the time you finish this lesson, you should be able to:

☐ Use basic terms for people

☐ Express *there is* and *there are*

☐ Talk about family members

☐ Express *here is ...*

☐ Begin to describe who people are and what they do

First, let's get started with some vocabulary. You'll hear the English first, and then you'll hear the Spanish. Repeat each new word or phrase every time you hear it. **¿Preparados?** [¿preh-pah-RAH-dohs?] *Ready?*

Vocabulary Builder 1

▶ 2B Vocabulary Builder 1 (CD 1, Track 12)

a person	una persona	oo-nah pehr-SOH-nah
a woman	una mujer	oo-nah moo-HEHR
There is … / There are …	Hay …	AY …
There's a woman.	Hay una mujer.	AY oo-nah moo-HEHR.
a man	un hombre	oon OHM-breh
a girl	una muchacha, una chica	oo-nah moo-CHAH-chah, oo-nah CHEE-kah
a boy	un muchacho, un chico	oon moo-CHAH-choh, oon CHEE-koh
a young boy/a child (male)	un niño	oon NEE-nyoh
a young girl/a child (female)	una niña	oo-nah NEE-nyah
There's a man, a woman, and a boy.	Hay un hombre, una mujer y un niño.	AY oon OHM-breh, oo-nah moo-HEHR, ee oon NEE-nyoh.

Ⅱ

✎ Vocabulary Practice 1

Fill in the blanks with the Spanish word to match the English translation. If you need help, just consult the list on the previous page.

a person _una persona_

a woman _una mujer_

There is … / There are … _Hay_

There's a woman. _Hay una mujer_

a man   *un hombre*

a girl   *una muchacha / una chica*

a boy   *un muchacho / un chico*

a young boy/a child (male)   *un niño*

a young girl/a child (female)   *una niña*

There's a man, a woman, and a boy.   *Hay un hombre, un mujer, y un niño*

Grammar Builder 1

▶ 2C Grammar Builder 1 (CD 1, Track 13)

Okay, let's take a break. You learned how to say *a person* (**una persona** [oo-nah pehr-SOH-nah]), *a woman* (**una mujer** [oo-nah moo-HEHR]), *a man* (**un hombre** [oon OHM-breh]), *a girl* (**una muchacha** [oo-nah moo-CHAH-chah] or **una chica** [oo-nah CHEE-kah]), *a boy* (**un muchacho** [oon moo-CHAH-choh] or **un chico** [oon CHEE-koh]), and *a young boy* or *young girl* (**un niño** [oon NEE-nyoh] or **una niña** [oo-nah NEE-nyah]). You probably noticed that the word **hay** [AY] means both *there is* and *there are*. It's spelled **h-a-y**, but the Spanish h is always silent, so whenever you see the letter **h** at the beginning of a word, just pretend it's not there. And did you notice that there are two words for the indefinite article *a* or *an,* **un** [OON] and **una** [OO-nah]? Spanish nouns are all either masculine or feminine. The masculine form of *a* or *an* is **un: un hombre, un muchacho.** The feminine form is **una: una mujer, una chica.**

It's easy to remember the gender of nouns like *man, woman, girl,* or *boy,* but in Spanish, all nouns have gender. This doesn't only apply to people; Spanish nouns from plants to houses to desks all have gender. A rule of thumb is that if the noun ends in **a**, it's probably feminine, and if it ends in **o**, it's probably masculine. But there are exceptions, and not all nouns end in **a** or **o**. It's best to memorize the gender of each new noun you learn. Speaking of new nouns, let's have some more vocabulary.

⏸

Vocabulary Builder 2

▶ 2D Vocabulary Builder 2 (CD 1, Track 14)

It's a family.	Es una familia.	ehs oo-nah fah-MEE-lyah.
Here is …	Aquí está …	ah-KEE ehs-TAH …
Here's the father.	Aquí está el padre.	ah-KEE ehs-TAH ehl PAH-dreh.
Here's the mother.	Aquí está la madre.	ah-KEE ehs-TAH lah MAH-dreh.
Here's the son.	Aquí está el hijo.	ah-KEE ehs-TAH ehl EE-hoh.
Here's the daughter.	Aquí está la hija.	ah-KEE ehs-TAH lah EE-hah.
Here's the brother.	Aquí está el hermano.	ah-KEE ehs-TAH ehl hehr-MAH-noh.
Here's the sister.	Aquí está la hermana.	ah-KEE ehs-TAH lah hehr-MAH-nah.

✎ Vocabulary Practice 2

Just like in Vocabulary Practice 1, fill in the blanks with the Spanish word to match the English translation. If you need help, just consult the list on the previous page.

It's a family. _Es una familia_

Here is … _aquí esta_

Here's the father. _el padre_

Here's the mother. _la madre_

Here's the son. _el hijo_

Here's the daughter. _la hija_

Here's the brother. _el hermano_

Here's the sister. _la hermana_

Grammar Builder 2

▶ 2E Grammar Builder 2 (CD 1, Track 15)

Let's pause there for a moment. First you learned how to say *a* or *an* in Spanish—
un for masculine nouns, and una for feminine nouns. Now you've just learned
how to say *the*, also known as the definite article. Again, gender is important. The
masculine form is **el** [EHL], and the feminine form is **la** [LAH]. So far you've learned
a few feminine nouns: **la familia** [lah fah-MEE-lyah] (*the family*), **la madre** [lah MAH-
dreh] (*the mother*), **la hija** [lah EE-hah] (*the daughter*), **la hermana** [lah ehr-MAH-nah]
(*the sister*), and **la persona** [lah pehr-SOH-nah] (*the person*). And you've learned a
few masculine nouns, too: **el padre** [ehl PAH-dreh] (*the father*), **el hijo** [ehl EE-hoh]
(*the son*), **el chico** [ehl CHEE-koh] (*the boy*), **el hermano** [ehl ehr-MAH-noh] (*the
brother*), **el hombre** [ehl OHM-breh] (*the man*), **el niño** [ehl NEE-nyoh] (*the child*).

⑪

✎ Work Out 1

Okay, let's put everything you've learned so far together in a short comprehension
exercise. Fill in the blank with the appropriate Spanish word. Use the English
translations as a guide. Be sure to try to complete the exercise before you listen
to the audio; the full Spanish phrases are read on the CD. When you're ready to
hear the answers, hit play on the CD. You'll hear the English first, and then the
Spanish, and then you should repeat the Spanish for practice.

▶ 2F Work Out 1 (CD 1, Track 16)

1. **Aquí** _está la familia Martínez_ . *Here is the Martínez family.*

2. **La señora Martínez** _es una mujer_ . *Mrs. Martínez is a woman.*

3. **El señor Martínez** _es un hombre_ . *Mr. Martínez is a man.*

4. **Pedro** _es un niño_ . *Pedro is a boy.*

5. Consuelo _es una niña_ . *Consuelo is a girl.*

6. La señora Martínez _es la madre_ . *Mrs. Martínez is the mother.*

7. El señor Martínez _es el padre_ . *Mr. Martínez is the father.*

8. Consuelo _es la hija_ . *Consuelo is the daughter.*

9. Pedro _es el hijo_ . *Pedro is the son.*

ANSWER KEY

1. Aquí está la familia Martínez. 2. La señora Martínez es una mujer. 3. El señor Martínez es un hombre. 4. Pedro es un niño. 5. Consuelo es una niña. 6. La señora Martínez es la madre. 7. El señor Martínez es el padre. 8. Consuelo es la hija. 9. Pedro es el hijo.

Bring It All Together

2G Bring It All Together (CD 1, Track 17)

Now let's bring it all together and add a little bit more vocabulary and structure.

Hello!
¡Saludos!
isah-LOO-dohs!

My name's Luis.
Me llamo Luis.
meh YAH-moh loo-EES.

I'm from Cancún.
Soy de Cancún.
soy deh kahn-KOON.

I'm Mexican.
Soy mexicano.
soy meh-hee-KAH-noh.

I have a small family.
Tengo una familia pequeña.
TEHN-goh oo-nah fah-MEE-lyah peh-KEH-nyah.

I have a father.
Tengo un padre.
TEHN-goh oon PAH-dreh.

He's a lawyer.
Él es abogado.
ehl ehs ah-boh-GAH-doh.

And I have a mother.
Y tengo una madre.
ee TEHN-goh oo-nah MAH-dreh.

She's a teacher.
Ella es maestra.
EH-yah ehs mah-EHS-trah.

And I have a sister.
Y tengo una hermana.
ee TEHN-goh oo-nah ehr-MAH-nah.

She's a student.
Ella es estudiante.
EH-yah ehs ehs-too-DYAHN-teh.

And I'm also a student.
Y yo también soy estudiante.
ee yoh tahm-BYEHN soy ehs-too-DYAHN-teh.

(II)

Take It Further
▷ 2H Take It Further (CD 1, Track 18)

Okay, you already knew a lot of that vocabulary, but there were a few new words, too, like **saludos** [sah-LOO-dohs], which literally means *greetings*. It's easy to figure out that the word **de** [deh] means *from* and that **mexicano** (m.)/**mexicana** (f.) [meh-hee-KAH-noh/meh-hee-KAH-nah] means *Mexican*. And did you notice that **soy** means *I am*? You also learned **él es** [ehl EHS] (*he is*) and **ella es** [EH-yah EHS] (*she is*). You'll learn more about that useful verb later. And speaking of useful verbs, you also heard Luis say **tengo ...** [TEHN-goh], meaning *I have*, as in **Tengo una familia pequeña** [TEHN-goh oo-nah fah-MEE-lyah peh-KEH-nyah], or *I have a small family*. Finally, you heard Luis say that his father is **un abogado** [oon ah-boh-GAH-doh], or *a lawyer*, his mother is **una maestra** [oo-nah mah-EHS-trah], or *a teacher*, and both he and his sister are *students*, **estudiantes** [ehs-too-dee-AHN-tehs]. We'll come back to all of that later.

(II)

✎ Work Out 2
▷ 2I Work Out 2 (CD 1, Track 19)

A. Now let's practice some of what you've learned. Translate the Spanish words below into English.

1. **una persona** _____ a person _____

2. **un niño** _____ a child/boy _____

3. **la familia** _____ The family _____

4. Hay una mujer. _There is a woman_

5. Mario es un hombre. _Mario is a man_

B. Now translate the following English phrases into Spanish.

1. *a boy* _Un chico / un muchacho_

2. *a woman* _una mujer_

3. *María is the sister.* _María es la hermana_

4. *Here's the son.* _aquí es la hijo_

5. *Josefina is the mother.* _Josefina es la madre_

C. Complete the sentences below using the English cues.

1. Tengo _una familia pequeño_ . *(a small family)*

2. Tengo _una madre_ . *(a mother)*

3. Tengo _un padre_ . *(a father)*

4. Tengo _una hermana_ . *(a sister)*

5. Tengo _un hijo_ . *(a son)*

ANSWER KEY
A. 1. *a person;* 2. *a young boy/a male child;* 3. *the family;* 4. *There's a woman.* 5. *Mario is a man.*
B. 1. **un chico/un muchacho;** 2. **una mujer;** 3. **María es la hermana.** 4. **Aquí está el hijo.** 5. **Josefina es la madre.**
C. 1. **Tengo una familia pequeña.** 2. **Tengo una madre.** 3. **Tengo un padre.** 4. **Tengo una hermana.** 5. **Tengo un hijo.**

✎ Drive It Home

A. Fill in the blanks with the proper definite article, either **el** or **la**, and then read each sentence out loud.

1. José es ___el___ padre de la niña..

2. ___el___ hermano es Carlos.

3. Aquí está ___el___ niño.

4. Marta es ___la___ madre de Roberto.

5. Clara es ___la___ hija del señor y la señora Martínez.

6. Aquí está ___la___ hermana.

B. Fill in the blanks with the indefinite article, either **un** or **una**, and then read each sentence out loud.

1. Hay ___un___ hombre.

2. Tengo ___un___ hijo.

3. Carlos es ___un___ niño.

4. Tengo ___una___ familia pequeña.

5. Margarita es ___una___ niña.

6. La señora Martínez es ___una___ mujer inteligente.

ANSWER KEY
A. 1, 2, 3: el; 4, 5, 6: la; B. 1, 2, 3: un; 4, 5, 6: una

Parting Words

¡Qué bien! [ikeh BYEHN!] *How nice!* You've finished the second lesson. You've learned the basic vocabulary you need to talk about your family. By now you should be able to:

☐ Use basic terms for people

☐ Express *there is* and *there are*

☐ Talk about family members

☐ Express *here is ...*

☐ Begin to describe who people are and what they do

Don't forget to practice and reinforce what you've learned by visiting **www.livinglanguage.com/languagelab** for flashcards, games, and quizzes for Lesson 2!

Take It Further

▶ 2J Take It Further (CD 1, Track 20)

You may, of course, want to extend the discussion a bit and talk about your *uncle* (**tío** [TEE-oh]), your *aunt* (**tía** [TEE-ah]), your *female cousin* (**prima** [PREE-mah]), or your *male cousin* (**primo** [PREE-moh]). And what family reunion would be complete without your *grandmother* (**abuela** [ah-BWEH-lah]) and *grandfather* (**abuelo** [ah-BWEH-loh])? If you're **un abuelo** or **una abuela**, that means you must have *a grandson* (**un nieto** [oon NYEH-toh]) or *a granddaughter* (**una nieta** [oo-nah NYEH-tah]). And if you're **un tío** or **una tía**, you must also have **un sobrino** [oon soh-BREE-noh] (*a nephew*) or **una sobrina** [oo-nah soh-BREE-nah] (*a niece*).

⏸

Word Recall

A. Let's review the family vocabulary from Lesson 2. Fill in the family tree with the correct Spanish word for each member of the family. Make sure you include the appropriate **el** or **la** before each word.

1. *el padre*
(Father)

2. *la modre*
(Mother)

3. *la hermana*
(Sister)

you

4. *el hermano*
(Brother)

B. Fill in the blank with the appropriate Spanish word for the member of the family.

1. La hermana de mi madre es mi ___tia___.

2. El hijo de mi tío es mi ___Primo___.

3. La ___Madre___ de mi padre es mi abuela.

4. Yo soy el nieto de mi ___abuelo___.

Lesson 3: Numbers

Lección tres: Los números
lehk-SYOHN TREHS: lohs NOO-meh-rohs

¡Hola! [¡OH-lah!] In this lesson, we'll deal with numbers. By the time you're finished with this lesson, you should be able to:

☐ Count from one to twenty

☐ Form the plurals of nouns

☐ Use personal pronouns in place of people's names

☐ Conjugate the verb **ser** [sehr] (*to be*)

☐ Express a person's age

☐ Count from twenty to one hundred

Let's get started as we did in the previous lessons, with some vocabulary. **Vamos a comenzar.** [BAH-mohs ah koh-mehn-ZAHR] *Let's begin.*

Vocabulary Builder 1

▶ 3B Vocabulary Builder 1 (CD 1, Track 22)

one, two, three	uno, dos, tres	OO-noh, DOHS, TREHS
four, five, six	cuatro, cinco, seis	KWAH-troh, SEEN-koh, SEH-ees
seven, eight, nine	siete, ocho, nueve	see-EH-teh, OH-choh, NWEH-beh
ten, eleven, twelve	diez, once, doce	dee-EHS, OHN-seh, DOH-seh
twelve cats	doce gatos	DOH-seh GAH-tohs
thirteen dogs	trece perros	TREH-seh PEH-rrohs
fourteen cousins	catorce primos	kah-TOHR-seh PREE-mohs
fifteen men	quince hombres	KEEN-seh OHM-brehs
sixteen women	dieciséis mujeres	dee-eh-see-SEH-ees moo-HEH-rehs
seventeen boys	diecisiete niños	dee-eh-see-see-EH-teh NEE-nyohs
eighteen mothers	dieciocho madres	dee-eh-see-OH-choh MAH-drehs
nineteen families	diecinueve familias	dee-eh-see-NWEH-beh fah-MEE-lyahs
twenty girls	veinte chicas	BAYN-teh CHEE-kahs

⏸

Everyday Life		At Work		Review Dialogues
Around Town	At a Restaurant		Entertainment	

✎ Vocabulary Practice 1

Fill in the blanks with the Spanish word to match the English translation. If you need help, just consult the list on the previous page.

one, two, three   Uno dos Tres

four, five, six   Quatro Cinco seis

seven, eight, nine   Siete Ocho nueve

ten, eleven, twelve   diez once doce

twelve cats   doce gatos

thirteen dogs   Trece perros

fourteen cousins   Catorce Primos

fifteen men   Quince hombres

sixteen women   dieciseis Mujeres

seventeen boys   diecisiete niños

eighteen mothers   dieciocho madres

nineteen families   diecinueve familias

twenty girls   veinte chicas.

Grammar Builder 1

▶ 3C Grammar Builder 1 (CD 1, Track 23)

Okay, let's stop there. So far in this lesson you've learned a lot of **números** [NOO-meh-rohs] (*numbers*). You also noticed some new nouns (**gatos** [GAH-tohs], *cats,* and **perros** [PEH-rrohs], *dogs*) and some other familiar ones: **familias** [fah-MEE-lee-ahs] (*families*), **madres** [MAH-drehs] (*mothers*), **niños** [NEE-nyohs] (*boys*), **mujeres** [moo-

HEH-rehs] (*women*), and hombres [OHM-brehs] (*men*). Notice that these nouns are in the plural form. The plural is fairly easy to form in Spanish. The general rule is that if a noun ends in a vowel, you simply have to add an -s at the end of the word. So the plural of maestra (*female teacher*) is maestras [mah-EHS-trahs], and the plural of padre (*father*) is padres [PAH-drehs]. On the other hand, if the noun ends in a consonant, you have to add -es. So the plural of mujer (*woman*) is mujeres, and the plural of señor [see-NYOHR] (*sir* or *Mr.*) is señores [see-NYOH-rehs].

And speaking of plural nouns, you should also know the plural forms of definite and indefinite articles. The plural forms of *the* are los (masculine) and las (feminine). The plural forms of *a* or *an* are unos (masculine) and unas (feminine), which mean *some*. You'll become more familiar with all this with some practice. But now let's move on.

Vocabulary Builder 2
3D Vocabulary Builder 2 (CD 1, Track 24)

I am	yo soy	yoh SOY
you are (informal)	tú eres	too EH-rehs
you are (formal)	usted es	oos-TEHD EHS
he is	él es	EHL EHS
she is	ella es	EH-yah EHS
we are (masculine/mixed group)	nosotros somos	noh-SOH-trohs SOH-mohs
we are (feminine)	nosotras somos	noh-SOH-trahs SOH-mohs
you (plural) are	ustedes son	oos-TEH-dehs SOHN
they are (masculine/mixed group)	ellos son	EH-yohs SOHN
they are (feminine)	ellas son	EH-yahs SOHN

✎ Vocabulary Practice 2

Just like in Vocabulary Practice 1, fill in the blanks with the Spanish word to match the English translation. If you need help, just consult the list on the previous page.

I am __yo soy__

you are (informal) __Tú eres__

you are (formal) __usted es__

he is __el es__

she is __ella es__

we are (masculine/mixed group) __nosotros somos__

we are (feminine) __nosotras somos__

you (plural) are __ustedes son__

they are (masculine/mixed group) __ellos son__

they are (feminine) __ellas son__

Grammar Builder 2

▶ 3E Grammar Builder 2 (CD 1, Track 25)

You've already learned tú (*you*, informal) and usted (*you*, formal). When talking to more than one person, use ustedes [oos-TEH-dehs]. In Spain, the forms vosotros [boh-SOH-trohs] (masculine) or vosotras [boh-SOH-trahs] (feminine) are also used for the informal plural *you*, but you won't hear them in the rest of the Spanish-speaking world. Now, you also noticed two forms of *we* and *they*—a masculine and a feminine form for each. But you may be wondering, what about mixed groups of men and women? Spanish uses the masculine forms ellos [EH-yohs], vosotros, and nosotros [noh-SOH-trohs] to refer to a mixed-gender group.

⏸

✎ Work Out 1

Okay, let's put everything you've learned so far together in a short comprehension exercise. Fill in the blank with the appropriate Spanish word. Use the English translations as a guide. Be sure to try to complete the exercise before you listen to the audio; the full Spanish phrases are read on the CD. When you're ready to hear the answers, hit play on the CD. You'll hear the English first, and then the Spanish, and then you should repeat the Spanish for practice.

▶ 3F Work Out 1 (CD 1, Track 26)

1. _Yo soy_ Carlos. *I'm Carlos.*

2. Yo tengo _Cinco hermanos_. *I have five brothers and sisters.*

3. Mis _tres hermanos son_ Paco, Ignacio y Juan. *My three brothers are Paco, Ignacio, and Juan.*

4. Mis _dos hermanas son_ Susana y Rosa. *My two sisters are Susana and Rosa.*

5. _Ellas son estudiantes_. *They're students. (feminine)*

6. _Nosotros somos_ una familia grande. *We're a big family.*

7. Nosotros tenemos _dos gatos y dos perros_. *We have two cats and two dogs.*

8. Nosotros también tenemos _once primos_. *We also have eleven cousins.*

ANSWER KEY

1. Yo soy Carlos. 2. Yo tengo cinco hermanos. 3. Mis tres hermanos son Paco, Ignacio y Juan. 4. Mis dos hermanas son Susana y Rosa. 5. Ellas son estudiantes. 6. Nosotros somos una familia grande. 7. Nosotros tenemos dos gatos y dos perros. 8. Nosotros también tenemos once primos.

ⅠⅠ

🔊 Bring It All Together
▶ 3G Bring It All Together (CD 1, Track 27)

Now let's bring it all together and add a little bit more vocabulary and structure.

I'm Julia.
Yo soy Julia.
yoh SOY HOO-lyah.

I'm thirty-nine years old.
Yo tengo treinta y nueve años.
yoh TEHN-goh TRAYN-tah **ee** NWEH-beh AH-nyohs.

I have two sons.
Yo tengo dos hijos.
yoh TEHN-goh DOHS EE-hohs.

Juan is fifteen years old.
Juan tiene quince años.
HWAHN tee-EH-neh KEEN-seh AH-nyohs.

Esteban is twelve years old.
Esteban tiene doce años.
ehs-TEH-bahn tee-EH-neh DOH-seh AH-nyohs.

They're good students.
Ellos son estudiantes buenos.
EH-yohs SOHN ehs-too-dee-AHN-tehs BWEH-nohs.

My father is sixty-two years old.
Mi padre tiene sesenta y dos años.
mee PAH-dreh tee-EH-neh seh-SEHN-tah ee DOHS AH-nyohs.

My mother is fifty-nine years old.
Mi madre tiene cincuenta y nueve años.
mee MAH-dreh tee-EH-neh seen-KWEHN-tah ee NWEH-beh AH-nyohs.

They live in Florida.
Ellos viven en la Florida.
EH-yohs bee-BEHN ehn lah floh-REE-dah.

My cousins are students.
Mis primos son estudiantes.
MEES PREE-mohs sohn ehs-too-dee-AHN-tehs.

And you (plural, formal) are also students.
Y ustedes también son estudiantes.
ee oo-STEH-dehs tahm-BYEHN sohn ehs-too-dee-AHN-tehs.

You and I are students of Spanish.
Tú y yo somos estudiantes de español.
TOO ee YOH SOH-mohs ehs-too-dee-AHN-tehs deh ehs-pah-NYOHL.

⏸

Take It Further

▶ 3H Take It Further (CD 1, Track 28)

You heard Julia say about her parents: **Ellos viven en la Florida,** or *They live in Florida.* The Spanish verb **vivir** [bee-BEER] means *to live.* We'll spend more time on verbs and their different forms later in the course. You also heard a verb that you heard before briefly, the verb **tener** [teh-NEHR], or *to have*. Interestingly, when you give your age in Spanish, you use the verb **tener**, so instead of being twenty years old, in Spanish you *have* those twenty years of experience. And speaking of numbers, you should also be familiar with the numbers **treinta** [TRAYN-tah] (*thirty*), **cuarenta** [kwah-REHN-tah] (*forty*), **cincuenta** [seen-KWEHN-tah] (*fifty*), **sesenta** [seh-SEHN-tah] (*sixty*), **setenta** [seh-TEHN-tah] (*seventy*), **ochenta** [oh-CHEHN-tah] (*eighty*), **noventa** [noh-BEHN-tah] (*ninety*), and **cien** [see-EHN] (*one hundred*). And what about all the numbers in between? Between numbers twenty-one and twenty-nine, use **veinti** [BAYN-tee] followed by the appropriate number to form one word: **veintiuno** [bayn-tee-OO-noh] (21), **veintidós** [bayn-tee-DOHS] (22), **veintitrés** [bayn-tee-TREHS] (23). And what about numbers thirty to one hundred? Simply place the word **y** [EE] (*and*) between the tens and the single digits to form a compound word: **treinta y uno** [TRAYN-tah ee OO-noh] (31), **cuarenta y cinco** [kwah-REHN-tah ee SEEN-koh] (45), **setenta y ocho** [seh-TEHN-tah ee OH-choh] (78), **ochenta y nueve** [oh-CHEHN-tah ee NWEH-beh] (89).

Ⓘ

✎ Work Out 2
▶ 3I Work Out 2 (CD 1, Track 29)

A. You'll see a number in Spanish; give the number that follows.

1. dos _____ 2 _____ Tres _____

2. diez _____ 10 _____ once _____

3. catorce _____ 14 _____ quince _____

4. cuatro _____ 4 _____ cinco _____

5. dieciocho _____ 18 _____ diecinueve _____

B. Now translate the following Spanish phrases into English.

1. **dieciséis mujeres** _A women_

2. **trece hombres** _13 Men_

3. **ocho familias** _8 Families_

4. **tres primos** _3 cousins_

5. **quince hijas** _15 sisters_

C. We'll give you a singular English noun; your job is to write out the plural form in Spanish. For example, if you see _a family_, the answer would be **unas familias**.

1. _a sister_ _unas hijas hermanas_

2. _the man_ _los hombres_

3. _a mother_ _unas madres_

4. _the dog_ _los perros_

5. _a brother_ _los hermanos_

Ⅱ

ANSWER KEY
A. 1. **tres**; 2. **once**; 3. **quince**; 4. **cinco**; 5. **diecinueve**
B. 1. _sixteen women_; 2. _thirteen men_; 3. _eight families_; 4. _three cousins_; 5. _fifteen daughters_
C. 1. **unas hermanas**; 2. **los hombres**; 3. **unas madres**; 4. **los perros**; 5. **unos hermanos**

✎ Drive It Home

Give the correct form of the verb ser (*to be*). Make sure to practice your pronunciation out loud.

1. Yo _____soy_____ americano.

2. Yo _____soy_____ de Nueva York.

3. Yo _____soy_____ el padre de Luis.

4. Yo _____soy_____ de Chicago.

5. Tú _____eres_____ de Nueva York.

6. Él _____es_____ de Nueva York.

7. Nosotros _____somos_____ de Nueva York.

8. Ellos _____son_____ de Nueva York.

ANSWER KEY
1 - 4: soy; 5. eres; 6. es; 7. somos; 8. son

Parting Words

¡Estupendo! [iehs-too-PEHN-doh!] *Great!* You've learned a lot of numbers in this lesson. By now you should be able to:

☐ Count from one to one hundred

☐ Form the plurals of nouns

☐ Use personal pronouns in place of people's names

☐ Conjugate the verb ser [sehr] (*to be*)

☐ Express a person's age

It might be a good idea to practice by counting out loud until you're comfortable with the numbers to one hundred.

Don't forget to practice and reinforce what you've learned by visiting **www.livinglanguage.com/ languagelab** for flashcards, games, and quizzes for Lesson 3!

Take It Further

3J Take It Further (CD 1, Track 30)

There are times when you may have to use higher numbers. *Two hundred* is doscientos [dohs-see-EHN-tohs], and *three hundred* is trescientos [trehs-see-EHN-tohs]. The rest of the numbers counting by hundreds, are cuatrocientos [KWAH-troh-see-EHN-tohs], quinientos [kee-nee-EHN-tohs], seiscientos [SEH-ees-see-EHN-tohs], setecientos [SEH-teh-see-EHN-tohs], ochocientos [OH-choh-see-EHN-tohs], and novecientos [NOH-beh-see-EHN-tohs], and *one thousand* is mil [MEEL]. Okay, that brings us to the end of Lesson 3. If you'd like to go back and review it, just listen to it as many times as you'd like. Or, move on to Lesson 4 if you're ready!

Word Recall

Now that you've learned your numbers, let's practice some basic math. Solve out these problems and say the numbers out loud. When saying the problems, use the following Spanish words: **más** (+, *plus*); **menos** (–, *minus*); **son** (=, *are/equals*)

1. *10 + 40 =* cincuenta
2. *13 – 1 =* doce
3. *79 + 2 =* ochenta y uno
4. *17 – 8 =* nueve
5. *33 + 42 =* setenta y cinco

ANSWER KEY
1. diez más cuarenta son cincuenta; 2. trece menos uno son doce; 3. setenta y nueve más dos son ochenta y uno; 4. diecisiete menos ocho son nueve; 5. treinta y tres más cuarenta y dos son setenta y cinco

Lesson 4: Around the House

Lección cuatro: En la casa

lehk-SYOHN KWAH-troh: ehn lah KAH-sah

¡Hola, amigos! [¡OH-lah, ah-MEE-gohs!] *Hello, friends!* By the time you reach the end of this lesson, you should be able to:

☐ Talk about your house

☐ Conjugate the verb **tener** (*to have*)

☐ Conjugate the verb **estar** (*to be*)

☐ Know the difference between **ser** and **estar** (*to be*)

☐ Use expressions like **me gusta** (*I like*)

☐ Recognize the difference between **esta** and **está**

Aquí vamos ... [ah-KEE BAH-mohs] (*Here we go ...*)

Vocabulary Builder 1

▶ 4B Vocabulary Builder 1 (CD 1, Track 32)

I have a nice house.	**Yo tengo una casa bonita.**	yoh TEHN-goh oo-nah KAH-sah boh-NEE-tah.
You have a large apartment. (informal)	**Tú tienes un apartamento grande.**	too tee-EH-nehs oon ah-pahr-tah-MEHN-toh GRAHN-deh.
You have a kitchen. (formal)	**Usted tiene una cocina.**	oo-STEHD tee-EH-neh oo-nah koh-SEE-nah.
She has two bathrooms.	**Ella tiene dos baños.**	EH-yah tee-EH-neh DOHS BAH-nyohs.
There are mirrors on the walls.	**Hay espejos en las paredes.**	AY ehs-PEH-hohs ehn lahs pah-REH-dehs.
We have a lot of clothes.	**Nosotros tenemos mucha ropa.**	noh-SOH-trohs teh-NEH-mohs MOO-chah ROH-pah.
You (plural) have an old clock.	**Ustedes tienen un reloj antiguo.**	oo-STEH-dehs tee-EHN-ehn oon reh-LOH ahn-TEE-gwoh.
They have three bathrooms.	**Ellos tienen tres baños.**	EH-yohs tee-EHN-ehn TREHS BAH-nyohs.
The boy has a bed.	**El niño tiene una cama.**	ehl NEE-nyoh tee-EH-neh oo-nah KAH-mah.
The woman has a dining room.	**La mujer tiene un comedor.**	lah moo-HEHR tee-EH-neh oon koh-meh-DOHR.
The room has no windows.	**La habitación no tiene ventanas.**	lah hah-bee-tah-SYOHN noh tee-EH-neh behn-TAH-nahs.
The living room has stairs.	**La sala tiene escaleras.**	lah SAH-lah tee-EH-neh ehs-kah-LEH-rahs.

⏸

✎ Vocabulary Practice 1

Fill in the blanks with the Spanish word missing in each sentence to match the English translation. If you need help, just consult the list on the previous page.

1. Yo tengo _____. *I have a nice house.*

2. Tú tienes _____. *You have a large apartment. (informal)*

3. Usted tiene _____. *You have a kitchen. (formal)*

4. Ella tiene _____. *She has two bathrooms.*

5. Hay espejos en _____. *There are mirrors on the walls.*

6. Nosotros tenemos _____. *We have a lot of clothes.*

7. El niño tiene _____. *The boy has a bed.*

8. La mujer tiene _____. *The woman has a dining room.*

9. La habitación no tiene _____. *The room has no windows.*

10. _____ tiene escaleras. *The living room has stairs.*

ANSWER KEY

1. una casa bonita; 2. un apartamento grande; 3. una cocina; 4. dos baños; 5. las paredes; 6. mucha ropa; 7. una cama; 8. un comedor; 9. ventanas; 10. La sala

Grammar Builder 1

▶ 4C Grammar Builder 1 (CD 1, Track 33)

You've just learned names for different parts of a house. **La cocina** [lah koh-SEE-nah], **el baño** [ehl BAH-nyoh], **la sala** [lah SAH-lah], and **el comedor** [ehl koh-meh-DOHR] are all rooms in **una casa** [oo-nah KAH-sah] or **un apartamento** [oon ah-par-tah-MEHN-toh]. You also learned the names of other objects that you would find in a house: **la pared** [lah pah-REHD] (*the wall*), **la ventana** [lah behn-TAH-nah] (*the window*), **las escaleras** [lahs ehs-kah-LEH-rahs] (*the stairs*), **la cama** [lah KAH-mah] (*the bed*), **el reloj** [ehl reh-LOH] (*the clock*), and **el espejo** [ehl ehs-PEH-hoh] (*the mirror*). You also heard different forms of the verb **tener** [teh-NEHR], or *to have*.

As we saw with the verb **ser** [sehr], each subject has a different form of the verb **tener**. These different forms are called a conjugation. The conjugation of the verb **tener** is:

yo tengo	**nosotros tenemos**
[YOH TEHN-goh]	[noh-SOH-trohs teh-NEH-mohs]
tú tienes	**vosotros tenéis**
[TOO tee-EH-nehs]	[boh-SOH-trohs teh-neh-EES]
él/ella/usted tiene	**ellos/ellas/ustedes tienen**
[EHL/EH-yah/oos-TEHD tee-EH-neh]	[EH-yohs/EH-yahs/oos-TEH-dehs tee-EHN-ehn]

Since there's a different form of the verb for each pronoun, you can drop the pronoun in Spanish. So, saying **Tengo una casa bonita** [TEHN-goh oo-nah KAH-sah boh-NEE-tah] is like saying **Yo tengo una casa bonita** [YOH TEHN-goh oo-nah KAH-sah boh-NEE-tah] because **tengo** is always used to refer to **yo**. Now let's move on to more vocabulary and phrases.

Ⓘ

Vocabulary Builder 2

▶ 4D Vocabulary Builder 2 (CD 1, Track 34)

I'm in the house.	**Yo estoy en la casa.**	YOH ehs-TOY ehn lah KAH-sah.
You're in New York. (informal, singular)	**Tú estás en Nueva York.**	TOO ehs-TAHS ehn NWEH-bah YORK.
And you're in Spain. (formal, singular)	**Y usted está en España.**	ee oos-TEHD ehs-TAH ehn ehs-PAH-nyah.
He's sick.	**Él está enfermo.**	ehl ehs-TAH ehn-FEHR-moh.

She's not in the room.	**Ella no está en la habitación.**	EH-yah noh ehs-TAH ehn lah hah-bee-tah-SYOHN.
We're happy.	**Nosotros estamos contentos.**	noh-SOH-trohs ehs-TAH-mohs kohn-TEHN-tohs.
They're tired. (masculine)	**Ellos están cansados.**	EH-yohs ehs-TAHN kahn-SAH-dohs.
They're not sad. (feminine)	**Ellas no están tristes.**	EH-yahs noh ehs-TAHN TREES-tehs.
You're in the kitchen. (plural, formal)	**Ustedes están en la cocina.**	oos-TEH-dehs ehs-TAHN ehn lah koh-SEE-nah.
Carolina and Tomás are in the garage.	**Carolina y Tomás están en el garaje.**	kah-roh-LEE-nah ee toh-MAHS ehs-TAHN ehn ehl gah-RAH-heh.
The children are in the backyard.	**Los niños están en el patio.**	lohs NEE-nyohs ehs-TAHN ehn ehl PAH-tee-oh.
Now they're quiet.	**Ahora están tranquilos.**	ah-OH-rah ehs-TAHN trahn-KEE-lohs.

⑪

✎ Vocabulary Practice 2

Just like in Vocabulary Practice 1, fill in the blanks with the Spanish word to match the English translation. If you need help, just consult the list on the previous page.

1. **Yo** _____ **en la casa.** *I'm in the house.*

2. **Tú** _____ **en Nueva York.** *You're in New York. (informal, singular)*

3. **Y usted** _____ **en España.** *And you're in Spain. (formal, singular)*

4. **Él** _____ **enfermo.** *He's sick.*

5. Ella _____ en la habitación. *She's not in the room.*

6. Nosotros _____ contentos. *We're happy.*

7. Ellos _____ cansados. *They're tired. (masculine)*

8. Ellas _____ tristes. *They're not sad. (feminine)*

9. Ustedes _____ en la cocina. *You're in the kitchen. (plural, formal)*

ANSWER KEY

1. estoy; 2. estás; 3. está; 4. está; 5. no está; 6. estamos; 7. están; 8. no están; 9. están

Grammar Builder 2

▶ 4E Grammar Builder 2 (CD 1, Track 35)

Let's take a closer look at what you've just learned. You probably noticed different variations of the verb estar [ehs-TAHR]. The different forms of the verb estar are:

yo estoy	nosotros estamos
[YOH ehs-TOY]	[noh-SOH-trohs ehs-TAH-mohs]
tú estás	vosotros estáis
[TOO ehs-TAHS]	[voh-SOH-trohs ehs-TAH-ees]
él/ella/usted está	ellos/ellas/ustedes están
[EHL/EH-yah/oos-TEHD ehs-TAH]	[EH-yohs/EH-yahs/oos-TEH-dehs ehs-TAHN]

The verb estar means *to be* in Spanish. But as you recall from Lesson 3, the verb ser also means *to be*. The verb ser is used to express a description, a nationality, or an occupation—something that's permanent or lasts for a while. The verb estar is used to express location and feelings, which tend to change more quickly. That's why the sentences from this lesson use estar—the phrases en la casa [ehn lah KAH-sah] (*in the house*), en Nueva York [ehn NWEH-bah YORK] (*in New York*), en España [ehn ehs-PAH-nyah] (*in Spain*), en la habitación [ehn lah hah-bee-tah-SYOHN] (*in the room*), enfermo [ehn-FEHR-moh] (*sick*), contento [kohn-TEHN-toh] (*happy*), and triste [TREES-teh] (*sad*) express either a person's location or how a person feels, two of the uses of the verb estar. In this lesson you also learned how to make negative sentences. To make a sentence negative, simply put the word no [NOH] in front of the verb: **Yo no estoy en México** [YOH noh ehs-TOY ehn MEH-hee-koh] (*I'm not in Mexico*); **Tú no estás cansada** [TOO noh ehs-TAHS kahn-SAH-dah] (*You're not tired* [f.]); **Ellos no están enfermos** [EH-yohs noh ehs-TAHN ehn-FEHR-mohs] (*They're not sick*).

Ⓘ

Take It Further

Let's take another look at one of the sentences above:

Tú no estás cansada.
TOO noh ehs-TAHS kahn-SAH-dah.
You're not tired.

The word for *tired*, **cansada**, ends in an **a** instead of an **o**. This is because it is a woman being described. Remember **encantado/encantada** and **bienvenido/bienvenida** in Lesson 1? Adjectives in Spanish change gender depending on what is being described.

Mi padre está enfermo.
mee PAH-dreh ehs-TAH ehn-FEHR-moh.
My father is sick.

Mi madre está enferma.
mee MAH-dreh ehs-TAH ehn-FEHR-mah.
My mother is sick.

You'll see more examples of these gender distinctions in later lessons on adjectives, but it's good to keep them in mind.

✎ Work Out 1

Okay, let's put everything you've learned so far together in a short comprehension exercise. Fill in the blank with the appropriate Spanish word. Use the English translations as a guide. Be sure to try to complete the exercise before you listen to the audio; the full Spanish phrases are read on the CD. When you're ready to hear the answers, hit play on the CD. You'll hear the English first, and then the Spanish, and then you should repeat the Spanish for practice.

▶ 4F Work Out 1 (CD 1, Track 36)

1. **Yolanda** _____. *Yolanda has a nice house.*

2. _____ **San Juan, Puerto Rico.** *The house is in San Juan, Puerto Rico.*

3. **Ella tiene muchas** _____. *She has many rooms.*

4. **También tiene** _____. *She also has a large family.*

5. **La hija** _____. *The daughter is sick.*

6. _____. *She's in bed.*

7. _____. *They're tired. (feminine)*

8. **El hijo y el padre** _____. *The son and the father are not sick.*

9. _____. *They're in the living room. (masculine)*

10. _____. *They're happy. (masculine)*

⏸

ANSWER KEY

1. Yolanda tiene una casa bonita. 2. La casa está en San Juan, Puerto Rico. 3. Ella tiene muchas habitaciones. 4. También tiene una familia grande. 5. La hija está enferma. 6. Ella está en la cama. 7. Ellas están cansadas. 8. El hijo y el padre no están enfermos. 9. Ellos están en la sala. 10. Ellos están contentos.

ᴄᴄ Bring It All Together

▶ 4G Bring It All Together (CD 1, Track 37)

Now let's bring it all together and add a little bit more vocabulary and structure.

I'm interested in this house.
Tengo interés en esta casa.
TEHN-goh een-teh-REHS ehn EHS-tah KAH-sah.

The house is in a nice neighborhood.
La casa está en un barrio bonito.
lah KAH-sah ehs-TAH ehn oon BAH-ree-oh boh-NEE-toh.

And it's near the city.
Y está cerca de la ciudad.
ee ehs-TAH SEHR-kah deh lah syoo-DAHD.

It's not far from the stores.
No está lejos de las tiendas.
NOH ehs-TAH LEH-hohs deh lahs tee-EHN-dahs.

It has three bedrooms.
Tiene tres habitaciones.
tee-EH-neh TREHS ah-bee-tah-SYOH-nehs.

It has an ideal size for our family.
Tiene un tamaño ideal para nuestra familia.
tee-EH-neh oon tah-MAH-nyoh ee-deh-AHL pah-rah nwehs-trah fah-MEE-lyah.

There's also a pool.
También hay una piscina.
tahm-BYEHN AY oo-nah pee-SEE-nah.

I like the color of the walls.
Me gusta el color de las paredes.
meh GOOS-tah ehl koh-LOHR deh lahs pah-REH-dehs.

I like the price very much.
Me gusta mucho el precio.
meh GOOS-tah MOO-choh ehl PREH-syoh.

It has a reasonable price.
Tiene un precio económico.
tee-EH-neh oon PREH-syoh eh-koh-NOH-mee-koh.

We're very happy.
Estamos muy contentos.
ehs-TAH-mohs MWEE kohn-TEHN-tohs.

Me too. I want this house!
Yo también. ¡Quiero esta casa!
YOH tahm-BYEHN. ikee-EH-roh ehs-tah KAH-sah!

⏸

Take It Further

▶ 4H Take It Further (CD 1, Track 38)

You were probably able to recognize words such as **interés** [een-teh-REHS] (*interest*), **ideal** [ee-deh-AHL] (*ideal*), **color** [koh-LOHR] (*color*), and **precio** [PREH-see-oh] (*price*) because they are cognates—words that sound close to or exactly like their English counterparts. You also learned that **lejos** means *far* and **cerca** means *near*. You also learned the words **piscina** (*pool*), **ciudad** (*city*), and **tienda** (*store*). You also heard that the house they would like to buy is located in **un barrio bonito**, *a nice* (or *pretty*) *neighborhood*. Finally, you were introduced to the expression **me gusta**, which means *I like* (singular). We'll learn these and other similar expressions later in the course.

⃞

One more thing: did you notice the difference in the dialogue above between the word **esta** and **está**?

Tengo interés en esta casa.
I'm interested in this house.

La casa está en un barrio bonito.
The house is in a nice neighborhood.

The first word, **esta**, means *this*, while the second word, **está**, is the third person singular of the verb **estar**. You'll learn more about demonstratives—words meaning *this, that, these, those*—such as **esta** later, but until you get the hang of the context, it's good to note the difference the accent makes in determining vocabulary differences so you don't get confused!

✎ Work Out 2

▶ 4I Work Out 2 (CD 1, Track 39)

A. Let's put everything together now and practice what you've learned. Form a sentence in Spanish using **tener** (*to have*) and the words given in English. For example, if you see *I/an apartment*, you'd answer **Yo tengo un apartamento.**

1. *She/a house* _____

2. *You (singular, formal)/a son* _____

3. *You (plural, formal)/three bedrooms* _____

4. *They (feminine)/a kitchen* _____

5. *You (singular, formal)/five windows* _____

B. Now create a sentence using the verb **estar** and the English cues. For example, if you see *she/sad,* you'd answer **Ella está triste.**

1. *They (masculine)/in Mexico* _____

2. *I/happy* _____

3. *He/tired* _____

4. *We (mixed group)/in the house* _____

5. *You (singular, informal)/sick* _____

C. Next, translate the following sentences from English to Spanish, then create the negative form of each sentence by using **no** in front of the verb. For example, if you see *I have an apartment*, you'd answer **Yo tengo un apartamento.**, followed by **Yo no tengo un apartamento.**

1. *She is sick.* _____

2. *I have a house.* _____

3. *He's happy.* _____

4. *They (mixed group) have a pool.* _____

5. *We are in the living room.* _____

(II)

ANSWER KEY
A. 1. **Ella tiene una casa.** 2. **Usted tiene un hijo.** 3. **Ustedes tienen tres habitaciones.** 4. **Ellas tienen una cocina.** 5. **Tú tienes cinco ventanas.**
B. 1. **Ellos están en México.** 2. **Yo estoy contenta.** or **Yo estoy contento.** 3. **Él está cansado.**
4. **Nosotros estamos en la casa.** 5. **Usted está enfermo.** or **Usted está enferma.**
C. 1. **Ella está enferma. Ella no está enferma.** 2. **Yo tengo una casa. Yo no tengo una casa.** 3. **Él está contento. Él no está contento.** 4. **Ellos tienen una piscina. Ellos no tienen una piscina.** 5. **Nosotros estamos en la sala. Nosotros no estamos en la sala.**

✎ Drive It Home

Write the correct form of the verb given in parentheses in the blanks provided. Make sure to practice the pronunciation out loud.

1. Mariana _____ un apartamento grande. (tener)

2. Tú y yo _____ un apartamento grande. (tener)

3. Usted _____ un apartamento grande. (tener)

4. Yo _____ enfermo/a. (estar)

5. Tú _____ enfermo/a. (estar)

6. Ellas _____ enfermas. (estar)

ANSWER KEY
1. tiene; 2. tenemos; 3. tiene; 4. estoy; 5. estás; 6. están

Parting Words

¡Buen trabajo! [¡BWEHN trah-BAH-hoh!] *Good job!* You've finished the lesson. By now you should be able to:

- ☐ Talk about your house
- ☐ Conjugate the verb **tener** (*to have*)
- ☐ Conjugate the verb **estar** (*to be*)
- ☐ Know the difference between **ser** and **estar** (*to be*)
- ☐ Use expressions like **me gusta** (*I like*)
- ☐ Recognize the difference between **esta** and **está**

Don't forget to practice and reinforce what you've learned by visiting **www.livinglanguage.com/ languagelab** for flashcards, games, and quizzes for Lesson 4!

Take It Further

⏵ 4J Take It Further (CD 1, Track 40)

In Spanish you use the verb **tener** to say that you're hungry, hot, cold, or sleepy. Instead of being hungry, in Spanish you say *I have hunger:* **tengo hambre** [tehn-goh AHM-breh]. Similar expressions are: **tengo calor** [tehn-goh kah-LOHR] (*I am hot*), **tengo frío** [tehn-goh FREE-oh] (*I am cold*), **tengo sueño** [tehn-goh SWEH-nyoh] (*I am sleepy*), **tengo sed** [tehn-goh SEHD] (*I am thirsty*), and **tengo interés en ...** [tehn-goh een-teh-REHS ehn ...] (*I'm interested in ...*).

⏸

Word Recall

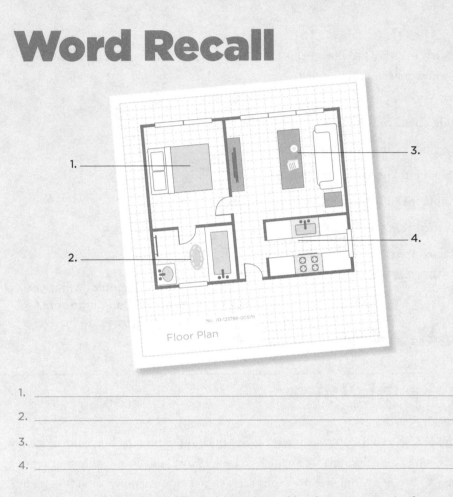

Floor Plan

1. _____
2. _____
3. _____
4. _____

Say the name of the room of the house indicated by the arrow. Begin the sentence by saying **La casa tiene ...** followed by the room of the house. Make sure that you use **un** or **una** before the room of the house.

ANSWER KEY

1. La casa tiene una habitación/un cuarto. 2. La casa tiene un baño. 3. La casa tiene una sala.
4. La casa tiene una cocina.

Lesson 5: Describing Things

Lección cinco: Las descripciones

lehk-SYOHN SEEN-koh: lahs dehs-kreep-see-OH-nehs

¡Y ahora llegamos a la lección cinco! [iee ah-OH-rah yeh-GAH-mohs ah lah lehk-SYOHN SEEN-koh!] *And here we are at Lesson 5!* By the time you're through with this lesson, the halfway point of *Essential Spanish*, you should be able to:

☐ Say the colors of specific items

☐ Talk about colors in singular and plural

☐ Describe size

☐ Use possessive adjectives such as *my* and *your*

☐ Say *I want, I need, it costs*

☐ Use other terms for clothing

Aquí vamos ... [ah-KEE BAH-mohs ...] *Here we go ...*

Vocabulary Builder 1

▶ 5B Vocabulary Builder 1 (CD 2, Track 2)

blue	azul	ah-ZOOL
red	rojo	ROH-hoh
green	verde	BEHR-deh
black	negro	NEH-groh
yellow	amarillo	ah-mah-REE-yoh
orange	anaranjado	ah-nah-rahn-HAH-doh
white	blanco	BLAHN-koh
gray	gris	GREES
brown	marrón	mah-RROHN
What color is … ?	¿De qué color es … ?	¿deh keh koh-LOHR ehs … ?
The apple is red.	La manzana es roja.	lah mahn-ZAH-nah ehs ROH-hah.
The elephants are gray.	Los elefantes son grises.	lohs eh-leh-FAHN-tehs sohn GREES-ehs.
The flowers are yellow.	Las flores son amarillas.	lahs FLOH-rehs sohn ah-mah-REE-yahs.

⏸

✎ Vocabulary Practice 1

Match each color below to its appropriate Spanish translation. If you need help, just consult the list on the previous page.

1. *black*   a. **gris**

2. *blue*   b. **marrón**

3. *brown*   c. **verde**

4. *gray*   d. **azul**

5. *green*

6. *orange*

7. *red*

8. *white*

9. *yellow*

e. anaranjado

f. amarillo

g. negro

h. blanco

i. rojo

ANSWER KEY
1. g; 2. d; 3. b; 4. a; 5. c; 6. e; 7. i; 8. h; 9; f

Grammar Builder 1

⏵ 5C Grammar Builder 1 (CD 2, Track 3)

As you learned earlier, all Spanish nouns are either masculine or feminine. Spanish adjectives agree in gender and number with the noun that they modify. For example, a feminine plural noun must be modified by a feminine plural adjective. As a general rule, if a masculine adjective ends in the letter -o, the feminine form changes from the letter -o to the letter -a. If the masculine form ends in any other letter, the feminine form is likely to be the same.

Let's take a look at some examples. The feminine forms of rojo, blanco, and negro are roja [ROH-hah], blanca [BLAHN-kah], and negra [NEH-grah] because these adjectives end in -o. On the other hand, the feminine forms of verde, gris, and azul stay the same.

Forming the plural is also very simple. If the adjective ends in a vowel, add -s. If it ends in a consonant, add -es. That's why the plurals of amarillo and anaranjado are amarillos [ah-mah-REE-yohs] and anaranjados [ah-nah-rahn-HAH-dohs], while the plurals of gris and azul are grises [GREES-ehs] and azules [ah-ZOO-lehs].

Now let's move on to some other descriptive adjectives.

⏸

Vocabulary Builder 2

▶ 5D Vocabulary Builder 2 (CD 2, Track 4)

big/my big house	grande/mi casa grande	GRAHN-deh/mee KAH-sah GRAHN-deh
small/your small apartment	pequeño/tu apartamento pequeño	peh-KEH-nyoh/too ah-pahr-tah-MEHN-toh peh-KEH-nyoh
long/her long skirt	largo/su falda larga	LAHR-goh/soo FAHL-dah LAHR-gah
short/my short pants	corto/mis pantalones cortos	KOHR-toh/mees pahn-tah-LOH-nehs KOHR-tohs
cheap/their cheap oven	barato/su horno barato	bah-RAH-toh/soo OHR-noh bah-RAH-toh
expensive/our expensive refrigerator	caro/nuestra nevera cara	KAH-roh/nwehs-trah neh-BEH-rah KAH-rah
wide/his wide shoes	ancho/sus zapatos anchos	AHN-choh/soos sah-PAH-tohs AHN-chohs
narrow/your narrow shirt	estrecho/tu camisa estrecha	ehs-TREH-choh/too kah-MEE-sah ehs-TREH-chah
new/our new car	nuevo/nuestro carro nuevo	NWEH-boh/nwehs-troh KAH-rroh NWEH-boh
old/your old TV	viejo/tu televisor viejo	bee-EH-hoh/too teh-leh-bee-SOHR bee-EH-hoh
pretty/my pretty tie	bonito/mi corbata bonita	boh-NEE-toh/mee kohr-BAH-tah boh-NEE-tah
ugly/her ugly dress	feo/su vestido feo	FEH-oh/soo behs-TEE-doh FEH-oh

�II

✎ Vocabulary Practice 2

We'll give you the adjective; you fill in the blank with its opposite. If you need help, just consult the list on the previous page.

1. grande _____

2. largo _____

3. feo _____

4. estrecho _____

5. caro _____

6. viejo _____

ANSWER KEY
1. pequeño; 2. corto; 3. bonito; 4. ancho; 5. barato; 6. nuevo

Grammar Builder 2

▶ 5E Grammar Builder 2 (CD 2, Track 5)

Okay, let's pause and talk about adjectives again. In this lesson you've learned common adjectives, such as **bonito** [boh-NEE-toh], **feo** [FEH-oh], **nuevo** [NWEH-boh], **viejo** [bee-EH-hoh], **caro** [KAH-roh], and **barato** [bah-RAH-toh]. You probably noticed that these words come after the noun they describe, so in Spanish, instead of saying *her nice car*, you would literally say *her car nice*.

By the way, don't confuse the noun **carro** [KAHR-rroh] (*car*) with the adjective **caro** [KAH-roh] (*expensive*). Can you hear the difference in pronunciation? **Carro**, **caro** [KAH-rroh, KAH-roh]. Speaking of **carros** [KAH-rrohs], in some Spanish-speaking countries, a car can also be **un coche** [oon KOH-cheh].

In this lesson you also heard several possessive adjectives. Possessive adjectives show who's in possession of something. *My* is **mi** [MEE], or **mis** [MEES] in the plural. *Your* (singular informal) is **tu** [TOO] or **tus** [TOOS]. **Su** [SOO] and **sus** [SOOS] can mean *his, her, its, their,* or *your* (plural or singular formal). **Nuestro** [NWEHS-troh] is *our*, and it changes like a regular adjective: **nuestro, nuestra, nuestros, nuestras** [NWEHS-troh, NWEHS-trah, NWEHS-trohs, NWEHS-trahs]. So *our shirts* is **nuestras camisas** [NWEHS-trahs kah-MEE-sahs] because the word **camisas** [kah-MEE-sahs] is feminine and plural.

Another way of expressing possession in Spanish is by simply using the word **de** [DEH] (*of*). So if you want to say *John's pants are blue,* you would say **Los pantalones de Juan son azules** [lohs pahn-tah-LOH-nehs deh HWAHN sohn ah-SOO-lehs].

To summarize the possessive pronouns:

	SINGULAR	PLURAL
my	mi	mis
your (sg. infml.)	tu	tus
his/her/its/their/your (pl./sg. fml.)	su	sus
our	nuestro/nuestra	nuestros/nuestras

✎ Work Out 1

Okay, let's put everything you've learned so far together in a short comprehension exercise. Fill in the blank with the appropriate Spanish word. Use the English translations as a guide. Be sure to try to complete the exercise before you listen to the audio; the full Spanish phrases are read on the CD. When you're ready to hear the answers, hit play on the CD. You'll hear the English first, and then the Spanish, and then you should repeat the Spanish for practice.

▶ 5F Work Out 1 (CD 2, Track 6)

1. **Los pantalones son** _____. *The pants are very cheap.*

2. **Las paredes de** _____ **son** _____. *The walls of my house are white.*

3. _____ **son** _____.
   My shirts are brown and gray.

4. _____ **son** _____ __. *Their cats are big and old.*

5. ____ _____ **es colombiana.** *Our friend is Colombian.*

6. _____ **es bonito.** *Your new dress is nice/pretty.*

7. _____ _____ ____ **son** _____ _____ _____. *Blue and yellow are my favorite colors.*

8. _____ **es muy** _____. *His tie is very wide.*

9. _____ _____ _____. *Our car is red, nice/pretty, and expensive.*

(II)

ANSWER KEY
1. Los pantalones son muy baratos. 2. Las paredes de mi casa son blancas. 3. Mis camisas son marrones y grises. 4. Sus gatos son grandes y viejos. 5. Nuestra amiga es colombiana. 6. Tu vestido nuevo es bonito. 7. El azul y el amarillo son mis colores favoritos. 8. Su corbata es muy ancha. 9. Nuestro carro/coche es rojo, bonito y caro.

◖ Bring It All Together

▷ 5G Bring It All Together (CD 2, Track 7)

Now let's do it one more time. Let's use what we've learned and add some more vocabulary and structure.

Good afternoon, sir.
Buenas tardes, señor.
BWEH-nahs TAHR-dehs, seh-NYOHR.

I need a new jacket.
Necesito una chaqueta nueva.
neh-seh-SEE-toh oo-nah chah-KEH-tah NWEH-bah.

There are a lot of clothes in various colors and styles.
Hay mucha ropa en varios colores y estilos.
AY MOO-chah ROH-pah ehn BAH-ree-ohs koh-LOH-rehs ee ehs-TEE-lohs.

I want a modern jacket.
Quiero una chaqueta moderna.
kee-EH-roh oo-nah chah-KEH-tah moh-DEHR-nah.

What size do you take?
¿Qué talla usa?
¿KEH TAH-yah OO-sah?

I take size medium.
Uso la talla mediana.
OO-soh lah TAH-yah meh-dee-AH-nah.

What color do you want?
¿Qué color desea?
¿KEH koh-LOHR deh-seh-AH?

My favorite color is gray.
Mi color favorito es el gris.
mee koh-LOHR fah-boh-REE-toh ehs ehl GREES.

There's a very nice jacket that's in style now.
Hay una chaqueta muy bonita y de moda.
AY oo-nah chah-KEH-tah MWEE boh-NEE-tah ee deh MOH-dah.

How much does it cost?
¿Cuánto cuesta?
¿KWAHN-toh KWEHS-tah?

It's very cheap—eighty-five dollars.
Es muy barata: ochenta y cinco dólares.
ehs MWEE bah-RAH-tah—oh-CHEHN-tah ee SEEN-koh DOH-lah-rehs.

I want it. Thanks a lot.
Yo la quiero. Muchas gracias.
yoh lah kee-EH-roh. MOO-chahs GRAH-syahs.

Ⓘ

Take It Further
▶ 5H Take It Further (CD 2, Track 8)

You probably figured out that **necesito** [neh-seh-SEE-toh] means *I need*, because it sounds like *necessity*. But that's not the only new verb that you saw. You heard the verb **quiero** [kee-EH-roh] (*I want* or *I love*), **uso** [OO-soh] (*I use,* or *I take* or *wear* when referring to sizes), and **cuesta** [KWEHS-tah] (*it costs*). We'll spend more time on verbs in a later lesson, but for now, you should remember that Spanish verbs change depending on the subject of the sentence, just like **ser**, **estar**, and **tener**. There were also a few other words that were easy to figure out: **mediana** [meh-dee-AH-nah] (*medium*), **estilo** [ehs-TEE-loh] (*style*), **moderno** [moh-DEHR-noh] (*modern*), and **chaqueta** [chah-KEH-tah] (*jacket*). Study these other nouns that are probably more difficult to remember: **ropa** [ROH-pah] (*clothes*), **talla** [TAH-yah] (*size*), and **moda** [MOH-dah] (*fashion*).

⏸

🖊 Work Out 2
▶ 5I Work Out 2 (CD 2, Track 9)

A. Translate the following words into Spanish and then create sentences beginning with **quiero**, *I want*. For example, if you see *a red jacket*, you would answer **Quiero una chaqueta roja.**

1. *a new car* _____

2. *a blue tie* _____

3. *a modern TV* _____

4. *a red flower* _____

5. *an expensive dress* _____

B. Let's practice possessive adjectives. You'll see an object in Spanish followed by its possessor. Repeat the object with the appropriate possessive adjective. For example, if you see object: **flores**, possessor: **ella**, you would answer **sus flores**.

1. *object:* **el carro,** *possessor:* (**él**) _____

2. *object:* la casa, *possessor:* (nosotros) _____

3. *object:* las manzanas, *possessor:* (yo) _____

4. *object:* los pantalones, *possessor:* (tú) _____

5. *object:* los zapatos, *possessor:* (nosotros) _____

C. Now translate the following phrases into Spanish.

1. *I need a large size.* _____

2. *I want a new style.* _____

3. *I take a large jacket.* _____

4. *I need a small car.* _____

5. *I want a new house.* _____

Ⅱ

ANSWER KEY
A. 1. **Quiero un carro nuevo.** 2. **Quiero una corbata azul.** 3. **Quiero un televisor moderno.** 4. **Quiero una flor roja.** 5. **Quiero un vestido caro.**
B. 1. **su carro**; 2. **nuestra casa**; 3. **mis manzanas**; 4. **tus pantalones**; 5. **nuestros zapatos**
C. 1. **Necesito una talla grande.** 2. **Quiero un estilo nuevo.** 3. **Uso una chaqueta grande.** 4. **Necesito un carro pequeño.** or **Necesito un coche pequeño.** 5. **Quiero una casa nueva.**

✎ Drive It Home

A. Let's practice Spanish adjectives. As you know, when using adjectives in Spanish you have to take into account the gender and number. Write down the correct form of the underlined adjective. As always, practice the pronunciation out loud.

1. **mis zapatos** _____ *my wide shoes*

2. **mis zapatos** _____ *my gray shoes*

3. **mis zapatos** _____ *my yellow shoes*

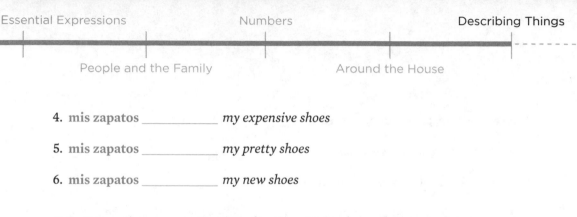

4. mis zapatos _____ *my expensive shoes*

5. mis zapatos _____ *my pretty shoes*

6. mis zapatos _____ *my new shoes*

B. Let's practice some possessive adjectives. Write down the appropriate possessive adjective in the space provided.

1. _____ apartamento bonito *(my)*

2. _____ apartamento bonito *(her)*

3. _____ apartamento bonito *(your, informal)*

4. _____ apartamento bonito *(our)*

5. _____ apartamento bonito *(your, formal)*

ANSWER KEY
A. 1. anchos; 2. grises; 3. amarillos; 4. caros; 5. bonitos; 6. nuevos
B. 1. mi; 2. su; 3. tu; 4. nuestro; 5. su

Parting Words

¡Qué bien! [¡KEH BYEHN!] This concludes our fifth lesson. By now, you should be able to:

☐ Say the colors of specific items

☐ Talk about colors in singular and plural

☐ Describe size

☐ Use possessive adjectives such as *my* and *your*

☐ Say *I want, I need, it costs*

Don't forget to practice and reinforce what you've learned by visiting **www.livinglanguage.com/ languagelab** for flashcards, games, and quizzes for Lesson 5!

Take It Further

▶ 5J Take It Further (CD 2, Track 10)

You've learned a lot of adjectives in this lesson, including descriptive words and colors. And speaking of colors, to express shades of the same color, use the words claro [KLAH-roh] (*light*) or oscuro [ohs-KOO-roh] (*dark*), as in azul claro [ah-SOOL KLAH-roh] (*light blue*) or verde oscuro [BEHR-deh ohs-KOO-roh] (*dark green*). And you're probably curious about some other colors too! Well, similar-sounding púrpura [poor-POO-rah] is *purple,* and violeta [bee-oh-LEH-tah] is *violet.* And speaking of similar colors, you might hear different variations on marrón [mahr-ROHN] (*brown*) in Spanish. The terms café [kah-FEH] and pardo [PAHR-doh] are other common ways of referring to this color. And what about metallic colors? *Gold* is dorado [doh-RAH-doh], while *silver* is plateado [plah-teh-AH-doh]. And finally, *pink* is rosado [roh-SAH-doh], as in Me gusta la pantera rosada [meh GOOS-tah lah pahn-TEH-rah roh-SAH-dah], or *I like the Pink Panther*. Yes, we say rosada [roh-SAH-dah] instead of rosado because notice that pantera [pahn-TEH-rah] is a feminine word!

⦾

Note: We hope that by now you have a good grasp of Spanish pronunciation from listening to the audio in conjunction with reading this book. From now on, there will be no phonetics included next to Spanish words. Refer to the section on pronunciation on page 166 if you get stuck over a certain word, and be sure to listen to the recordings to help you get it right!

Word Recall

Write out the item of clothing that you need based on the clues provided. Make sure that you use the appropriate indefinite article. Start each phrase with *Necesito …*

1. *short pants* _____

2. *black skirt* _____

3. *expensive tie* _____

4. *new shoes* _____

5. *blue jacket* _____

ANSWER KEY
1. Necesito unos pantalones cortos. 2. Necesito una falda negra. 3. Necesito una corbata cara.
4. Necesito unos zapatos nuevos. 5. Necesito una chaqueta azul.

Quiz 1

Prueba corta 1

Now let's see how you've done so far. In this section you'll find a short quiz testing what you learned in Lessons 1–5. After you've answered all of the questions, score your quiz and see how you did! If you find that you need to go back and review, please do so before continuing on to Lesson 6.

You'll get a second quiz after Lesson 10, followed by a final review with five dialogues and comprehension questions.

Let's get started!

A. Match the following English words to the correct Spanish translations:

1. el patio   a. *the kitchen*

2. la habitación   b. *the house/home*

3. la cocina   c. *the room*

4. la piscina   d. *the backyard*

5. la casa   e. *the pool*

B. Translate the following English expressions into Spanish.

1. *What is your name? (formal)* _____

2. *May I please …?* _____

3. *My name is …* _____

4. *Let me introduce you to …* _____

5. *Do you speak English? (formal)* _____

C. Form the plural of each of the phrases below:

1. tu habitación bonita _____

2. mi pared blanca _____

3. nuestro carro grande _____

4. su televisor viejo _____

5. nuestra prima contenta _____

D. Fill in the table with the correct forms of **tener** (*to have*):

I have	*1.*
you have (informal)	*2.*
she has	*3.*
you have (formal)	*4.*
they have (masculine)	*5.*

How Did You Do?

Give yourself a point for every correct answer, then use the following key to determine whether or not you're ready to move on:

0–7 points: It's probably best to go back and study the lessons again to make sure you understood everything completely. Take your time; it's not a race! Make sure you spend time reviewing the vocabulary and reading through each Grammar Builder section carefully.

8–16 points: If the questions you missed were in sections A or B, you may want to review the vocabulary from previous lessons again; if you missed answers mostly in sections C or D, check the Grammar Builder sections to make sure you have your grammar basics down.

17–20 points: Feel free to move on to Lesson 6! You're doing a great job.

 **points**

Lesson 6: Around Town

Lección seis: Por la ciudad

Welcome to Lesson 6. In this lesson, you'll learn to ask questions and get directions. You'll also get the basic vocabulary that you'll need to get around town. By the time you're through with this lesson, you should be able to:

☐ Ask for directions to the post office or bakery

☐ Understand when someone tells you to *turn right* or *go straight ahead*

☐ Ask questions such as *where?*, *how?*, *why?*, and *when?* and give answers

Let's start by taking a look at some key sentences.

Vocabulary Builder 1

▶ 6B Vocabulary Builder 1 (CD 2, Track 12)

Where is the post office?	**¿Dónde está el correo?**
It's two blocks from here.	**Está a dos cuadras de aquí.**
Continue straight.	**Continúa recto.**
Turn left.	**Gira a la izquierda.**
Turn right.	**Gira a la derecha.**
Stop at the traffic light.	**Para en el semáforo.**
What street are you looking for?	**¿Qué calle buscas?**
In what supermarket do you shop?	**¿En qué supermercado compras?**
Which is the main avenue?	**¿Cuál es la avenida principal?**

⏸

✎ Vocabulary Practice 1

Fill in the blanks with the Spanish word to match the English translation. If you need help, just consult the list on the previous page.

1. *Where is the post office?* _____

2. *It's two blocks from here.* _____

3. *Continue straight.* _____

4. *Turn left.* _____

5. *Turn right.* _____

6. *Stop at the traffic light.* _____

ANSWER KEY
1. ¿Dónde está el correo? 2. Está a dos cuadras de aquí. 3. Continúa recto. 4. Gira a la izquierda.
5. Gira a la derecha. 6. Para en el semáforo.

Grammar Builder 1

▶ 6C Grammar Builder 1 (CD 2, Track 13)

Let's focus now on question words. Now you know how to ask *where* (*¿dónde?*), *what* (*¿qué?*), and *which* (*¿cuál?*). Note that *¿cuál?* is singular, and there's a plural form, *¿cuáles?*

You've also seen some important nouns, such as **correo** (*post office*), **supermercado** (*supermarket*), **cuadra** (*block*), **calle** (*street*), **avenida** (*avenue*), and **semáforo** (*traffic light*).

You also learned how to tell someone to *continue straight* (**continúa recto**), to *turn left* (**gira a la izquierda**), or to *turn right* (**gira a la derecha**). And last but not least, in this lesson you've seen a good number of verbs.

In addition to **continuar** (*to continue*) and **girar** (*to turn*), you also learned **comprar** (*to buy*), **buscar** (*to look for*), and **parar** (*to stop*). We'll get back to verbs later.

⑪

Vocabulary Builder 2

▶ 6D Vocabulary Builder 2 (CD 2, Track 14)

How do you get to the bakery?	¿Cómo llegas a la panadería?
I arrive by bus.	Yo llego en autobús.
When do you work in the store?	¿Cuándo trabajas en la tienda?
Who do you watch TV with?	¿Con quién miras la televisión?
Why do you listen to the radio?	¿Por qué escuchas la radio?
How many languages do you speak at work?	¿Cuántos idiomas hablas en el trabajo?

⑪

✎ Vocabulary Practice 2

Just like in Vocabulary Practice 1, fill in the blank with the Spanish word to match the English translation. If you need help, just consult the list on the previous page.

1. *How do you get to the bakery?*

   _____

2. *I arrive by bus.*

   _____

3. *When do you work in the store?*

   _____

4. *Who do you watch TV with?*

   _____

5. *Why do you listen to the radio?*

   _____

6. *How many languages do you speak at work?*

   _____

ANSWER KEY

1. ¿Cómo llegas a la panadería? 2. Yo llego en autobús. 3. ¿Cuándo trabajas en la tienda? 4. ¿Con quién miras la televisión? 5. ¿Por qué escuchas la radio? 6. ¿Cuántos idiomas hablas en el trabajo?

Grammar Builder 2

▶ 6E Grammar Builder 2 (CD 2, Track 15)

Now you know how to ask *how* (¿cómo?), *when* (¿cuándo?), *why* (¿por qué?), *who* (¿quién?), and *how many* (¿cuántos?, or ¿cuántas? in the feminine).

Notice that **¿quiénes?** is the plural version of **¿quién?** Use the plural form when asking a question that refers to more than one person, such as:

¿Quiénes son tus amigos?
Who are your friends?

Also notice that **¿cuántas?** is the feminine version of **¿cuántos?** Use **¿cuántas?** when referring to feminine objects, as in:

¿Cuántas casas hay en la calle?
How many houses are on the street?

We also went over some new nouns. You heard **panadería** (*bakery*), **televisión** (*television*), **radio** (*radio*), **autobús** (*bus*), **trabajo** (*work*), and **idioma** (*language*).

You also learned some very important verbs: **llegar** (*to arrive*), **trabajar** (*to work*), **mirar** (*to watch*), **escuchar** (*to listen*), and **hablar** (*to speak*).

⏸

✎ Work Out 1

Okay, let's put everything you've learned so far together in a short comprehension exercise. Fill in the blank with the appropriate Spanish word. Use the English translations as a guide. Be sure to try to complete the exercise before you listen to the audio; the full Spanish phrases are read on the CD. When you're ready to hear the answers, hit play on the CD. You'll hear the English first, and then the Spanish, and then you should repeat the Spanish for practice.

▶ 6F Work Out 1 (CD 2, Track 16)

1. _____, por favor, ¿_____

_____? *Excuse me (informal) please, where's the pharmacy?*

2. ¿Qué farmacia _____? *What pharmacy do you need?*

3. _____ la Farmacia Figueroa. *I'm looking for Figueroa Pharmacy.*

4. _____. *Continue straight.*

5. ¿_____? *How many blocks?*

6. Cinco cuadras, _____. *Five blocks, more or less.*

7. ¿_____? *Which street is it on?*

8. La Farmacia Figueroa _____ _____.

Figueroa Pharmacy is on Figueroa Street.

9. ¡_____! ¡Es muy fácil! _____. *Of course! That's easy! Thanks.*

ANSWER KEY
1. Disculpa, por favor, ¿dónde está la farmacia? 2. ¿Qué farmacia necesitas? 3. Yo busco la Farmacia Figueroa. 4. Continúa recto. 5.¿Cuántas cuadras? 6. Cinco cuadras, más o menos. 7.¿En qué calle está? 8. La Farmacia Figueroa está en la calle Figueroa. 9. ¡Claro! ¡Es muy fácil! Gracias.

Bring It All Together

6G Bring It All Together (CD 2, Track 17)

Now let's try a similar conversation between a tourist and the concierge of a hotel.

I need to go to the airport today.
Necesito ir al aeropuerto hoy.

How would you like to go?
¿Cómo quiere ir?

You can go by subway, taxi, or bus.
Puede ir en metro, en taxi o en autobús.

Where's the subway station?
¿Dónde está la estación de metro?

Do I need a taxi to get there?
¿Necesito un taxi para llegar?

It's not far. It's near here.
No está lejos. Está cerca de aquí.

How much does the ticket cost?
¿Cuánto cuesta el billete?

The subway ticket costs three pesos.
El billete en metro cuesta tres pesos.

Ⓘ

✎ Work Out 2
▶ 6H Work Out 2 (CD 2, Track 18)

A. Now let's practice. First, translate the following phrases from Spanish to English.

1. **una panadería** _____

2. **cerca** _____

3. **un idioma** _____

4. **una maleta** _____

5. lejos _____

B. Now let's translate some question words from English to Spanish.

1. *How?* _____

2. *When?* _____

3. *What?* _____

4. *Why?* _____

5. *Who?* _____

C. Good job. Now translate the following questions from English into Spanish.

1. *Which is the subway station?*

_____

2. *Where is the subway station?*

_____

3. *What subway station are you looking for?*

_____

4. *How many subway stations are there?*

_____

Ⅱ

ANSWER KEY
A. 1. *a bakery*; 2. *near*; 3. *a language*; 4. *a suitcase*; 5. *far*
B. 1. ¿Cómo? 2. ¿Cuándo? 3. ¿Qué? 4. ¿Por qué? 5. ¿Quién? or ¿Quiénes?
C. 1. ¿Cuál es la estación de metro? 2. ¿Dónde está la estación de metro? 3. ¿Qué estación de metro buscas? 4. ¿Cuántas estaciones de metro hay?

✎ Drive It Home

Choose the correct Spanish question word out of the two choices in parentheses. Pay close attention to the underlined words since they provide a very good hint. As always, make sure that you practice the pronunciation out loud.

1. ¿_____ es la muchacha? La muchacha es _Sarita_. **(Quién/Por qué)**

2. ¿_____ es la muchacha? La muchacha es _rubia_. **(Cómo/Por qué)**

3. ¿_____ es la muchacha? La muchacha es _de Nueva York_.

   (De dónde/Cómo)

4. ¿_____ está tu casa? Mi casa está _cerca de aquí_. **(Cuándo/Dónde)**

5. ¿_____ es tu casa? Mi casa es _bonita_. **(Cómo/Quién)**

6. ¿_____ casas tienes? Yo tengo _dos casas_. **(Dónde/Cuántas)**

ANSWER KEY
1. Quién; 2. Cómo; 3. De dónde; 4. Dónde; 5. Cómo; 6. Cuántas

Parting Words

¡Enhorabuena! _Congratulations!_ You've finished **la lección seis**. In this lesson you've learned how to ask questions, **las preguntas**. In addition to **las preguntas**, you also learned useful vocabulary associated with errands and going around town. By now, you should be able to:

☐ Ask for directions to the post office or bakery

☐ Understand when someone tells you to _turn right_ or _go straight ahead_

☐ Ask questions such as _where?_, _how?_, _why?_, and _when?_ and give answers

Don't forget to practice and reinforce what you've learned by visiting **www.livinglanguage.com/ languagelab** for flashcards, games, and quizzes for Lesson 6!

Take It Further

▶ 6I Take It Further (CD 2, Track 19)

And speaking of places around town, you may want to expand your vocabulary and talk about **el centro comercial** (*the shopping mall*) or **la estación de tren** (*the train station*). You may be interested in knowing that **la peluquería** is *the hair salon* and **la barbería** is *the barbershop*. If you're feeling hungry, you may want to stop by **la heladería** (*the ice cream parlor*), **el restaurante** (*the restaurant*), or **la cafetería** (*the diner/cafeteria*). And no town would be complete without **una gasolinera** (*a gas station*), **una iglesia** (*a church*), or **un templo** (*a temple*).

⏸

Word Recall

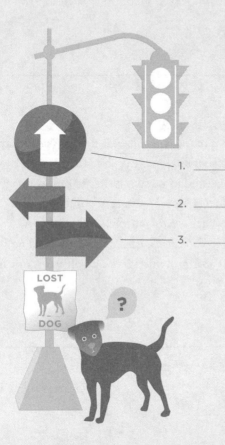

1. _____

2. _____

3. _____

Look at the arrows above. What are they indicating? Give the Spanish expression that you would use to tell someone to continue straight ahead, turn left or right.

ANSWER KEY
1. **Continúa recto.** 2. **Gira a la izquierda.** 3. **Gira a la derecha.**

Lesson 7: Everyday Life

Lección siete: La vida diaria

¡Hola! In this lesson, you'll learn about la vida diaria, *everyday life*. By the end of the lesson, you'll be able to:

☐ Say *I speak* and *I listen*

☐ Talk about traveling and walking in the present tense

☐ Say *I read* and *I understand*

☐ Conjugate verbs such as to eat, to learn, and to write

☐ Use verbs to talk about your everyday life

Let's get started!

Vocabulary Builder 1

▶ 7B Vocabulary Builder 1 (CD 2, Track 21)

I listen to the radio.	**Yo escucho la radio.**
You travel a lot. (singular informal)	**Tú viajas mucho.**
You speak Spanish. (singular formal)	**Usted habla español.**
He walks far.	**Él camina lejos.**
She buys a lot of gifts.	**Ella compra muchos regalos.**
We pay with a credit card.	**Nosotros pagamos con tarjeta de crédito.**
They use cash.	**Ellos usan efectivo.**
They arrive at work early.	**Ellos llegan al trabajo temprano.**
You dance well. (plural formal)	**Ustedes bailan bien.**
You help in church. (singular informal)	**Tú ayudas en la iglesia.**
Pablo and Marta study Spanish.	**Pablo y Marta estudian español.**

⏸

✎ Vocabulary Practice 1

Fill in the blank with the Spanish word to match the English translation. If you need help, just consult the list on the previous page.

1. Yo _____ la radio. *I listen to the radio.*

2. Tú _____ mucho. *You travel a lot. (singular informal)*

3. Usted _____ español. *You speak Spanish. (singular formal)*

4. Ella _____ muchos regalos. *She buys a lot of gifts.*

5. Nosotros _____ con tarjeta de crédito. *We pay with a credit card.*

6. **Ellos** _____ **al trabajo temprano.** *They arrive at work early.*

7. **Ustedes** _____ **bien.** *You dance well. (plural formal)*

ANSWER KEY
1. escucho; 2. viajas; 3. habla; 4. compra; 5. pagamos; 6. llegan; 7. bailan

Grammar Builder 1

▶ 7C Grammar Builder 1 (CD 2, Track 22)

Let's focus on the new verbs that you just heard. You learned the verbs escuchar (*to listen*), viajar (*to travel*), hablar (*to speak*), caminar (*to walk*), comprar (*to buy*), pagar (*to pay*), usar (*to use*), llegar (*to arrive*), bailar (*to dance*), and estudiar (*to study*). You've probably noticed that all these verbs end in -ar.

There are three main categories of regular verbs in Spanish: verbs that end in -ar, verbs that end in -er, and verbs that end in -ir. Spanish verbs are conjugated, meaning that they change form according to their subject.

Let's focus on the conjugation of -ar verbs. Just drop the -ar and add -o when the subject is yo. Add -as when the subject is tú, -a when it's él, ella, or usted, -amos when it's nosotros or nosotras, -áis when it's vosotros or vosotras, and -an when it's ellos, ellas, or ustedes.

Let's hear how this works with hablar (*to speak*):

HABLAR *(TO SPEAK)*			
yo	hablo	nosotros/nosotras	hablamos
tú	hablas	vosotros/vosotras*	habláis
él/ella/Ud.	habla	ellos/ellas/Uds.	hablan

*Remember that vosotros is the plural form of *you* that is only used in Spain. In the rest of the Spanish-speaking world, ustedes is preferred.

Now let's turn our attention to some other important Spanish verbs.

To summarize:

-AR VERB ENDINGS			
yo	-o	nosotros/nosotras	-amos
tú	-as	vosotros/vosotras	-áis
él/ella/Ud.*	-a	ellos/ellas/Uds.	-an

*You will often see usted and ustedes abbreviated as Ud. and Uds. Note that these words are only capitalized when they appear in their abbreviated form.

Some common regular -ar verbs: hablar (*to speak*), escuchar (*to listen*), viajar (*to travel*), caminar (*to walk*), comprar (*to buy*), pagar (*to pay*), usar (*to use*), llegar (*to arrive*), bailar (*to dance*), and estudiar (*to study*).

Vocabulary Builder 2

▶ 7D Vocabulary Builder 2 (CD 2, Track 23)

I read the newspaper.	Yo leo el periódico.
You eat very little. (singular informal)	Tú comes muy poco.
You live in the United States. (singular formal)	Usted vive en los Estados Unidos.
He opens the door.	Él abre la puerta.
She understands the question.	Ella comprende la pregunta.
We learn Spanish at home.	Nosotros aprendemos español en casa.
They write on the computer.	Ellos escriben en la computadora.
They sell their products online.	Ellos venden sus productos por Internet.
Do you answer in Spanish? (singular informal)	¿Tú respondes en español?

⏸

✎ Vocabulary Practice 2

Just like in Vocabulary Practice 1, fill in the blank with the Spanish word to match the English translation. If you need help, just consult the list on the previous page.

1. Yo _____ el periódico. *I read the newspaper.*

2. Tú _____ muy poco. *You eat very little. (singular informal)*

3. Usted _____ en los Estados Unidos. *You live in the United States.*

   (singular formal)

4. Ella _____ la pregunta. *She understands the question.*

5. Nosotros _____ español en casa. *We learn Spanish at home.*

6. Ellos _____ en la computadora. *They write on the computer.*

7. ¿Tú _____ en español? *Do you answer in Spanish?*

   (singular informal)

ANSWER KEY
1. leo; 2. comes; 3. vive; 4. comprende; 5. aprendemos; 6. escriben; 7. respondes

Grammar Builder 2

▶ 7E Grammar Builder 2 (CD 2, Track 24)

Let's take a look at another set of verbs. In this section you heard the verbs **leer** (*to read*), **comer** (*to eat*), **vivir** (*to live*), **abrir** (*to open*), **comprender** (*to understand*), **aprender** (*to learn*), **escribir** (*to write*), **vender** (*to sell*), and **responder** (*to answer*).

The verbs that you heard in this section are from the other two main categories: **-er** ending verbs and **-ir** ending verbs. These two categories follow a different set of endings from **-ar** verbs.

When conjugating -er verbs, drop the -er and add -o when the subject is yo, -es when it's tú, -e when it's él, ella, or usted, -emos when it's nosotros or nosotras, -éis when it's vosotros or vosotras, and -en when it's ellos, ellas, or ustedes. Let's hear how this works with comer (*to eat*):

COMER *(TO EAT)*			
yo	como	nosotros/nosotras	comemos
tú	comes	vosotros/vosotras	coméis
él/ella/Ud.	come	ellos/ellas/Uds.	comen

And what about -ir ending verbs? The conjugation of -ir verbs is the same as -er verbs, with two exceptions: add -imos when the subject is nosotros or nosotras, and -ís when it's vosotros or vosotras. Let's hear how this works with vivir (*to live*):

VIVIR *(TO LIVE)*			
yo	vivo	nosotros/nosotras	vivimos
tú	vives	vosotros/vosotras	vivís
él/ella/Ud.	vive	ellos/ellas/Uds.	viven

You also heard a couple of questions in the previous listening exercise. Spanish questions are very easy to form, because just by raising the intonation of the statement, you can form a question. It's that simple! An alternate way is by switching the order of the subject and the verb and raising the intonation.

To summarize:

-ER VERB ENDINGS			
yo	-o	nosotros/nosotras	-emos
tú	-es	vosotros/vosotras	-éis
él/ella/Ud.	-e	ellos/ellas/Uds.	-en

Some common regular **-er** verbs: **comer** (*to eat*), **leer** (*to read*), **comprender** (*to understand*), **aprender** (*to learn*), **vender** (*to sell*), and **responder** (*to answer*).

-IR VERB ENDINGS			
yo	-o	nosotros/nosotras	-imos
tú	-es	vosotros/vosotras	-ís
él/ella/Ud.	-e	ellos/ellas/Uds.	-en

Some common regular **-ir** verbs: **vivir** (*to live*), **abrir** (*to open*), and **escribir** (*to write*).

✎ Work Out 1

Okay, let's put everything you've learned so far together in a short comprehension exercise. Fill in the blank with the appropriate Spanish word. Use the English translations as a guide. Be sure to try to complete the exercise before you listen to the audio; the full Spanish phrases are read on the CD. When you're ready to hear the answers, hit play on the CD. You'll hear the English first, and then the Spanish, and then you should repeat the Spanish for practice.

▶ 7F Work Out 1 (CD 2, Track 25)

1. _____ _____ **en la ciudad.** *I live in the city.*

2. _____ **al trabajo temprano.** *I arrive at work early.*

3. _____ **el tren.** *María uses the train.*

4. _____ **en el autobús.** *I read on the bus.*

5. _____ **en mi casa.** *I learn Spanish at home.*

6. _____ ___ **bastante.** *We understand quite a bit.*

Ⅱ

ANSWER KEY
1. Yo vivo en la ciudad. 2. Yo llego al trabajo temprano. 3. María usa el tren. 4. Yo leo en el autobús.
5. Yo aprendo español en mi casa. 6. Nosotros comprendemos bastante.

 Bring It All Together

▶ 7G Bring It All Together (CD 2, Track 26)

Now let's bring it all together and add a little bit more vocabulary and structure.

I live a very busy life.
Yo vivo una vida muy agitada.

I work and I also attend the university.
Yo trabajo y asisto a la universidad también.

I also take classes at your university.
Yo tomo clases en tu universidad también.

What days do you go?
¿Qué días vas?

I go twice a week.
Voy dos días a la semana.

At what time do you get there?
¿A qué hora llegas?

I only go at night.
Yo voy solamente por las noches.

⏸

✎ Work Out 2

▶ 7H Work Out 2 (CD 2, Track 27)

A. Let's practice -ar, -ir, and -er verb conjugations. Fill in the empty spaces in each verb chart below.

COMPRAR 1. _____			
yo	compro	nosotros/nosotras	compramos
tú	2. _____	vosotros/vosotras	3. _____
él/ella/Ud.	compra	ellos/ellas/Uds.	4. _____

5. _____ *(TO OPEN)*			
yo	6. _____	nosotros/nosotras	8. _____
tú	abres	vosotros/vosotras	abrís
él/ella/Ud.	7. _____	ellos/ellas/Uds.	9. _____

VENDER *(TO SELL)*			
yo	10. _____	nosotros/nosotras	13. _____
tú	11. _____	vosotros/vosotras	14. _____
él/ella/Ud.	12. _____	ellos/ellas/Uds.	15. _____

B. Now translate the following phrases into Spanish.

1. *I live in the city.*

_____

2. *We learn Spanish at home.*

_____

3. *You read the newspaper. (formal)*

_____

4. *They speak English and Spanish.*

_____

5. *We arrive early.*

_____

(II)

ANSWER KEY
A. 1. to buy; 2. compras; 3. compráis; 4. compran; 5. abrir; 6. abro; 7. abre; 8. abrimos; 9. abren; 10. vendo; 11. vendes; 12. vende; 13. vendemos; 14. vendéis; 15. venden
B. 1. Yo vivo en la ciudad. 2. Nosotros aprendemos español en casa. 3. Usted lee el periódico. 4. Ellos hablan inglés y español. 5. Nosotros llegamos temprano.

✎ Drive It Home

We've learned a lot about verb conjugations in this lesson. Let's practice the verb vivir. Fill in the blanks with the appropriate form of the verb. And don't forget to say the sentences out loud.

1. Yo _____ en los Estados Unidos.

2. ¿Tú _____ en una casa grande?

3. Mi padre _____ en California.

4. Nosotros _____ en un apartamento.

5. Ustedes _____ en un apartamento bonito.

6. Paco y Marta _____ en una casa pequeña.

ANSWER KEY
A. 1. vivo; 2. vives; 3. vive; 4. vivimos; 5. viven; 6. viven

Parting Words

You've finished Lesson 7, **una lección muy importante**. In this lesson you've learned how to use regular Spanish verbs. By now you should be able to:

☐ Say *I speak* and *I listen*

☐ Talk about traveling and walking in the present tense

☐ Say *I read* and *I understand*

☐ Conjugate verbs such as *to eat, to learn,* and *to write*

 Don't forget to practice and reinforce what you've learned by visiting **www.livinglanguage.com/ languagelab** for flashcards, games, and quizzes for Lesson 7!

Take It Further

⊳ 7I Take It Further (CD 2, Track 28)

You've learned three categories of verbs and how to conjugate them. There are, of course, many verbs in Spanish. You may want to expand your vocabulary and include other action words, such as **preguntar** (*to ask*), **mirar** (*to look at*), **contestar** (*to answer*), **llevar** (*to carry* or *to wear*), **beber** (*to drink*), **prometer** (*to promise*), **correr** (*to run*), **decidir** (*to decide*), or **describir** (*to describe*).

Word Recall

You've seen a lot of verbs so far. How many of them do you remember? Read the following phrases. Identify the infinitive form of the verb of each sentence and translate it into English.

1. Yo escucho la radio. _____

2. Tú estás cansado. _____

3. Nosotros compramos los regalos. _____

4. Tú ayudas a tus amigos. _____

5. Ustedes caminan mucho. _____

6. Las muchachas comen muy poco. _____

7. Ella tiene una casa muy bonita. _____

8. Mis camisas son blancas y bonitas. _____

ANSWER KEY
1. escuchar, *to listen*; 2. estar, *to be*; 3. comprar, *to buy*; 4. ayudar, *to help*; 5. caminar, *to walk*;
6. comer, *to eat*; 7. tener, *to have*; 8. ser, *to be*

Lesson 8: At a Restaurant

Lección ocho: En un restaurante

Bienvenidos a la lección ocho. By the end of this lesson, you should have the skills under your belt to get by in a restaurant, including being able to:

☐ Say *this* and *that*

☐ Use basic terms for food

☐ Make basic requests using the expression *could you …*

☐ Express *I'd like* and *I want*

☐ Use requests and food terms to order in a restaurant

Pues vamos a comenzar … *So let's begin …*

Vocabulary Builder 1

▶ 8B Vocabulary Builder 1 (CD 2, Track 30)

this restaurant	este restaurante
this dinner	esta cena
this fish	este pescado
these salads	estas ensaladas
these chickens	estos pollos
that breakfast	ese desayuno
that drink	esa bebida
those breads	esos panes
that lunch over there	aquel almuerzo
those desserts over there	aquellos postres
that meat over there	aquella carne
those soups over there	aquellas sopas

⊪

✎ Vocabulary Practice 1

Fill in the blank with the Spanish word to match the English translation. If you
need help, just consult the list on the previous page.

1. esta _____ this dinner

2. este _____ this fish

3. estas _____ these salads

4. ese _____ that breakfast

5. esa _____ that drink

6. aquel _____ *that lunch over there*

7. aquellos _____ *those desserts over there*

8. aquellas _____ *those soups over there*

ANSWER KEY
1. cena; 2. pescado; 3. ensaladas; 4. desayuno; 5. bebida; 6. almuerzo; 7. postres; 8. sopas

Grammar Builder 1

▶ 8C Grammar Builder 1 (CD 2, Track 31)

Notice that demonstratives like este (*this*) or aquel (*that*) agree with nouns, like adjectives do. Also note that there's a three-way split between *this*, *that*, and *that over there*. Let's take a closer look.

To refer to a singular object that is near you, use este (masculine) or esta (feminine). To refer to nearby plural objects, use estos (masculine) or estas (feminine).

To refer to objects that are near the person you're talking to, use ese, esa, esos, or esas.

Finally, to refer to objects that are far from both you and the other person, use aquel, aquella, aquellos, or aquellas.

Ⓘ

To summarize:

THIS/THESE (NEAR THE SPEAKER)		
	Masculine	Feminine
Singular	este	esta
Plural	estos	estas

THAT/THOSE (NEAR THE LISTENER)

	Masculine	Feminine
Singular	ese	esa
Plural	esos	esas

THAT/THOSE (FAR FROM THE SPEAKER AND THE LISTENER)

	Masculine	Feminine
Singular	aquel	aquella
Plural	aquellos	aquellas

Vocabulary Builder 2

▶ 8D Vocabulary Builder 2 (CD 2, Track 32)

Sofía, call the waitress, please.	Sofía, llama a la camarera, por favor.
Could you get me the menu?	¿Me podría traer la carta?
I'd like to pay the bill.	Yo quisiera pagar la cuenta.
Is service included?	¿Está incluido el servicio?
Ricardo, order the chocolate dessert.	Ricardo, pide el postre de chocolate.
Luisa, eat more fruit.	Luisa, come más fruta.
Use another credit card, sir.	Señor, use otra tarjeta de crédito.
I'd like to pay cash.	Me gustaría pagar en efectivo.
Pay at the cash register.	Pague en la caja.

⊘

✎ Vocabulary Practice 2

Translate the following phrases from English to Spanish. If you need help, just consult the list on the previous page.

1. *Sofía, call the waitress, please.*

   _____

2. *Could you get me the menu?*

   _____

3. *I'd like to pay the bill.*

   _____

4. *Is service included?*

   _____

5. *Ricardo, order the chocolate dessert.*

   _____

6. *Luisa, eat more fruit.*

   _____

7. *Use another credit card, sir.*

   _____

8. *I'd like to pay cash.*

   _____

ANSWER KEY

1. Sofía, llama a la camarera, por favor. 2. ¿Me podría traer la carta? 3. Yo quisiera pagar la cuenta.
4. ¿Está incluido el servicio? 5. Ricardo, pide el postre de chocolate. 6. Luisa, come más fruta.
7. Señor, use otra tarjeta de crédito. 8. Me gustaría pagar en efectivo.

Grammar Builder 2

▶ 8E Grammar Builder 2 (CD 2, Track 33)

Let's pause for a moment and talk about different courtesy expressions. You just heard the expressions me gustaría and yo quisiera. Use these expressions followed by the infinitive of the verb whenever you want to say *I'd like*. So, for example, if you want to say *I'd like to drink more water*, you would say:

Me gustaría beber más agua.
Yo quisiera beber más agua.

Another useful word is podría (*could you*). For example:

¿Podría traer la cuenta?
Could you bring the check?

¿Podría traer más pan?
Could you bring more bread?

To give commands, once again you have to conjugate: just drop the -ar, -er, or -ir from the infinitive of the verb and add a specific ending. The endings vary according to how familiar you are with the person and whether you're using an -ar, -er, or -ir verb.

Add -e to -ar verbs and -a to -er and -ir verbs when talking to someone you don't know very well.

Add -a to -ar verbs and -e to -er and -ir verbs when talking to a friend.

Let's take the verb hablar (*to speak*), for instance. Use hable when giving a command to someone you don't know well. Use habla when talking to your friend.

As for **-er** or **-ir** ending verbs, using the verb escribir (*to write*) as an example, use the polite form escriba when talking to someone you don't know very well and escribe when talking to your friend. It's that easy!

To summarize:

COMMANDS - DROP THE ENDING AND ADD ...		
	Familiar	Polite
-AR verbs	-a (Habla.)	-e (Hable.)
-ER/-IR verbs	-e (Escribe.)	-a (Escriba.)

Take It Further

In Spanish, the overly polite request form seen above with words like gustaría, quisiera, and podría is not necessarily required. You will sound just as polite expressing wishes and making requests using me gusta, yo quiero, and me puede instead of me gustaría, yo quisiera, and podría.

Me gusta pagar en efectivo.
I'd like to pay in cash.

Yo quiero pagar la cuenta.
I want to pay the bill.

¿Me puede traer la cuenta?/¿Me trae la cuenta?
Can you bring the check?

✎ Work Out 1

Okay, let's put everything you've learned so far together in a short comprehension exercise. Fill in the blank with the appropriate Spanish word.

Use the English translations as a guide. Be sure to try to complete the exercise before you listen to the audio; the full Spanish phrases are read on the CD. When you're ready to hear the answers, hit play on the CD. **Escucha y repite.** *Listen and repeat.* You'll hear the English first, and then the Spanish, and then you should repeat the Spanish for practice.

▷ 8F Work Out 1 (CD 2, Track 34)

1. _____, **por favor.** *I'd like the check, please.*

2. _____ **con tarjeta de crédito.** *I'd like to pay with a credit card.*

3. **Pedro,** _____. *Pedro, drink more water.*

4. **Mariela,** _____ **por favor.** *Mariela, speak more slowly please.*

5. _____, **señor.** *Listen carefully, sir.*

6. _____. *Write down your name and your phone number.*

7. _____, **Lucrecia.** *Ask for the check, Lucrecia.*

8. _____ **y yo pago la cuenta.** *Pay the tip and I'll pay the check.*

⏸

ANSWER KEY
1. Quisiera la cuenta, por favor. 2. Me gustaría pagar con tarjeta de crédito. 3. Pedro, bebe más agua. 4. Mariela, habla más despacio por favor. 5. Escuche atentamente, señor. 6. Escriba su nombre y su número de teléfono. 7. Pide la cuenta, Lucrecia. 8. Paga la propina y yo pago la cuenta.

 Bring It All Together

▶ 8G Bring It All Together (CD 2, Track 35)

Now let's bring it all together and add a little bit more vocabulary and structure.

This restaurant has very good prices.
Este restaurante tiene precios muy buenos.

And a glass of wine is free with dinner.
Y una copa de vino es gratis con la cena.

I'd like to order beef, Patricia.
Me gustaría pedir carne de res, Patricia.

No, order the fish. It's excellent here.
No, pide el pescado. Es excelente aquí.

They have mixed, green, potato, rice, and fruit salads.
Tienen ensalada mixta, verde, de papa, de arroz y de frutas.

And the desserts are fantastic.
Y los postres son fantásticos.

Sir, we're ready to order.
Señor, estamos listos para pedir.

⏸

✎ Work Out 2

▶ 8H Work Out 2 (CD 2, Track 36)

A. Fill out the chart with the corresponding demonstrative adjectives in Spanish.

	NEAR THE SPEAKER	NEAR THE OTHER PERSON	FAR FROM BOTH
masculine singular	este niño	1. _____ niño	aquel niño
feminine singular	2. _____ niña	esa niña	3. _____ niña
masculine plural	4. _____ niños	5. _____ niños	aquellos niños
feminine plural	estas niñas	6. _____ niñas	7. _____ niñas

B. Now translate the following English phrases into Spanish.

1. *this bread* _____

2. *that waitress* _____

3. *those credit cards* _____

4. *those restaurants over there* _____

5. *I'd like the check, please.* _____

6. *I need change for the tip.* _____

7. *I'd like to use my credit card.* _____

(II)

ANSWER KEY
A. 1. ese; 2. esta; 3. aquella; 4. estos; 5. esos; 6. esas; 7. aquellas
B. 1. este pan; 2. esa camarera; 3. esas tarjetas de crédito; 4. aquellos restaurantes; 5. Quisiera la cuenta, por favor. 6. Necesito cambio para la propina. 7. Me gustaría usar mi tarjeta de crédito.

✎ Drive It Home

Make Spanish commands using the clues below. Don't forget to add **por favor** at the end.

1. **hablar despacio (tú)** _____

2. **hablar en español (tú)** _____

3. **hablar más (tú)** _____

4. **hablar despacio (usted)** _____

5. **hablar en español (usted)** _____

6. **hablar más (usted)** _____

ANSWER KEY
1. Habla despacio, por favor. 2. Habla en español, por favor. 3. Habla más, por favor. 4. Hable despacio, por favor. 5. Hable en español, por favor. 6. Hable más, por favor.

Parting Words

So you've made it through another lesson successfully! In this lesson we covered commands, polite expressions, and food vocabulary. By now, you should be able to:

☐ Say *this* and *that*

☐ Use basic terms for food

☐ Make basic requests using the expression *could you …*

☐ Express *I'd like* and *I want*

☐ Use requests and food terms to order in a restaurant

 Don't forget to practice and reinforce what you've learned by visiting **www.livinglanguage.com/ languagelab** for flashcards, games, and quizzes for Lesson 8!

Take It Further

▶ 8I Take It Further (CD 2, Track 37)

There are probably a lot of other food items that you might be interested in knowing. You may want to know the names of common fruits and vegetables, such as **manzana** (*apple*), **pera** (*pear*), **uvas** (*grapes*), **plátanos** (*bananas*), **lechuga** (*lettuce*), **cebolla** (onion), and **tomate** (*tomato*). And of course you may want to accompany your meal with **agua** (*water*), **jugo** (*juice*), **leche** (*milk*), **cerveza** (*beer*), **vino blanco** (*white wine*), or **vino tinto** (*red wine*). **¡Buen provecho!** *Enjoy the meal!*

⑪

Word Recall

You have learned a lot of vocabulary so far. Let's see how much you remember. Match the Spanish phrase on the left with its logical response on the right.

1. ¿Quién es ella?
2. ¿De qué color es la falda?
3. ¿Cuánto cuesta?
4. ¿Me permites usar el teléfono?
5. Te presento a Carlos.
6. ¿Cómo está usted?

a. Mucho gusto.
b. ¡Claro que sí!
c. Estoy bien, gracias.
d. Es amarilla.
e. No mucho, es barata.
f. Es la hija de Patricia.

ANSWER KEY
1. f; 2. d; 3. e; 4. b; 5. a; 6. c

Lesson 9: At Work

Lección nueve: En el trabajo

¡Y ahora llegamos a la lección nueve! *And now we arrive at Lesson 9!* In this lesson we'll talk about work, **el trabajo**. By the end of the lesson, you should be able to:

☐ Talk about professions and occupations

☐ Express *to go* and *to know*

☐ Ask for and tell time

☐ Talk about particular days of the week

☐ Use time expressions to talk about your working life

Speaking of time, **es hora de comenzar**. *It's time to begin.*

Vocabulary Builder 1

▶ 9B Vocabulary Builder 1 (CD 2, Track 39)

I'm going to the doctor's office.	**Yo voy al consultorio del médico.**
I need to talk to my lawyer.	**Necesito hablar con mi abogado.**
The engineer knows the project well.	**El ingeniero conoce bien el proyecto.**
The receptionist and I are going to eat in the cafeteria.	**La recepcionista y yo vamos a comer en la cafetería.**
I know the secretary from your office.	**Yo conozco a la secretaria de tu oficina.**
I don't know if Paco's son is a pharmacist or an accountant.	**No sé si el hijo de Paco es farmacéutico o contable.**
The architect knows about art and math.	**El arquitecto sabe de arte y matemáticas.**
The teacher knows his students well.	**El maestro conoce bien a sus alumnos.**
The store clerk doesn't know the price of the pants.	**La dependienta no sabe el precio de los pantalones.**
I share my office with the new office worker.	**Yo comparto mi despacho con el oficinista nuevo.**
The representative goes to many offices.	**El representante va a muchas oficinas.**

⏸

✎ Vocabulary Practice 1

Fill in the blank with the Spanish word to match the English translation. If you need help, just consult the list on the previous page.

1. **Yo voy al** _____ .

   I'm going to the doctor's office.

2. Necesito hablar con mi _____. *I need to talk to my lawyer.*

3. _____ conoce bien el proyecto.

The engineer knows the project well.

4. _____ y yo vamos a comer en la cafetería.

The receptionist and I are going to eat in the cafeteria.

5. No sé si el hijo de Paco es _____ o _____.

I don't know if Paco's son is a pharmacist or an accountant.

6. _____ sabe de arte y matemáticas.

The architect knows about art and math.

7. _____ conoce bien a sus alumnos.

The teacher knows his students well.

8. Yo comparto mi _____ con el oficinista nuevo.

I share my office with the new office worker.

ANSWER KEY
1. consultorio del médico; 2. abogado; 3. El ingeniero; 4. La recepcionista; 5. farmacéutico/
contable; 6. El arquitecto; 7. El maestro; 8. despacho

Grammar Builder 1

▶ 9C Grammar Builder 1 (CD 3, Track 1)

Now you know several terms for professions. You heard abogado (*lawyer*),
ingeniero (*engineer*), and secretario (*secretary*), among others. Remember that
the feminine form of these nouns is formed by changing the final -o to -a. You also
heard several new verbs. Up to this lesson we've concentrated mostly on regular
Spanish verbs. Regular verbs follow a predictable pattern: you simply drop the
-ar, -er, or -ir, and replace it with the specific ending that goes with the subject.

In this lesson you heard three verbs that are not regular: **ir** (*to go*), **saber** (*to know*), and **conocer** (also *to know*). Notice the irregular forms of the verb **ir**:

IR *(TO GO)*			
yo	voy	nosotros/nosotras	vamos
tú	vas	vosotros/vosotras	vais
él/ella/Ud.	va	ellos/ellas/Uds.	van

The verbs **saber** and **conocer** both mean *to know*, but they're used to express different things.

Use **saber** to say that you know facts, have information, or know how to do something. Here are the different forms of the verb **saber**:

SABER *(TO KNOW [FACTS, INFORMATION])*			
yo	sé	nosotros/nosotras	sabemos
tú	sabes	vosotros/vosotras	sabéis
él/ella/Ud.	sabe	ellos/ellas/Uds.	saben

Use **conocer** to say that you're acquainted with a person, place, or thing. Its forms are:

CONOCER *(TO KNOW [PEOPLE, PLACES])*			
yo	conozco	nosotros/nosotras	conocemos
tú	conoces	vosotros/vosotras	conocéis
él/ella/Ud.	conoce	ellos/ellas/Uds.	conocen

Finally, did you notice that in the sentence …

Yo conozco a la secretaria de tu oficina.
I know the secretary from your office.

… you use **a** after **conozco**? In Spanish, with verbs other than **tener** (*to have*), if the direct object is a person, you use this construction, called **a personal**.

Tú conoces a María.
You know María.

Yo veo a la profesora.
I see the professor.

Escuchamos a la maestra.
We listen to the teacher.

Vocabulary Builder 2
9D Vocabulary Builder 2 (CD 3, Track 2)

I work from Monday through Friday.	**Yo trabajo de lunes a viernes.**
They don't go to work on Mondays.	**Ellos no van al trabajo los lunes.**
He goes to the university at 4:00 p.m.	**Él va a la universidad a las cuatro de la tarde.**
I get to work at 9:00 a.m.	**Llego al trabajo a las nueve de la mañana.**
She goes to the gym on Tuesdays and Thursdays at 7:00 p.m.	**Ella va al gimnasio los martes y los jueves a las siete de la noche.**
I don't have school on Wednesdays.	**No tengo clases los miércoles.**
I get up at a quarter to six in the morning.	**Me levanto a las seis menos cuarto de la mañana.**
She goes to her house at 8:10.	**Ella va a su casa a las ocho y diez.**
We go to the station at 5:30 p.m.	**Nosotros vamos a la estación a las cinco y media de la tarde.**
I don't work on weekends.	**Yo no trabajo los fines de semana.**
You go to the office Saturdays and Sundays.	**Tú vas a la oficina los sábados y los domingos.**
What time is it?	**¿Qué hora es?**
At what time is it?	**¿A qué hora es?**

✎ Vocabulary Practice 2

Just like in Vocabulary Practice 1, fill in the blank with the Spanish word or words to match the English translation. If you need help, just consult the list on the previous page.

1. Yo trabajo de _____ a _____.

   I work from Monday through Friday.

2. Llego al trabajo _____.

   I get to work at 9:00 a.m.

3. Ella va al gimnasio _____ _____ a las

   siete de la noche. *She goes to the gym on Tuesdays and Thursdays at 7:00 p.m.*

4. No tengo clases _____.

   I don't have school on Wednesdays.

5. Me levanto _____

   _____. *I get up at a quarter to six in the morning.*

6. Tú vas a la oficina _____.

   You go to the office Saturdays and Sundays.

7. ¿_____? *What time is it?*

8. ¿_____ _____? *At what time is it?*

ANSWER KEY
1. lunes/viernes; 2. a las nueve de la mañana; 3. los martes y los jueves; 4. los miércoles; 5. a las seis menos cuarto de la mañana; 6. los sábados y los domingos; 7. Qué hora es; 8. A qué hora es

Grammar Builder 2

▶ 9E Grammar Builder 2 (CD 3, Track 3)

In this section you learned the days of the week: lunes (*Monday*), martes
(*Tuesday*), miércoles (*Wednesday*), jueves (*Thursday*), viernes (*Friday*), sábado
(*Saturday*), and domingo (*Sunday*). To tell the time, start with either es la (for *one
o'clock*) or son las (for other hours).

Es la una.
It's one o'clock.

Son las tres.
It's three o'clock.

The time past the hour is expressed by y (*and*) followed by the number of
minutes. Use y media to say *half past* and y cuarto to say *quarter past*. After half
past, use menos followed by the number of minutes. For example:

Son las dos menos cuarto.
It's a quarter to two.

Finally, say de la mañana to express times in the morning, de la tarde in the
afternoon, and de la noche at night or in the evening. To say at a particular time,
use a (*at*), as in a la una (*at one o'clock*) or a las cinco (*at five o'clock*).

⏸

✎ Work Out 1

Okay, let's put everything you've learned so far together in a short comprehension
exercise. Fill in the blank with the appropriate Spanish word. Use the English
translations as a guide. Be sure to try to complete the exercise before you listen
to the audio; the full Spanish phrases are read on the CD. When you're ready to

hear the answers, hit play on the CD. You'll hear the English first, and then the Spanish, and then you should repeat the Spanish for practice.

▶ 9F Work Out 1 (CD 3, Track 4)

1. _____. *I go to work at seven.*

2. _____ *inglés y español.*

   You (singular informal) know how to speak English and Spanish.

3. _____*a tu médico. I don't know your doctor.*

4. ¿_____?

   What time do you (singular informal) go to work?

5. Ricardo _____ *este fin de semana. Ricardo works this weekend.*

6. ¿_____ **a la oficina del abogado** _____?

   Are you (singular informal) going to the lawyer's office this Wednesday?

7. ¿_____? *What time is it?*

8. _____.

   It's three thirty in the afternoon.

⏸

ANSWER KEY

1. Yo voy al trabajo a las siete. 2. Tú sabes hablar inglés y español. 3. Yo no conozco a tu médico.
4. ¿A qué hora vas al trabajo? 5. Ricardo trabaja este fin de semana. 6. ¿Vas a la oficina del abogado
el miércoles? 7. ¿Qué hora es? 8. Son las tres y media de la tarde.

🔊 Bring It All Together

▶ 9G Bring It All Together (CD 3, Track 5)

Let's do it again … We'll use everything we've learned with a bit more vocabulary.

Do you (singular informal) know a good accountant?
¿Conoces a un buen contable?

Yes, let's go to mine. He's very good.
Sí, vamos al mío. Es muy bueno.

I don't know how to do my tax return.
No sé hacer la planilla de impuestos.

Yes, of course. I'm going to call him on the phone.
Sí, claro. Voy a llamarlo por teléfono.

What day are you (singular informal) going?
¿Qué día vas?

I have an appointment for Thursday afternoon.
Tengo cita el jueves por la tarde.

I can go on Thursday too.
Yo puedo ir el jueves también.

I leave work at four.
Salgo del trabajo a las cuatro.

I can go at a quarter to five.
Yo puedo ir a las cinco menos cuarto.

My appointment is for a quarter past four.
Mi cita es a las cuatro y cuarto.

Take It Further

▷ 9H Take It Further (CD 3, Track 6)

So, you heard a person looking for help with taxes (**los impuestos**). Tax return is **la planilla de impuestos**, and appointment is **la cita**. You also heard someone using the verb **ir** to express an action in the future. This expression is used the same way as in English, as in **Voy a llamarlo**—I'm going to call him. You also heard two new verbs, **salgo** and **puedo**. **Salgo** comes from the verb **salir**, which means to leave or to go out, and **puedo** comes from **poder**, which means to be able to.

Work Out 2

▷ 9I Work Out 2 (CD 3, Track 7)

A. Translate each sentence from English into Spanish.

1. *It's two o'clock in the afternoon.*

_____

2. *It's one fifteen in the afternoon.*

_____

3. *It's half past nine in the morning.*

_____

4. *It's a quarter to ten in the evening.*

_____

5. *It's six ten in the morning.*

_____

B. Now, give the form of the verb that matches the pronoun.

1. **conocer, nosotros** _____

2. **ir, ellos** _____

3. **conocer, yo** _____

4. **ir, nosotros** _____

5. **saber, yo** _____

6. **saber, tú** _____

C. Now decide whether **conozco**, **sé**, or **voy** is correct in front of the following phrases. For example, if you hear **a la madre de Rosa**, you would say **conozco**. **Yo conozco a la madre de Rosa.**

1. **al trabajo a las seis** _____

2. **hablar español** _____

3. **a Lucía** _____

4. **a la estación** _____

5. **al señor Fortuno** _____

(II)

ANSWER KEY
A. 1. Son las dos de la tarde. 2. Es la una y cuarto de la tarde. 3. Son las nueve y media de la mañana.
4. Son las diez menos cuarto de la noche. 5. Son las seis y diez de la mañana.
B. 1. conocemos; 2. van; 3. conozco; 4. vamos; 5. sé; 6. sabes
C. 1. voy/Yo voy al trabajo a las seis. 2. sé/Yo sé hablar español. 3. conozco/Yo conozco a Lucía.
4. voy/Yo voy a la estación. 5. conozco/Yo conozco al señor Fortuno.

✎ Drive It Home

Let's practice those irregular verbs that we learned. Give the correct form of the verb **ir** (*to go*).

1. Yo _____ al consultorio del médico.

2. Ella _____ al consultorio del médico.

3. Tú _____ al consultorio del médico.

4. Nosotros ___ _____ al consultorio del médico.

5. Usted _____ al consultorio del médico.

6. Ustedes _____ al consultorio del médico.

ANSWER KEY
1. voy; 2. va; 3. vas; 4. vamos; 5. va; 6. van

Parting Words

This concludes **la lección nueve**. By now, you should be able to:

☐ Talk about professions and occupations

☐ Express *to go* and *to know*

☐ Ask for and tell time

☐ Talk about particular days of the week

Don't forget to practice and reinforce what you've learned by visiting **www.livinglanguage.com/languagelab** for flashcards, games, and quizzes for Lesson 9!

Take It Further

▶ 9J Take It Further (CD 3, Track 8)

In this lesson you were introduced to the days of the week and you also learned how to say the time of the day. You may also want to know that **mediodía** is *noon*, **medianoche** is *midnight*, and **año** is *year*. And speaking of **años**, you will surely recognize many of these **meses** (*months*) right away: **enero** (*January*), **febrero** (*February*), **marzo** (*March*), **abril** (*April*), **mayo** (*May*), **junio** (*June*), **julio** (*July*), **agosto** (*August*), **septiembre** (*September*), **octubre** (*October*), **noviembre** (*November*), and **diciembre** (*December*).

Ⅱ

Word Recall

¡Hola!

1. _____

2. _____

3. _____

4. _____

5. _____

¿Qué hora es? Look at the clocks above and say the appropriate time in Spanish.

ANSWER KEY
1. Es la una. 2. Es la una y diez. 3. Son las tres y media. 4. Son las cinco menos cuarto. 5. Son las seis menos cinco.

Lesson 10: Entertainment

Lección diez: Las diversiones

Bienvenidos a la última lección, la lección diez. In this final lesson of *Essential Spanish*, you'll learn how to talk about hobbies and entertainment. By the end of this lesson, you should be able to:

☐ Say *I like, I don't like, I'm interested in*, and *I'm bored by*

☐ Talk about film and music

☐ Say *to leave* or *to go out, to bring* or *to take something*, and *to hear*

☐ Talk about sports

☐ Use your Spanish to express you interest in hobbies and entertainment

Let's get started!

Vocabulary Builder 1

▶ 10B Vocabulary Builder 1 (CD 3, Track 10)

Let's go to the movies.	**Vamos al cine.**
What type of movie do you like?	**¿Qué tipo de película prefieres?**
I'm interested in comedies.	**Me interesan las comedias.**
I don't like serious dramas.	**No me gustan los dramas serios.**
Are you interested in documentaries?	**¿Te interesan los documentales?**
Do you like adventure films?	**¿Te gustan las películas de aventuras?**
I love romantic films.	**Me encantan las películas románticas.**
We can go to the theater.	**Podemos ir al teatro.**
I like plays.	**Me gustan las obras de teatro.**
We can see a musical.	**Podemos ver un musical.**
Let's go to the concert.	**Vamos al concierto.**
Are you interested in classical music?	**¿Te interesa la música clásica?**

⏸

✎ Vocabulary Practice 1

Fill in the blank with the Spanish word to match the English translation. If you need help, just consult the list on the previous page.

1. **Vamos** _____. *Let's go to the movies.*

2. **¿Qué** _____ **prefieres?** *What type of movie do you like?*

3. **Me interesan** _____. *I'm interested in comedies.*

4. **Me encantan** _____. *I love romantic films.*

5. **Podemos ir** _____. *We can go to the theater.*

6. **Me gustan** _____. *I like plays.*

7. **Vamos** _____. *Let's go to the concert.*

8. **¿Te interesa** _____? *Are you interested in classical music?*

ANSWER KEY
1. al cine; 2. tipo de película; 3. las comedias; 4. las películas románticas; 5. al teatro; 6. las obras de teatro; 7. al concierto; 8. la música clásica

Grammar Builder 1

▶ 10C Grammar Builder 1 (CD 3, Track 11)

You've just learned the Spanish term for *movies* (**el cine**), *a play* (**una obra de teatro**), *an adventure movie* (**una película de aventuras**), *classical music* (**la música clásica**), and *concert* (**un concierto**).

You also learned expressions that are used to express likes and dislikes. Use **me gusta** or **me gustan** when you want to say that you like something. Just keep in mind that **me gusta** is followed by a verb or a singular noun while **me gustan** is followed by a plural noun.

Use **me encanta** or **me encantan** to emphasize that you really like something. Again, **me encanta** is followed by a verb or a singular noun, and **me encantan**, a plural noun.

Other similar expressions are **me interesa** or **me interesan** (*I'm interested in*) and **me aburre** or **me aburren** (*I'm bored by*).

In all these cases, if you substitute **me** with **te**, you're making a statement about the person you're talking to. So **Te interesa la música clásica** means *You're interested in classical music.* And one last thing: put **no** in front of **me** or **te** to make negative statements, as in **No te interesa la música clásica.**

Ⓘ

To summarize:

	SINGULAR	PLURAL
I/You like	me/te gusta	me/te gustan
I/You really like	me/te encanta	me/te encantan
I'm/You're interested in	me/te interesa	me/te interesan
I'm/You're bored by	me/te aburre	me/te aburren

Vocabulary Builder 2

▶ 10D Vocabulary Builder 2 (CD 3, Track 12)

We're going to the baseball game.	**Vamos al partido de béisbol.**
I'm leaving for the stadium now.	**Salgo para el estadio ahora.**
The game starts at five.	**El partido comienza a las cinco.**
I'm bringing my two children.	**Traigo a mis dos niños.**
I'm meeting my friends there.	**Yo encuentro a mis amigos allí.**
My favorite team wins the game.	**Mi equipo favorito gana el partido.**
The other team loses.	**El otro equipo pierde.**
They play very well.	**Ellos juegan muy bien.**
The players return to the field.	**Los jugadores vuelven al campo.**
I hear the game on the radio.	**Yo oigo el partido por la radio.**

⏸

✎ Vocabulary Practice 2

Just like in Vocabulary Practice 1, fill in the blank with the Spanish word to match the English translation. If you need help, just consult the list on the previous page.

1. **Vamos al partido** _____. *We're going to the baseball game.*

2. **Salgo para** _____ **ahora.** *I'm leaving for the stadium now.*

3. _____ comienza a las cinco. *The game starts at five.*

4. _____ a mis dos niños. *I'm bringing my two children.*

5. _____ gana el partido. *My favorite team wins the game.*

6. El otro equipo _____ . *The other team loses.*

7. _____ vuelven al campo. *The players return to the field.*

8. _____ el partido por la radio. *I hear the game on the radio.*

ANSWER KEY
1. de béisbol; 2. el estadio; 3. El partido; 4. Traigo; 5. Mi equipo favorito; 6. pierde; 7. Los jugadores; 8. Yo oigo

Grammar Builder 2
▶ 10E Grammar Builder 2 (CD 3, Track 13)

Okay, so we've just gone over a few new verbs. The verb salir means *to leave* or *to go out*, traer means *to bring* or *to take something*, and oír means *to hear*. What these verbs have in common is how they are irregular when the subject is yo.

Notice the yo conjugation of these three verbs:

salgo
traigo
oigo

Did you notice that they all end in -go? You also heard the verbs jugar (*to play*), volver (*to return*), perder (*to lose*), encontrar (*to find, to meet up with*), and comenzar (*to begin*). Let's take, for instance, the verb encontrar. Listen carefully to its conjugation:

ENCONTRAR *(TO FIND, TO MEET UP WITH)*			
yo	encuentro	nosotros/nosotras	encontramos
tú	encuentras	vosotros/vosotras	encontráis
él/ella/Ud.	encuentra	ellos/ellas/Uds.	encuentran

Notice how the o in **encontrar** becomes **ue** in all forms except when the subject is **nosotros** or **vosotros**. This irregularity is common to all these verbs; that's why they're called stem-changing verbs.

There are different types of stem-changing verbs. **Jugar** is a **u**-to-**ue** stem-changing verb: **yo juego**.

Volver and **encontrar** change from **o** to **ue**: **vuelvo, encuentro**.

Perder and **comenzar** change from **e** to **ie**: **pierdo, comienzo**.

This may sound confusing at first, but with a little bit of practice you'll be able to master it. Remember, stem-changing verbs are irregular in all forms except when the subject is **nosotros** or **vosotros**.

(II)

To summarize:

Let's look again at the three types of stem-changing verbs.

U **TO UE:** JUGAR *(TO PLAY)*			
yo	juego	nosotros/nosotras	jugamos
tú	juegas	vosotros/vosotras	jugáis
él/ella/Ud.	juega	ellos/ellas/Uds.	juegan
O **TO UE:** VOLVER *(TO RETURN)*			
yo	vuelvo	nosotros/nosotras	volvemos
tú	vuelves	vosotros/vosotras	volvéis

O **TO UE:** VOLVER *(TO RETURN)*			
él/ella/Ud.	vuelve	ellos/ellas/Uds.	vuelven

E **TO IE:** PERDER *(TO LOSE)*			
yo	pierdo	nosotros/nosotras	perdemos
tú	pierdes	vosotros/vosotras	perdéis
él/ella/Ud.	pierde	ellos/ellas/Uds.	pierden

Work Out 1

Okay now, **vamos a practicar**. Fill in the blank with the appropriate Spanish word. Use the English translations as a guide. Be sure to try to complete the exercise before you listen to the audio; the full Spanish phrases are read on the CD. When you're ready to hear the answers, hit play on the CD. **Escucha la frase en inglés y después en español. Repite la frase en español.**

▶ 10F Work Out 1 (CD 3, Track 14)

1. _____. *I love baseball.*

2. _____ este fin de semana.

   My favorite team is playing this weekend.

3. _____.

   I'm leaving for the stadium with Paco.

4. _____.

   She prefers to watch the games on TV.

5. _____ las comedias y las películas de aventuras.

   You're interested in comedies and adventure films.

6. **Los Tigres** _____. *The Tigers win the game.*

7. **Los Leones** _____. *The Lions lose.*

8. _____ **por la radio.**

I hear the game on the radio.

9. _____ **en el estadio Calderón.**

The game starts at four at the Calderón Stadium.

⏸

ANSWER KEY

1. **Me encanta el béisbol.** 2. **Mi equipo favorito juega este fin de semana.** 3. **Yo salgo para el estadio con Paco.** 4. **Ella prefiere mirar los partidos por televisión.** 5. **Te interesan las comedias y las películas de aventuras.** 6. **Los Tigres ganan el partido.** 7. **Los Leones pierden.** 8. **Yo oigo el partido por la radio.** 9. **El partido comienza a las cuatro en el estadio Calderón.**

🎧 Bring It All Together
▶ 10G Bring It All Together (CD 3, Track 15)

Now listen to this conversation.

Are you going to the Real Madrid game?
¿Vas al partido del Real Madrid?

I love soccer. What time is it?
Me encanta el fútbol. ¿A qué hora es?

It's tomorrow afternoon.
Es mañana por la tarde.

It depends; I don't have tickets.
Depende; no tengo billetes.

We can go to the stadium today and buy them.
Podemos ir hoy al estadio y comprarlos.

It's going to be an exciting game.
Va a ser un partido emocionante.

Real Madrid has some great players.
El Real Madrid tiene unos jugadores magníficos.

I think this year they'll win the Cup again.
Pienso que este año vuelven a ganar la Copa.

But they say that Fernández has an injury to his leg.
Pero dicen que Fernández tiene una lesión en la pierna.

I hope they win!
¡Ojalá que ganen!

I hope so!
¡Yo espero que sí!

⏸

Take It Further

▶ 10H Take It Further (CD 3, Track 16)

Let's take a look at some of the new vocabulary. You probably knew that **fútbol** refers to *soccer*. American-style football is barely known in Spanish speaking countries; it's known as **fútbol americano**. The word **billete** means *ticket*. They are hoping that the game will be **emocionante** (*exciting*) because the team has some **jugadores magníficos** (*great players*). They are certainly hoping so because there's a rumor that Fernández received **una lesión** (*an injury*) to his *leg*, or **pierna**.

Finally, you heard one of the friends say **¡Ojalá que ganen!** to express a wish. The expression **ojalá que** is followed by the subjunctive of the verb **ganar**.

The subjunctive is something that you'll learn as you continue more advanced studies of Spanish. As one of the friends says in the dialogue, **¡Yo espero que sí!**—*I hope so!*

✎ Work Out 2
▶ 101 Work Out 2 (CD 3, Track 17)

A. Translate the following into Spanish.

1. *soccer* _____

2. *the player* _____

3. *the movies* _____

4. *the movie* _____

5. *the stadium* _____

6. *I like football.* _____

7. *I don't like adventure movies.* _____

8. *You love the theater.* _____

9. *I'm interested in classical music.* _____

10. *The concert bores me.* _____

B. Now conjugate the following verbs with the subjects that follow.

1. salir, yo _____

2. comenzar, el partido _____

3. oír, yo _____

4. jugar, los jugadores _____

5. volver, yo _____

⑪

ANSWER KEY
A. 1. el fútbol; 2. el jugador; 3. el cine; 4. la película; 5. el estadio; 6. Me gusta el fútbol americano.
7. No me gustan las películas de aventura. 8. Te encanta el teatro. 9. Me interesa la música clásica.
10. Me aburre el concierto.
B. 1. salgo; 2. comienza; 3. oigo; 4. juegan; 5. vuelvo

✎ Drive It Home

Write the conjugation of the verbs in parentheses. Then translate the sentence to English.

1. Yo _____ a mis amigos. (encontrar)

2. Yo _____ al béisbol muy bien. (jugar)

3. Yo _____ para el estadio. (salir)

4. Ella _____ el partido. (perder)

5. Nosotros _____ el partido. (perder)

6. Ustedes _____ el partido. (perder)

ANSWER KEY
1. encuentro/*I find my friends.* 2. juego/*I play baseball well.* 3. salgo/*I'm leaving for the stadium.*
4. pierde/*She loses the game.* 5. perdemos/*We lose the game.* 6. pierden/*You (pl.) lose the game.*

Parting Words

¡Muy bien! You've just finished Lesson 10. By now you should be able to:

- ☐ Say *I like, I don't like, I'm interested in*, and *I'm bored by*
- ☐ Talk about film and music
- ☐ Say *to leave* or *to go out, to bring* or *to take something*, and *to hear*
- ☐ Talk about sports
- ☐ Use your Spanish to express you interest in hobbies and entertainment

Don't forget to practice and reinforce what you've learned by visiting **www.livinglanguage.com/languagelab** for flashcards, games, and quizzes for Lesson 10!

Take It Further

(▶) 10J Take It Further (CD 3, Track 18)

You may want to expand your vocabulary by learning these other verbs that end in -**go** in the **yo** form: **hacer** (*to do* or *to make*: **yo hago**), **poner** (*to put* or *to place*: **yo pongo**), **caer** (*to fall*: **yo caigo**), **decir** (*to tell*: **yo digo**), and **venir** (*to come*: **yo vengo**). You also learned stem-changing verbs. These other stem-changing verbs will come in handy. **Dormir** (*to sleep*: **yo duermo**) and **recordar** (*to remember*: **yo recuerdo**) are other examples of o-to-**ue** stem-changing verbs. **Entender** (*to understand*: **yo entiendo**) and **pensar** (*to think*: **yo pienso**) are e-to-**ie** stem-changing verbs. I hope you start putting them into practice soon, maybe even in *Complete Spanish*!

(II)

Word Recall

You have learned a lot of words related to leisure and entertainment. Say whether you like the activities below (me gusta/n). You may want to be more specific by saying whether you find them very appealing (me encanta/n), interesting (me interesa/n), or dislike them altogether and find them boring (me aburre/n).

1. el béisbol _____

2. la música clásica _____

3. el fútbol _____

4. las películas de aventuras _____

5. las obras de teatro _____

ANSWER KEY
1. Me gusta/Me encanta/Me interesa/Me aburre el béisbol.
2. Me gusta/Me encanta/Me interesa/Me aburre la música clásica.
3. Me gusta/Me encanta/Me interesa/Me aburre el fútbol.
4. Me gustan/Me encantan/Me interesan/Me aburren las películas de aventuras.
5. Me gustan/Me encantan/Me interesan/Me aburren las obras de teatro.

Quiz 2

Prueba corta 2

Now let's review! In this section you'll find a final quiz testing what you learned in Lessons 1–10. Once you've completed it, score yourself to see how well you've done. If you find that you need to go back and review, please do so before continuing on to the final section with review dialogues and comprehension questions.

A. Match the Spanish expressions on the left to the correct English translations on the right.

1. ¿Qué hora es?   a. *Who is it?*

2. ¿Cuándo es?   b. *What is it?*

3. ¿Dónde está?   c. *When is it?*

4. ¿Qué es?   d. *Where is it?*

5. ¿Quién es?   e. *What time is it?*

B. Rewrite the following times using numbers instead of words. For example, you might write *7 p.m., 2:25 p.m., 9:47 a.m.,* etc.

1. Es la una y media de la tarde. _____

2. Son las nueve menos cuarto de la noche. _____

3. Son las ocho y nueve minutos de la mañana. _____

4. Son las doce y veinte y cinco de la tarde. _____

5. Son las diez menos diez de la noche. _____

C. Fill in the blanks with the appropriate Spanish adjective in the correct form.

1. No me gustan las comedias; prefiero las películas _____. *I don't like comedies; I prefer serious movies.*

2. Los pantalones son muy _____. ¡Cuestan ciento cincuenta euros! *The pants are expensive. They cost 150 euros!*

3. El apartamento tiene cuatro habitaciones; es un apartamento muy _____. *The apartment has four bedrooms; it's a very large apartment.*

4. Mi abuelo tiene noventa y tres años. ¡Es un hombre _____! *My grandfather is 93 years old. He is an old man!*

5. La bandera americana es _____, blanca y _____. *The American flag is red, white, and blue.*

D. Conjugate the verbs in parentheses in the correct form and then translate each sentence into English.

1. Nosotros _____ (trabajar) en una oficina.

2. Usted _____ (beber) mucho café.

3. Ellas _____ (buscar) el autobús.

4. Tú _____ (viajar) a Perú en enero.

5. Ustedes _____ (leer) el periódico los domingos.

E. Write the following irregular verbs in the correct form and then translate each sentence into English.

1. Nosotros _____ (ir) al cine esta noche.

2. Yo _____ (saber) hablar inglés y español.

3. El equipo argentino _____ (perder) el partido.

4. Tú _____ (jugar) el fútbol muy bien.

5. Yo _____ (conocer) a la madre de Juan.

F. Choose the right verb, conjugate it, and give its English translation.

1. María _____ española. (ser/estar)

2. Yo no _____ hablar italiano. (saber/conocer)

3. ¿Por qué tomas aspirina? ¿_____ enfermo? (ser/estar)

4. Ellos siempre _____ una copa de vino tinto con la cena. (beber/comer)

5. Estamos contentos porque nuestro equipo favorito siempre

_____. (ganar/perder)

ANSWER KEY
A. 1. e; 2. c; 3. d; 4. b; 5. a
B. 1. *1:30 p.m.*; 2. *8:45 p.m.*; 3. *8:09 a.m.*; 4. *12:25 p.m.*; 5. *9:50 p.m.*
C. 1. serías; 2. caros; 3. grande; 4. viejo; 5. roja, azul
D. 1. trabajamos/*We work in an office.* 2. bebe/*You (formal) drink a lot of coffee.* 3. buscan/*They (fem) look for the bus.* 4. viajas/*You (informal) travel to Peru in January.* 5. leen/*You (pl) read the newspaper on Sundays.*
E. 1. vamos/*We're going to the movies tonight.* 2. sé/*I know how to speak English and Spanish.* 3. pierde/ *The Argentinian team loses the game.* 4. juegas/*You (informal) play soccer very well.* 5. conozco/*I know Juan's mother.*
F. 1. es/*Maria is Spanish.* 2. sé/*I don't know how to speak Italian.* 3. estás/*Why are you taking aspirin? Are you sick?* 4. beben/*They always drink a glass of red wine with dinner.* 5. gana/*We're happy because our favorite team always wins.*

How Did You Do?

Give yourself a point for every correct answer, then use the following key to determine whether or not you're ready to move on:

0–11 points: It's probably best to go back and study the lessons again. Take as much time as you need to. Review the vocabulary lists and carefully read through each Grammar Builder section.

12–24 points: If the questions you missed were in sections A, B, or C, you may want to review the vocabulary again; if you missed answers mostly in sections D, E, or F, check the Grammar Builder sections to make sure you have your conjugations and other grammar basics down.

25–30 points: Feel free to move on to the Review Dialogues! Great job!

 **points**

Review Dialogues
¡Bienvenidos! *Welcome!*

Here's your chance to practice all the vocabulary and grammar you've mastered in ten lessons of *Essential Spanish* with these five everyday dialogues. Don't forget to listen to the audio as you review these dialogues! You'll hear the dialogue in Spanish first, then in Spanish and English. Next, for practice, you'll do some role play by taking part in the conversation yourself!

Dialogue 1
TALKING ABOUT THE FAMILY

First, try to read (and listen to!) the whole dialogue in Spanish. Then read and listen to the Spanish and English together. How much did you understand? Next, take part in the role play exercise in the audio and answer the comprehension exercises here in the book.

▶ Spanish Only - 11A Dialogue 1 Spanish (CD 3, Track 20); Spanish and English - 11B Dialogue I Spanish and English (CD3, Track 21); Role Play Exercise - 11C Dialogue 1 Exercise (CD 3, Track 22)

Marcos:	**Lucrecia, ¿cómo está tu primo Mario?**
	Lucrecia, how's your cousin Mario?
Lucrecia:	**Está bien, gracias. Yo hablo con Mario todas las semanas.**
	He's fine, thanks. I talk to Mario every week.
Marcos:	**¿Sabes que Mario estudia en la universidad de Francisco?**
	Do you know that Mario studies at Francisco's school?
Lucrecia:	**¿Quién? ¿Tu hermano Francisco? ¡Qué coincidencia!**
	Who? Your brother Francisco? What a coincidence!
Marcos:	**Sí, pero Francisco estudia en la Facultad de Ciencias Económicas.**
	Yes, but Francisco is in the School of Economics.

Lucrecia:	**Mario estudia ingeniería. Está en su tercer año. ¿Y Francisco?** *Mario is in engineering. He's in his third year. What about Francisco?*
Marcos:	**Está en su segundo año de finanzas.** *He's in his second year of Finance.*
Lucrecia:	**¿Cuántos años tiene?** *How old is he?*
Marcos:	**Ahora tiene diecinueve años. Y Mario tiene …** *He's nineteen now. And Mario is …*
Lucrecia:	**… veinte años.** *… twenty years old.*
Marcos:	**Él siempre fue un estudiante muy bueno. Mario es inteligente y responsable.** *He was always a very good student. Mario is smart and responsible.*
Lucrecia:	**Y tu hermano también.** *And so is your brother.*
Marcos:	**¡Gracias! Francisco dice que ellos comen juntos en la cafetería de la universidad.** *Thanks! Francisco says that they have lunch together in the university's cafeteria.*
Lucrecia:	**¡Mi tía Julia va a estar tan contenta!** *My aunt Julia will be so happy!*
Marcos:	**¿Por qué no vamos todos a cenar el viernes?** *Why don't we all go have dinner on Friday?*
Lucrecia:	**De acuerdo. Yo llamo por teléfono a Mario esta tarde.** *All right. I'll call Mario this afternoon.*
Marcos:	**Y yo hablo con Francisco.** *And I'll talk to Francisco.*

Lucrecia:	El viernes es un buen día; ¿a las ocho de la noche?
	Friday's a good day; what about eight p.m.?
Marcos:	De acuerdo. Te llamo mañana con los detalles.
	Okay. I'll call you tomorrow with the details.

✎ Dialogue 1 Practice

Now let's check your comprehension of the dialogue and review what you learned in Lessons 1–10 with the following exercises. Ready?

A. In this dialogue you saw some vocabulary terms for members of the family. Let's review them again. Don't forget to translate the definite articles!

1. *the male cousin* _____ _____

2. *the sister* _____

3. *the grandfather* _____

4. *the nephew* _____

5. *the daughter* _____ _____

6. *the granddaughter* _____

7. *the niece* _____

8. *the brother* _____

B. In this dialogue you saw the phrase **Ahora tiene diecinueve años** (*He is now nineteen years old*, or literally, *has nineteen years*). You also learned numbers in Spanish. Say how old these people are based on the clues below.

1. **Marcos** *(12)* _____

2. **Luisa** *(22)* _____

3. **Mi hijo** *(15)* _____

4. **Ernesto** *(34)* _____

5. **Margarita** *(46)* _____

6. **Mi tía** *(60)* _____

7. **El señor Gómez** *(58)* _____

8. **Mi abuela** *(77)* _____

ANSWER KEY

A. 1. el primo; 2. la hermana; 3. el abuelo; 4. el sobrino; 5. la hija; 6. la nieta; 7. la sobrina;
8. el hermano

B. 1. **Marcos tiene doce años.** 2. **Luisa tiene veintidós años.** 3. **Mi hijo tiene quince años.** 4. **Ernesto
tiene treinta y cuatro años.** 5. **Margarita tiene cuarenta y seis años.** 6. **Mi tía tiene sesenta años.**
7. **El señor Gómez tiene cincuenta y ocho años.** 8. **Mi abuela tiene setenta y siete años.**

◖ Dialogue 2
AN APPOINTMENT WITH A REAL ESTATE AGENT

As with Dialogue 1, first read and listen to the whole dialogue in Spanish.
Then read and listen to the Spanish and English together. How much did you
understand? Next, take part in the role play exercise in the audio and answer the
comprehension exercises here in the book.

▶ Spanish Only - 12A Dialogue 2 Spanish (CD 3, Track 23); Spanish and English - 12B
Dialogue 2 Spanish and English (CD 3, Track 24); Role Play Exercise - 12C Dialogue 2
Exercise (CD 3, Track 25)

Ricardo:	**Buenos días, señora Rodríguez.**
	Good morning, Ms. Rodríguez.
Agente:	**Bienvenido, señor Cepeda. ¿Qué necesita?**
	Welcome, Mr. Cepeda. What would you like?
Ricardo:	**Tengo interés en un apartamento en el área. Estoy aquí de**
	vacaciones con mi familia.

I'm interested in an apartment in the area. I'm here on vacation with my family.

Agente: Pues tenemos muchos. ¿Qué tipo de apartamento busca?

Well, we have a lot. What type of apartment are you looking for?

Ricardo: Bueno, buscamos un apartamento de playa. Pero lo necesitamos tres semanas.

Well, we're looking for a beach apartment. But we need it for three weeks.

Agente: Sí, no es problema. Hay mucha variedad. ¿Para cuántas personas?

Yes, that's not a problem. There's a lot of choice. For how many people?

Ricardo: Yo quiero un apartamento de dos habitaciones. Es para mí, mi esposa y dos niños.

I want a two-bedroom apartment. It's for me, my wife, and two children.

Agente: Tengo uno muy bonito con vista al mar. Un momento … Es de dos habitaciones, ah, pero no tiene muebles.

I have a very nice one with an ocean view. Hold on … It's a two-bedroom, oh, but it doesn't have furniture.

Ricardo: ¡Qué pena! Necesitamos un apartamento amueblado.

That's too bad! We need a furnished apartment.

Agente: No se preocupe … ¡tenemos muchos más!

Don't worry … we have many more!

Ricardo: Necesitamos un apartamento amueblado de dos habitaciones, cocina y vista al mar.

We need a furnished apartment, with two bedrooms, a kitchen, and an ocean view.

Agente: Nuestros apartamentos tienen garaje también.

Our apartments have a garage too.

Ricardo: Perfecto, ¿cuándo podemos visitar los apartamentos?

Perfect, when can we visit them?

Agente:	¿Cuándo puede usted?
	When can you go?
Ricardo:	Hoy o mañana, pero prefiero hoy.
	Today or tomorrow, but I would prefer today.
Agente:	¡Pues vamos ahora!
	Let's go now, then!

(II)

✎ Dialogue 2 Practice

In that dialogue, you saw a lot of vocabulary relating to rooms and objects in the house.

A. First, let's review rooms in a house. Match the following Spanish words to the English correct translations.

1. *the dining room*	a. la cocina
2. *the backyard*	b. el baño
3. *the garage*	c. la casa
4. *the kitchen*	d. la habitación
5. *the house*	e. el patio
6. *the living room*	f. el comedor
7. *the bathroom*	g. el garaje
8. *the bedroom*	h. la sala

B. Now, let's review the objects in a house. Match the following Spanish words to the correct English translations.

1. *the wall*	a. las ventanas
2. *the bed*	b. la piscina
3. *the pool*	c. los muebles
4. *the stairs*	d. el reloj

5. *the clock*   e. las escaleras

6. *the windows*   f. el horno

7. *the furniture*   g. la pared

8. *the oven*   h. la cama

ANSWER KEY
A. 1. f; 2. e; 3. g; 4. a; 5. c; 6. h; 7. b; 8. d
B. 1. g; 2. h; 3. b; 4. e; 5. d; 6. a; 7. c; 8. f

Dialogue 3
A TOUR OF THE NEW HOUSE

As with the first two dialogues, first read and listen to the whole dialogue in Spanish. Then read and listen to the Spanish and English together. How much did you understand? Next, take part in the role play exercise in the audio and answer the comprehension exercises here in the book.

▶ Spanish Only - 13A Dialogue 3 Spanish (CD 3, Track 26); Spanish and English - 13B Dialogue 3 Spanish and English (CD 3, Track 27); Role Play Exercise - 13C Dialogue 3 Exercise (CD 3, Track 28)

Pedro: **Me gusta mucho tu casa nueva.**
               I like your new house very much.

Ana: **Gracias, Pedro. La casa es muy cómoda y bonita.**
               Thanks, Pedro. The house is very comfortable and nice.

Pedro: **¿Cuántas habitaciones tiene?**
               How many rooms does it have?

Ana: **Es muy grande. Tiene cuatro dormitorios.**
               It's very big. It has four bedrooms.

Pedro: **¡Y la sala! Es tan grande ...**
               And the living room! It's so large ...

Ana: **Ah, y tiene tres baños, cocina, comedor, garaje, oficina … ¡hasta una piscina!**

Oh, and it has three bathrooms, a kitchen, a dining room, a garage, an office … even a pool!

Pedro: **Es la casa ideal para una familia de seis personas.**

It's the ideal house for a family of six.

Ana: **Estoy muy contenta con la decisión.**

I'm very happy with the decision.

Pedro: **Me gusta mucho el color de las paredes.**

I like the color of the walls a lot.

Ana: **Bueno, hay paredes de varios colores, depende de la habitación.**

Well, there are walls of different colors, depending on the room.

Pedro: **Me gusta el azul claro para la habitación de Carlitos.**

I like light blue for Carlitos's bedroom.

Ana: **Y ese rosado va muy bien con la habitación de Anita.**

And that pink goes very well in Anita's bedroom.

Pedro: **Y ahora necesitas comprar los muebles.**

And now you need to buy the furniture.

Ana: **Bueno, tengo muebles para las habitaciones, pero necesito comprar para la sala y el comedor.**

Well, I have furniture for the bedrooms, but I need to buy (furniture) for the living room and dining room.

Pedro: **¿Qué estilo prefieres?**

What style do you prefer?

Ana: **Yo prefiero un estilo moderno, ¡pero económico también!**

I prefer a modern style, but economical too!

✎ Dialogue 3 Practice

You saw a variety of verbs in that dialogue, so for this exercise, let's practice verbs.

A. Each phrase below is from the dialogue and contains one verb. Identify the verb and then write its **_infinitive_** form in the blank space provided, followed by its English translation. (There may be several English translations for a verb; just write down one.) For example, if the phrase was **como mucho**, you would write down **comer** (*to eat*).

1. **es muy cómoda y bonita** _____

2. **tiene cuatro dormitorios** _____

3. **estoy muy contenta** _____

4. **ese rosado va muy bien** _____

5. **ahora necesitas comprar** _____

6. **qué estilo prefieres** _____

B. Now conjugate each of the verbs in the **nosotros** form. For example, if the verb was **comer**, you would write **nosotros comemos**.

1. **es muy cómoda y bonita** _____

2. **tiene cuatro dormitorios** _____

3. **estoy muy contenta** _____

4. **ese rosado va muy bien** _____

5. **ahora necesitas comprar** _____

6. **qué estilo prefieres** _____

ANSWER KEY

A. 1. **ser** *(to be)*; 2. **tener** *(to have)*; 3. **estar** *(to be)*; 4. **ir** *(to go)*; 5. **necesitar** *(to need)*;
6. **preferir** *(to prefer)*

B. 1. **nosotros somos**; 2. **nosotros tenemos**; 3. **nosotros estamos**; 4. **nosotros vamos**; 5. **nosotros necesitamos**; 6. **nosotros preferimos**

❝ Dialogue 4
GETTING DIRECTIONS TO A RESTAURANT

Let's try another dialogue.

▶ Spanish Only - 14A Dialogue 4 Spanish (CD 3, Track 29); Spanish and English - 14B
Dialogue 4 Spanish and English (CD3, Track 30); Role Play Exercise - 14C Dialogue 4
Exercise (CD 3, Track 31)

Angélica:	**Gabriel, ¿conoces el restaurante nuevo de la avenida Colón?**
	Gabriel, do you know the new restaurant on Colón Avenue?
Gabriel:	**¿Qué tipo de restaurante es?**
	What type of restaurant is it?
Angélica:	**Es de comida italiana. Se llama Restaurante Monte Vesubio.**
	It's Italian food. It's called Mount Vesuvius Restaurant.
Gabriel:	**¿Aceptan tarjetas de crédito?**
	Do they take credit cards?
Angélica:	**Sí, y es económico también.**
	Yes, and it's also inexpensive.
Gabriel:	**¿Dónde está?**
	Where is it?
Angélica:	**Está muy cerca de aquí. Continúa recto en la calle Magallanes y gira a la derecha en el semáforo.**
	It's very near here. Continue straight ahead on Magallanes Street and turn right at the traffic light.
Gabriel:	**¿El semáforo de la avenida Bolívar?**
	The traffic light at Bolívar Avenue?
Angélica:	**No, gira a la derecha en el semáforo de la avenida Martí.**

No, turn right at the traffic light on Martí Avenue.

Gabriel: **Bien, entonces continúo recto en esta calle, paso Bolívar y giro a la derecha en Martí.**

Fine, so I'll continue straight on this street, pass Bolívar, and turn right on Martí.

Angélica: **Exacto. Pasa el correo y el supermercado. Lo vas a encontrar allí.**

Exactly. Go by the post office and the supermarket. You'll find it there.

Gabriel: **¿Está a la derecha o a la izquierda?**

Is it on the right or left side?

Angélica: **El restaurante está a la izquierda, después de la farmacia.**

The restaurant is on the left, after the pharmacy.

Gabriel: **Gracias, es muy fácil. Voy mañana con mi familia.**

Thanks, that's very easy. I'm going tomorrow with my family.

Angélica: **¡Ah! Y puedes ir en autobús también; el restaurante está enfrente de la parada.**

Oh! And you can also go by bus; the restaurant is across from the bus stop.

Gabriel: **Es verdad, el cuarenta y cuatro pasa por la avenida Colón.**

That's right, the number forty-four goes by Colón Avenue.

✎ Dialogue 4 Practice

In that dialogue, Angélica recommended a restaurant to Gabriel.

A. First, let's review our comprehension of the dialogue. Choose the correct word that best describes the action that took place.

1. **Gabriel no _____ (conoce/escucha) el restaurante.**

2. **Angélica recomienda un restaurante _____ (viejo/nuevo).**

3. **El Monte Vesubio** _____ (acepta/es) **un restaurante italiano.**

4. **El restaurante es económico; no necesita** _____ (pagar/tener) **mucho.**

5. **En el restaurante puede usar** _____ (la pared/la tarjeta de crédito).

6. **El restaurante está** _____ (lejos/cerca).

7. **Es** _____ (fácil/difícil) **ir al restaurante.**

8. **El restaurante está enfrente de** _____ (la parada/el correo).

B. Below are some of the vocabulary words you saw in the dialogue. Next to each one, write **un** or **una** and then translate the phrase into English.

1. _____ **restaurante**

2. _____ **comida**

3. _____ **tarjeta de crédito**

4. _____ **calle**

5. _____ **semáforo**

6. _____ **correo**

7. _____ **farmacia**

8. _____ **parada**

ANSWER KEY
A. 1. conoce; 2. nuevo; 3. es; 4. pagar; 5. la tarjeta de crédito; 6. cerca; 7. fácil; 8. la parada
B. 1. un restaurante (*a restaurant*); 2. una comida (*a meal, a food*); 3. una tarjeta de crédito (*a credit card*); 4. una calle (*a street*); 5. un semáforo (*a traffic light*); 6. un correo (*a post office*); 7. una farmacia (*a pharmacy*); 8. una parada (*a stop*)

Dialogue 5
AT A STORE

Last one! You're almost done with *Essential Spanish*.

▶ Spanish Only - 15A Dialogue 5 Spanish (CD 3, Track 32); Spanish and English - 15B Dialogue 5 Spanish and English (CD 3, Track 33); Role Play Exercise - 15C Dialogue 5 Exercise (CD 3, Track 34)

Camila:	**Esos pantalones son muy bonitos, Iván.**
	Those pants are very nice, Iván.
Iván:	**Sí, pero no tienen mi talla. Me gustan estos pantalones también.**
	Yes, but they don't have my size. I like these pants too.
Camila:	**Sí, el color es muy bonito.**
	Yes, and the color is very pretty.
Iván:	**Me gusta mucho el azul oscuro, pero no los tienen en mi talla.**
	I like dark blue a lot, but they don't have them in my size.
Camila:	**Vamos a buscar más; hay mucha variedad de pantalones aquí.**
	Let's look for more; there's a good variety of pants here.
Iván:	**Ah, mira estos pantalones negros. ¡Qué elegantes!**
	Oh, look at these black pants. How elegant!
Camila:	**Sí, pero son pequeños.**
	Yes, but they're small.
Iván:	**Necesito la talla treinta y cuatro.**
	I need size thirty-four.
Camila:	**Y estos son treinta y dos.**
	And these are thirty-two.
Iván:	**¿Y éstos?**
	How about these?
Camila:	**Mira el precio. Son muy caros.**
	Look at the price. They're very expensive.
Iván:	**¿Cuánto cuestan?**

How much are they?

Camila: **Doscientos dólares. Pero mira éstos. Son talla treinta y cuatro y**
               cuestan setenta dólares.
               Two hundred dollars. But look at these. They're size thirty-four and
               cost seventy dollars.

Iván: **Me gustan mucho. ¿Aceptan tarjetas de crédito?**
               I like them a lot. Do they take credit cards?

Camila: **Seguro que sí. Vamos a pagar.**
               I'm sure they do. Let's pay.

Iván: **Mira, la caja está allí.**
               Look, the cash register is over there.

✎ Dialogue 5 Practice

A. In this dialogue you heard Camila and Juan talk about clothes that they liked.
   Let's practice expressing likes and dislikes. How would you say the following
   phrases? Keep in mind that **me gusta** is used for singular nouns and **me gustan**
   is used for the plural. Also, remember that adjectives must match the gender and
   number of the item that they describe. For example, *I like the white shoes* would
   be **Me gustan los zapatos blancos.**

1. *I like the color.* _____

2. *I like the pants.* _____

3. *I like the size.* _____

4. *I like light blue.* _____

5. *I like the black shirt* _____

6. *I like dark green.* _____

7. *I like the price.* _____

8. *I like the expensive shoes.* _____

B. In this dialogue you saw the phrase **El color es muy bonito.** Let's transform the phrase using the clues below. For example, if you see the word *pants*, change it into **Los pantalones son bonitos.** Let's begin …
   El color es muy bonito.

1. *the skirt* _____

2. *expensive* _____

3. *the pants* _____

4. *cheap* _____

5. *the price* _____

6. *the shirt* _____

7. *light blue* _____

ANSWER KEY

A. 1. **Me gusta el color.** 2. **Me gustan los pantalones.** 3. **Me gusta la talla.** 4. **Me gusta el azul claro.** 5. **Me gusta la camisa negra.** 6. **Me gusta el verde oscuro.** 7. **Me gusta el precio.** 8. **Me gustan los zapatos caros.**

B. 1. **La falda es muy bonita.** 2. **La falda es muy cara.** 3. **Los pantalones son muy caros.** 4. **Los pantalones son muy baratos.** 5. **El precio es muy barato.** 6. **La camisa es muy barata.** 7. **La camisa es azul clara.**

Pronunciation Guide

If you've ever had trouble with English spelling, or if you've ever come across an unfamiliar word and had no idea how to pronounce it, you'll be happy to know that neither of these things is likely to be an issue in Spanish. Spanish spelling is phonetic, meaning that things are pronounced the way they're written. The rules for stress—which SYL-la-ble gets the EM-pha-sis—are very regular in Spanish, and any irregularities are marked in spelling with an accent mark. We'll cover all of that little by little, but let's get started with an overview of Spanish pronunciation.

1. VOWELS

Each vowel in Spanish is pronounced clearly and distinctly, and each vowel has one and only one pronunciation. A vowel may be written with an accent, as in *sí* or *América*, but this never changes the pronunciation of that vowel. It may mark stress, as in *América*, or it may only serve to distinguish between two words, as in *sí* (*yes*) and *si* (*if*). Let's look at each vowel, starting with simple vowels.

a	like *a* in *father*	a, amigo, la, las, pan, habla, Santiago
e	like *ay* in *day*, but cut off before the *ee*	él, de, en, padre, tren, este, Mercedes
i	like *i* in *police*	mí, amiga, hiciste, cinco, Chile, Sevilla
o	like *o* in *no*, but cut off before the *oo*	no, dos, hombre, costar, ocho, teléfono, Colombia
u	like *u* in *rule*	uno, tú, mucho, azúcar, Honduras, puro

Vowels can also appear in pairs, which are called diphthongs. A diphthong is usually a combination of a weaker vowel (**i** or **u**) and a more prominent one.

ai, ay	like *i* in *bide*	aire, hay, traigo, ¡ay!

au	like *ou* in *house*	restaurante, autobús, automóvil, Mauricio
ei, ey	like *ay* in *day*	seis, ley, treinta, rey
ia, ya	like *ya* in *yard*	gracias, comercial, estudiar, ya
ie, ye	like *ye* in *yet*	pie, quiero, tiene, yerba, abyecto
io, yo	like *yo* in *yoga*	yo, acción, despacio, estudio
iu, yu	like *u* in *united*	ciudad, yuca, yugo, yunta
oi, oy	like *oy* in *toy*	estoy, hoy, oiga, voy
ua	like *wa* in *want*	cuatro, Juan, ¿cuál?, ¿cuánto?
ue	like *we* in *west*	nueve, fuego, puerta, cuesta, bueno
uo	like *wo* in *woe*	continuo, antiguo, mutuo, superfluo
ui, uy	like *we* in *week*	muy, ruido, cuidado, huir

2. CONSONANTS

b	like *b* in *boy* at the beginning of a word	bueno, brazo, bajo, barca, bocadillo
b	between vowels for some speakers, as above, but the lips don't touch	Cuba, haber, beber, cobayo, deber, ubicar
c	like *k* in *kite* before consonants, a, o, and u	Cristóbal, cosa, casa, cuánto, cuál, truco

c	like *s* in *sea* before e and i	cerca, servicio, cierto, fácil, posición
ch	like *ch* in *choose*	charlar, chico, muchacho, ocho, mucho
d	at the beginning of a word or after n, like *d* in *day*, but with the tongue touching the back of the upper teeth	día, despegar, durante, cuándo, donde, mando
d	between vowels, like *th* in *thin*	media, nada, todo, poder, freiduría, prometido
f	like *f* in *father*	familia, Francisco, Federico, formulario
g	like *g* in *go* before consonants, a, o, and u	grande, Gloria, gustar, gusano, goloso, ganar, vengo
g	like the strong *h* in *hope* before e or i	general, Gibraltar, girar, rígido, urgente
gü	like *gw* in *Gwen*	vergüenza, lengüeta, cigüeña
h	silent	hablo, hay, hubo, ahora, hombre, deshonroso
j	like the strong *h* in *hope*	julio, jabón, mejor, José, tarjeta, jefe, trujar
ll	like *y* in *yes*	llamo, pollo, llama, llover, allí, llaves, trulla
m	like *m* in *met*	mismo, Marco, mano, Manuel, pluma, mandar

n	like *n* in *not*	nunca, no, Nicaragua, Argentina, nombre
ñ	like *ni* in *onion*	español, mañana, muñeca, ñame, gañir
p	like *p* in *pear*	para, pueblo, postre, Panamá, Perú
qu	like *k* in *kite*	que, querer, paquete, saquen, quemar, quizás
r	at the beginning of a word, a trilled sound made with the tongue against the ridge behind the upper teeth	rico, rubio, Ramón, Rosa, rincón, red, risa
r	otherwise like the tapped *d* in *ladder*	América, pero, quisiera, aire, libre, brazo, caro
rr	like word-initial r, a trilled sound made with the tongue against the ridge behind the upper teeth	perro, carro, tierra, horror, irritar, terrible
s	like *s* in *see* (never like *z* in *zone*)	casa, sucio, San Salvador, soltero, vasto, rosa
t	like *t* in *take*, but with the tongue touching the back of the upper teeth	tocar, fruta, tú, teclado, traje, tener
v	like *b* in *boy* at the beginning of a word	vaso, veinte, vivir, vivo, veramente
y	like *y* in *yes*; on its own, like *ee* in *teen*	ayer, ayudo, Bayamo, poyo

| z | like *s* in *see* | zona, diez, luz, marzo, azul, azúcar |

3. STRESS

There are three simple rules to keep in mind when it comes to stress. First, if a word ends in any consonant other than -n or -s, the last syllable receives the stress.

cuidad, capaz, notabilidad, navegar, familiar, refrigerador

Second, if a word ends in a vowel or in -n or -s, the penultimate (second-to-last) syllable receives the stress.

amigo, hablan, derechos, cubierto, portorriqueño, examen, libros

Note that diphthongs with the weak vowels i or u count as one syllable, so the stress will regularly fall before them.

academia, continuo, manubrio, sanitario, justicia

Combinations with two strong vowels count as two syllables.

tarea, menudeo, banqueteo, barbacoa

Any time stress doesn't follow these rules, an accent is used.

inglés, teléfono, tomó, práctico, drogaría, todavía, título, farmacéutico, petróleo, revés, apagón

4. REGIONAL SPANISH PRONUNCIATION

The Spanish pronunciation that you'll learn in this course is standard Latin American Spanish. There are certainly some local differences in pronunciation that you will probably come across, the most commonly known being the difference between Latin American and European Spanish. The major difference in pronunciation is that the sound *th*, as in *thin*, is much more common in Spain. In Latin America, this sound is typically only found in *d* when it comes between vowels.

media, nada, todo, poder, puedo

These words are pronounced with a *th* in Spain, too. But in Spain, c before i or e and z is also pronounced like *th* in *thin*.

cerca, servicio, cierto, fácil, docena, diez, voz, luz, marzo, azul, razón

There are some noticeable differences in local varieties of Spanish found in Latin America and Spain, as well. You don't need to worry about imitating these differences; the standard pronunciation you'll learn in this course will serve you perfectly well. But you may notice, for example, that in some countries or regions the combination ll is pronounced like the *lli* in *million*, the *j* in *juice*, the *sh* in *show*, or the *s* in *pleasure*. The semivowel y may have a similar range of pronunciation. In some countries, particularly in the Caribbean, final s may be dropped altogether, if not the entire last syllable! You may even hear r pronounced as something similar to l. There's certainly nothing wrong with any of these variations, although as a student, you'll probably find it useful to concentrate on the standard pronunciation offered in this course first.

Grammar Summary

Keep in mind that there are always at least some exceptions to every grammar rule.

1. ARTICLES

	DEFINITE		INDEFINITE	
	Singular	Plural	Singular	Plural
Masculine	el	los	un	unos
Feminine	la	las	una	unas

Note: **El** is used before a feminine noun beginning with stressed **a** (or **ha**). The article **lo** is used before parts of speech other than nouns when they are used as nouns. **Unos** (**unas**) is often used to mean *some* or *a few*.

2. CONTRACTIONS

de + el = del (*from/of the*)
a + el = al (*to the*)

3. PLURALS

a. Nouns ending in an unstressed vowel or diphthong add -s.
b. Nouns ending in a stressed vowel or diphthong add -es.
c. Nouns ending in a consonant add -es.
d. Nouns ending in -z change the z to c and then add -es.

4. POSSESSION

Possession is shown by the preposition **de**: **el libro de Juan** (*Juan's book*).

5. ADJECTIVES

Adjectives agree with the nouns they modify in both gender and number.

a. If the masculine singular ending is -o, the feminine singular is -a, the masculine plural is -os, and the feminine plural is -as.

b. If the masculine singular ending is not -o, there is no change in the feminine singular, and both genders are -es in the plural.

6. COMPARISON

The regular comparative is formed with **más** (*more*) or **menos** (*less*), and the regular superlative is formed with the definite article + **más** (*the most*) or **menos** (*the least*).

7. PRONOUNS

	SUBJECT	DIRECT OBJECT	INDIRECT OBJECT	PREPOSITIONAL	REFLEXIVE
1st sg.	yo	me	me	mí	me
2nd sg.	tú	te	te	ti	te
3rd m. sg.	él	lo	le	él	se
3rd f. sg.	ella	la	le	ella	se
2nd sg., fml.	usted	lo/la	le	usted	se
1st pl.	nosotros/ nosotras	nos	nos	nosotros	nos
2nd pl.	vosotros/ vosotras	os	os	vosotros	os
3rd m. pl.	ellos	los	les	ellos	se

	SUBJECT	DIRECT OBJECT	INDIRECT OBJECT	PREPOSITIONAL	REFLEXIVE
3rd f. pl.	ellas	las	les	ellas	se
2nd pl., fml.	ustedes	los/las	les	ustedes	se

8. QUESTION WORDS

¿Qué?	What?	¿Cuál? ¿Cuáles?	What?/ Which one?
¿Por qué?	Why?	¿Quién? ¿Quiénes?	Who?
¿Cómo?	How?	¿Dónde?	Where?
¿Cuánto? ¿Cuánta? ¿Cuántos? ¿Cuántas?	How much?/How many?	¿Cuándo?	When?

9. ADVERBS

Spanish -mente corresponds to -ly in English. It is added to the feminine form of the adjective.

10. DEMONSTRATIVES

ADJECTIVES		PRONOUNS			
Masculine	Feminine	Masculine	Feminine	Neuter	
este	esta	éste	ésta	esto	*this*
ese	esa	ése	ésa	eso	*that*
aquel	aquella	aquél	aquélla	aquello	*that (farther removed)*
estos	estas	éstos	éstas	estos	*these*
esos	esas	ésos	ésas	esos	*those*
aquellos	aquellas	aquéllos	aquéllas	aquellos	*those (farther removed)*

11. *IF* SENTENCES

IF THE MAIN CLAUSE HAS A VERB IN THE:	THE SI *(IF)* CLAUSE HAS A VERB IN THE:
Present	*Present/Future*
Future	*Present*
Imperfect	*Imperfect*
Preterite	*Preterite*
Conditional	*Imperfect Subjunctive (-ra or -se)*
Past Conditional	*Past Perfect Subjunctive (hubiera or hubiese)*

If the subject of the main clause and the subject of the *if* clause are the same, it's possible to replace a verb in the subjunctive with an infinitive. In this case si is replaced by de.

12. SUBJUNCTIVE

The subjunctive is used:

a. with verbs of desire, request, suggestion, permission, approval and disapproval, judgment, opinion, uncertainty, emotion, surprise, fear, denial, and so on. It is often used in a dependent clause introduced by **que** (*that*).

b. in affirmative or negative commands in the polite form, in negative commands in the familiar form, in *let's* suggestions, and in indirect or third person commands with *let* (*him/her/them*).

c. in **si** (*if*) conditional clauses that are unreal or contrary to fact.

d. after impersonal verbs that do not express certainty.

e. after certain conjunctions that never introduce statements of accomplished fact (**antes de que, aunque, como si**, etc.). Other conjunctions may or may not introduce a statement of accomplished fact. When they do, they take the indicative; otherwise they take the subjunctive (**a menos que, a pesar de que**, etc.).

f. to refer to indefinites like **ningún** (*no*) or **alguien** (*someone*) when there's a doubt about that person's existence.

g. after compounds with **-quiera** (*-ever*): **quienquiera** (*whoever*), **dondequiera** (*wherever*), **cualquier** (*whatever, whichever*).

comer
to eat

yo	nosotros/as
tú	vosotros/as
él/ella/usted	ellos/ellas/ustedes

Present

como	comemos
comes	coméis
come	comen

Present Progressive

estoy comiendo	estamos comiendo
estás comiendo	estáis comiendo
está comiendo	están comiendo

Preterite

comí	comimos
comiste	comisteis
comió	comieron

Imperfect

comía	comíamos
comías	comíais
comía	comían

Future

comeré	comeremos
comerás	comeréis
comerá	comerán

Conditional

comería	comeríamos
comerías	comeríais
comería	comerían

Imperative

come	comed
coma	

Subjunctive

coma	comamos
comas	comáis
coma	coman

conducir
to drive

yo	nosotros/as
tú	vosotros/as
él/ella/usted	ellos/ellas/ustedes

Present		Present Progressive	
conduzco	conducimos	estoy conduciendo	estamos conduciendo
conduces	conducís	estás conduciendo	estáis conduciendo
conduce	conducen	está conduciendo	están conduciendo

Preterite		Imperfect	
conduje	condujimos	conducía	conducíamos
condujiste	condujisteis	conducías	conducíais
condujo	condujeron	conducía	conducían

Future		Conditional	
conduciré	conduciremos	conduciría	conduciríamos
conducirás	conduciréis	conducirías	conduciríais
conducirá	conducirán	conduciría	conducirían

Imperative		Subjunctive	
		conduzca	conduzcamos
conduce	conducid	conduzcas	conduzcáis
conduzca		conduzca	conduzcan

conocer
to know

yo	nosotros/as
tú	vosotros/as
él/ella/usted	ellos/ellas/ustedes

Present

conozco	conocemos
conoces	conocéis
conoce	conocen

Present Progressive

estoy conociendo	estamos conociendo
estás conociendo	estáis conociendo
está conociendo	están conociendo

Preterite

conocí	conocimos
conociste	conocisteis
conoció	conocieron

Imperfect

conocía	conocíamos
conocías	conocíais
conocía	conocían

Future

conoceré	conoceremos
conocerás	conoceréis
conocerá	conocerán

Conditional

conocería	conoceríamos
conocerías	conoceríais
conocería	conocerían

Imperative

conoce	conoced
conozca	

Subjunctive

conozca	conozcamos
conozcas	conozcáis
conozca	conozcan

dar
to give

yo	nosotros/as
tú	vosotros/as
él/ella/usted	ellos/ellas/ustedes

Present

doy	damos
das	dais
da	dan

Present Progressive

estoy dando	estamos dando
estás dando	estáis dando
está dando	están dando

Preterite

di	dimos
diste	disteis
dio	dieron

Imperfect

daba	dábamos
dabas	dabais
daba	daban

Future

daré	daremos
darás	daréis
dará	darán

Conditional

daría	daríamos
darías	daríais
daría	darían

Imperative

da	dad
dé	

Subjunctive

dé	demos
des	deis
dé	den

deber
to have to, must

yo	nosotros/as
tú	vosotros/as
él/ella/usted	ellos/ellas/ustedes

Present

debo	debemos
debes	debéis
debe	deben

Present Progressive

estoy debiendo	estamos debiendo
estás debiendo	estáis debiendo
está debiendo	están debiendo

Preterite

debí	debimos
debiste	debisteis
debió	debieron

Imperfect

debía	debíamos
debías	debíais
debía	debían

Future

deberé	deberemos
deberás	deberéis
deberá	deberán

Conditional

debería	deberíamos
deberías	deberíais
debería	deberían

Imperative

debe	debed
deba	

Subjunctive

deba	debamos
debas	debáis
deba	deban

escoger
to choose

yo	nosotros/as
tú	vosotros/as
él/ella/usted	ellos/ellas/ustedes

Present

escojo	escogemos
escoges	escogéis
escoge	escogen

Present Progressive

estoy escogiendo	estamos escogiendo
estás escogiendo	estáis escogiendo
está escogiendo	están escogiendo

Preterite

escogí	escogimos
escogiste	escogisteis
escogió	escogieron

Imperfect

escogía	escogíamos
escogías	escogíais
escogía	escogían

Future

escogeré	escogeremos
escogerás	escogeréis
escogerá	escogerán

Conditional

escogería	escogeríamos
escogerías	escogeríais
escogería	escogerían

Imperative

escoge	escoged
escoja	

Subjunctive

escoja	escojamos
escojas	escojáis
escoja	escojan

estar
to be

yo	nosotros/as
tú	vosotros/as
él/ella/usted	ellos/ellas/ustedes

Present

estoy	estamos
estás	estáis
está	están

Present Progressive

estoy estando	estamos estando
estás estando	estáis estando
está estando	están estando

Preterite

estuve	estuvimos
estuviste	estuvisteis
estuvo	estuvieron

Imperfect

estaba	estábamos
estabas	estábais
estaba	estaban

Future

estaré	estaremos
estarás	estaréis
estará	estarán

Conditional

estaría	estaríamos
estarías	estaríais
estaría	estarían

Imperative

está	estad
esté	

Subjunctive

esté	estemos
estés	estéis
esté	estén

hablar
to speak, to talk

yo	nosotros/as
tú	vosotros/as
él/ella/usted	ellos/ellas/ustedes

Present		Present Progressive	
hablo	hablamos	estoy hablando	estamos hablando
hablas	habláis	estás hablando	estáis hablando
habla	hablan	está hablando	están hablando

Preterite		Imperfect	
hablé	hablamos	hablaba	hablábamos
hablaste	hablasteis	hablabas	hablabais
habló	hablaron	hablaba	hablaban

Future		Conditional	
hablaré	hablaremos	hablaría	hablaríamos
hablarás	hablaréis	hablarías	hablaríais
hablará	hablarán	hablaría	hablarían

Imperative		Subjunctive	
		hable	hablemos
habla	hablad	hables	habléis
hable		hable	hablen

hacer
to do, to make

yo	nosotros/as
tú	vosotros/as
él/ella/usted	ellos/ellas/ustedes

Present

hago	hacemos
haces	hacéis
hace	hacen

Present Progressive

estoy haciendo	estamos haciendo
estás haciendo	estáis haciendo
está haciendo	están haciendo

Preterite

hice	hicimos
hiciste	hicisteis
hizo	hicieron

Imperfect

hacía	hacíamos
hacías	hacíais
hacía	hacían

Future

haré	haremos
harás	haréis
hará	harán

Conditional

haría	haríamos
harías	haríais
haría	harían

Imperative

haz	haced
haga	

Subjunctive

haga	hagamos
hagas	hagáis
haga	hagan

ir
to go

yo	nosotros/as
tú	vosotros/as
él/ella/usted	ellos/ellas/ustedes

Present		Present Progressive	
voy	vamos	estoy yendo	estamos yendo
vas	vais	estás yendo	estáis yendo
va	van	está yendo	están yendo

Preterite		Imperfect	
fui	fuimos	iba	íbamos
fuiste	fuisteis	ibas	ibais
fue	fueron	iba	iban

Future		Conditional	
iré	iremos	iría	iríamos
irás	iréis	irías	iríais
irá	irán	iría	irían

Imperative		Subjunctive	
		vaya	vayamos
ve	id	vayas	vayáis
vaya		vaya	vayan

pedir
to ask for

yo	nosotros/as
tú	vosotros/as
él/ella/usted	ellos/ellas/ustedes

Present

pido	pedimos
pides	pedís
pide	piden

Present Progressive

estoy pidiendo	estamos pidiendo
estás pidiendo	estáis pidiendo
está pidiendo	están pidiendo

Preterite

pedí	pedimos
pediste	pedisteis
pidió	pidieron

Imperfect

pedía	pedíamos
pedías	pedíais
pedía	pedían

Future

pediré	pediremos
pedirás	pediréis
pedirá	pedirán

Conditional

pediría	pediríamos
pedirías	pediríais
pediría	pedirían

Imperative

pide	pedid
pida	

Subjunctive

pida	pidamos
pidas	pidáis
pida	pidan

pensar
to think

yo	nosotros/as
tú	vosotros/as
él/ella/usted	ellos/ellas/ustedes

Present

pienso	pensamos
piensas	pensáis
piensa	piensan

Present Progressive

estoy pensando	estamos pensando
estás pensando	estáis pensando
está pensando	están pensando

Preterite

pensé	pensamos
pensaste	pensasteis
pensó	pensaron

Imperfect

pensaba	pensábamos
pensabas	pensabais
pensaba	pensaban

Future

pensaré	pensaremos
pensarás	pensaréis
pensará	pensarán

Conditional

pensaría	pensaríamos
pensarías	pensaríais
pensaría	pensarían

Imperative

piensa	pensad
piense	

Subjunctive

piense	pensemos
pienses	penséis
piense	piensen

poder
to be able to, can

yo	nosotros/as
tú	vosotros/as
él/ella/usted	ellos/ellas/ustedes

Present

puedo	podemos
puedes	podéis
puede	pueden

Present Progressive

estoy pudiendo	estamos pudiendo
estás pudiendo	estáis pudiendo
está pudiendo	están pudiendo

Preterite

pude	pudimos
pudiste	pudisteis
pudo	pudieron

Imperfect

podía	podíamos
podías	podíais
podía	podían

Future

podré	podremos
podrás	podréis
podrá	podrán

Conditional

podría	podríamos
podrías	podríais
podría	podrían

Imperative

puede	poded
pueda	

Subjunctive

pueda	podamos
puedas	podáis
pueda	puedan

poner
to put

yo	nosotros/as
tú	vosotros/as
él/ella/usted	ellos/ellas/ustedes

Present		Present Progressive	
pongo	ponemos	estoy poniendo	estamos poniendo
pones	ponéis	estás poniendo	estáis poniendo
pone	ponen	está poniendo	están poniendo

Preterite		Imperfect	
puse	pusimos	ponía	poníamos
pusiste	pusisteis	ponías	poníais
puso	pusieron	ponía	ponían

Future		Conditional	
pondré	pondremos	pondría	pondríamos
pondrás	pondréis	pondrías	pondríais
pondrá	pondrían	pondría	pondrían

Imperative		Subjunctive	
		ponga	pongamos
pon	poned	pongas	pongáis
ponga		ponga	pongan

querer
to want

yo	nosotros/as
tú	vosotros/as
él/ella/usted	ellos/ellas/ustedes

Present

quiero	queremos
quieres	queréis
quiere	quieren

Present Progressive

estoy queriendo	estamos queriendo
estás queriendo	estáis queriendo
está queriendo	están queriendo

Preterite

quise	quisimos
quisiste	quisisteis
quiso	quisieron

Imperfect

quería	queríamos
querías	queríais
quería	querían

Future

querré	querremos
querrás	querréis
querrá	querrán

Conditional

querría	querríamos
querrías	querríais
querría	querrían

Imperative

quiere	quered
quiera	

Subjunctive

quiera	queramos
quieras	queráis
quiera	quieran

saber
to know

yo	nosotros/as
tú	vosotros/as
él/ella/usted	ellos/ellas/ustedes

Present

sé	sabemos
sabes	sabéis
sabe	saben

Present Progressive

estoy sabiendo	estamos sabiendo
estás sabiendo	estáis sabiendo
está sabiendo	están sabiendo

Preterite

supe	supimos
supiste	supisteis
supo	supieron

Imperfect

sabía	sabíamos
sabías	sabíais
sabía	sabían

Future

sabré	sabremos
sabrás	sabréis
sabrá	sabrán

Conditional

sabría	sabríamos
sabrías	sabríais
sabría	sabrían

Imperative

sabe	sabed
sepa	

Subjunctive

sepa	sepamos
sepas	sepáis
sepa	sepan

Essential Spanish

salir
to go out

yo	nosotros/as
tú	vosotros/as
él/ella/usted	ellos/ellas/ustedes

Present

salgo	salimos
sales	salís
sale	salen

Present Progressive

estoy saliendo	estamos saliendo
estás saliendo	estáis saliendo
está saliendo	están saliendo

Preterite

salí	salimos
saliste	salisteis
salió	salieron

Imperfect

salía	salíamos
salías	salíais
salía	salían

Future

saldré	saldremos
saldrás	saldréis
saldrá	saldrán

Conditional

saldría	saldríamos
saldrías	saldríais
saldría	saldrían

Imperative

sal	salid
salga	

Subjunctive

salga	salgamos
salgas	salgáis
salga	salgan

ser
to be

yo	nosotros/as
tú	vosotros/as
él/ella/usted	ellos/ellas/ustedes

Present

soy	somos
eres	sois
es	son

Present Progressive

estoy siendo	estamos siendo
estás siendo	estáis siendo
está siendo	están siendo

Preterite

fui	fuimos
fuiste	fuisteis
fue	fueron

Imperfect

era	éramos
eras	erais
era	eran

Future

seré	seremos
serás	seréis
será	serán

Conditional

sería	seríamos
serías	seríais
sería	serían

Imperative

sé	sed
sea	

Subjunctive

sea	seamos
seas	seáis
sea	sean

tener
to have

yo	nosotros/as
tú	vosotros/as
él/ella/usted	ellos/ellas/ustedes

Present		Present Progressive	
tengo	tenemos	estoy teniendo	estamos teniendo
tienes	tenéis	estás teniendo	estáis teniendo
tiene	tienen	está teniendo	están teniendo

Preterite		Imperfect	
tuve	tuvimos	tenía	teníamos
tuviste	tuvisteis	tenías	teníais
tuvo	tuvieron	tenía	tenían

Future		Conditional	
tendré	tendremos	tendría	tendríamos
tendrás	tendréis	tendrías	tendríais
tendrá	tendrán	tendría	tendrían

Imperative		Subjunctive	
		tenga	tengamos
ten	tened	tengas	tengáis
tenga		tenga	tengan

traer
to bring

yo	nosotros/as
tú	vosotros/as
él/ella/usted	ellos/ellas/ustedes

Present		Present Progressive	
traigo	traemos	estoy trayendo	estamos trayendo
traes	traéis	estás trayendo	estáis trayendo
trae	traen	está trayendo	están trayendo

Preterite		Imperfect	
traje	trajimos	traía	traíamos
trajiste	trajisteis	traías	traíais
trajo	trajeron	traía	traían

Future		Conditional	
traeré	traeremos	traería	traeríamos
traerás	traeréis	traerías	traeríais
traerá	traerán	traería	traerían

Imperative		Subjunctive	
		traiga	traigamos
trae	traed	traigas	traigáis
traiga		traiga	traigan

venir
to come

yo	nosotros/as
tú	vosotros/as
él/ella/usted	ellos/ellas/ustedes

Present		Present Progressive	
vengo	venimos	estoy viniendo	estamos viniendo
vienes	venís	estás viniendo	estáis viniendo
viene	vienen	está viniendo	están viniendo

Preterite		Imperfect	
vine	vinimos	venía	veníamos
viniste	vinisteis	venías	veníais
vino	vinieron	venía	venían

Future		Conditional	
vendré	vendremos	vendría	vendríamos
vendrás	vendréis	vendrías	vendríais
vendrá	vendrán	vendría	vendrían

Imperative		Subjunctive	
		venga	vengamos
ven	venid	vengas	vengáis
venga		venga	vengan

ver
to see

yo	nosotros/as
tú	vosotros/as
él/ella/usted	ellos/ellas/ustedes

Present

veo	vemos
ves	veis
ve	ven

Present Progressive

estoy viendo	estamos viendo
estás viendo	estáis viendo
está viendo	están viendo

Preterite

vi	vimos
viste	visteis
vio	vieron

Imperfect

veía	veíamos
veías	veíais
veía	veían

Future

veré	veremos
verás	veréis
verá	verán

Conditional

vería	veríamos
verías	veríais
vería	verían

Imperative

ve	ved
vea	

Subjunctive

vea	veamos
veas	veáis
vea	vean

Essential Spanish

vivir
to live

yo	nosotros/as
tú	vosotros/as
él/ella/usted	ellos/ellas/ustedes

Present		Present Progressive	
vivo	vivimos	estoy viviendo	estamos viviendo
vives	vivís	estás viviendo	estáis viviendo
vive	viven	está viviendo	están viviendo

Preterite		Imperfect	
viví	vivimos	vivía	vivíamos
viviste	vivisteis	vivías	vivíais
vivió	vivieron	vivía	vivían

Future		Conditional	
viviré	viviremos	viviría	viviríamos
vivirás	viviréis	vivirías	viviríais
vivirá	vivirán	viviría	vivirían

Imperative		Subjunctive	
		viva	vivamos
vive	vivid	vivas	viváis
viva		viva	vivan

Glossary

Note that the following abbreviations will be used in this glossary: (m.) = masculine, (f.) = feminine, (sg.) = singular, (pl.) = plural, (fml.) = formal/polite, (infml.) = informal/familiar. If a word has two grammatical genders, (m./f.) or (f./m.) is used.

Spanish-English

A

a *to, at*
  a las cinco *at five (o'clock)*
  ¿A qué hora es? *At what time is it?*
  A ver ... *Let's see ...*
  de ... a ... *from ... through ...*
abdomen (m.) *abdomen*
abogado/abogada (m./f.) *lawyer*
abonado/abonada (m./f.) *subscriber*
  línea (f.) **de abonado digital (DSL)** *DSL*
abrigo (m.) *overcoat*
abril (m.) *April*
abrir *to open*
  abrir la puerta *to open the door*
abrochar *to fasten*
  abrocharse el cinturón de seguridad *to buckle up*
absolutamente *absolutely*
absoluto/absoluta (m./f.) *absolute*
  en absoluto *absolutely not*
absurdo/absurda (m./f.) *absurd*
abuela (f.) *grandmother*
abuelo (m.) *grandfather*
  abuelos (pl.) *grandfathers, grandparents*
aburrido/aburrida (m./f.) *bored, boring*
aburrir *to bore*
aburrirse *to be bored, to get bored*
  Me aburre/aburren ... (sg./pl.) *I'm bored by ...*
acabar *to finish*
  acabar de ... *to have just ... (done something)*
academia (f.) *school, academy*
académico/académica (m./f.) *academic*
accidente (m.) *accident*
aceite (m.) *oil*

aceptar *to accept*
acera (f.) *sidewalk*
aconsejar *to advise*
  aconsejar que ... *to advise that/to ...*
acostarse *to go to bed*
actor (m.) *actor*
actriz (f.) *actress*
actualmente *at the present time*
acuerdo (m.) *agreement*
  De acuerdo. *All right.*
acupuntura (f.) *acupuncture*
además *moreover*
Adiós. *Good-bye.*
adjuntar *to attach*
  adjuntar un documento *to attach a file*
adjunto/adjunta (m./f.) *enclosed*
  documento (m.) **adjunto** *attachment*
adolescente (m.) *adolescent, teenager*
adulto/adulta (m./f.) *adult*
aerolínea (f.) *airline*
aeropuerto (m.) *airport*
afeitar *to shave*
  navaja (f.) **de afeitar** *razor*
afeitarse *to shave (oneself)*
afición (f.) *hobby*
aficionado/aficionada (m./f.) *fan*
afuera *outside*
afueras (f. pl.) *outskirts*
agencia (f.) *agency*
agente (m./f.) *agent*
agitado/agitada (m./f.) *agitated, rough*
agosto (m.) *August*
agradable (m./f.) *pleasant*
agradecer *to be thankful*
  Le agradezco su ayuda. *Thank you for your help.*
agrio/agria (m./f.) *sour*
agua (f.) *water*

agua mineral *mineral water*
el agua *the water*
las aguas *the waters*
aguacate (m.) *avocado*
aguja (f.) *needle*
ahí *there*
ahora *now*
  ahora mismo *right now*
ahorrar *to save*
ahumado/ahumada (m./f.) *smoked*
ajedrez (m.) *chess*
ajustado/ajustada (m./f.) *tight*
al (a + el) *to the* (m.)/*at the* (m.)
albornoz (m.) *robe*
alcalde (m.) *mayor*
alcaldía (f.) *municipal building*
alcoba (f.) *bedroom, room*
aldea (f.) *village*
alegrarse *to be glad*
  alegrarse de que … *to be glad that …*
alegre (m./f.) *happy*
alemán (m.) *German (language)*
alemán/alemana (m./f.) *German*
alergia (f.) *allergy*
alérgico/alérgica (m./f.) *allergic*
alfombra (f.) *carpet*
álgebra (f.) *algebra*
algo *something, somewhat*
  ¿Algo más? *Anything else?*
algodón (m.) *cotton*
alguien *somebody, someone*
  alguien más *somebody else*
algún/alguno/alguna (before m. sg. nouns/
  m. sg./f. sg.) *some, something*
algunos/algunas (m. pl./f. pl.) *some, something*
allí *there*
almorzar *to have lunch*
almuerzo (m.) *lunch*
¿Aló? *Hello? (on the phone)*
alquilar *to rent*
alto (m.) *stop, height*
  ¡Alto! *Stop!*
alto/alta (m./f.) *tall, high*
  tener la tensión alta *to have high blood
    pressure*
alumno/alumna (m./f.) *student*
amanecer (m.) *dawn*
  al amanecer *at dawn*

amar *to love*
amargo/amarga (m./f.) *bitter, sour*
amarillo/amarilla (m./f.) *yellow*
  páginas (f. pl.) amarillas *yellow pages*
americana (f.) *jacket*
americano/americana (m./f.) *American*
amigo/amiga (m./f.) *friend*
amueblado/amueblada (m./f.) *furnished*
anaranjado/anaranjada (m./f.) *orange (color)*
ancho/ancha (m./f.) *wide, baggy*
andar *to walk*
andén (m.) *sidewalk, platform*
  por el andén *on the sidewalk*
anexo (m.) *attachment*
  anexo al correo electrónico *e-mail
    attachment*
angosto/angosta (m./f.) *narrow*
anillo (m.) *ring*
año (m.) *year*
  año pasado *last year*
  año que viene *next year*
  año entrante *next year*
  ¿Cuántos años tiene? *How old are you
    (sg. fml.)/is he/is she?*
  este año *this year*
  los años cincuenta *the fifties*
  segundo año *second year*
  tercer año *third year*
  tener … años *to be … years old*
anoche *last night*
anotar *to record, to write down*
  anotar un gol *to score a goal*
antes *before*
  antes de … *before …*
  lo antes posible *as soon as possible*
antigüedad (f.) *antique*
  tienda (f.) de antigüedades *antique store*
antigüedades (f. pl.) *antiques*
antiguo/antigua (m./f.) *old*
antipático/antipática (m./f.) *unfriendly*
apagar *to turn off*
  apagar las luces *to turn off the lights*
aparador (m.) *cupboard*
apartamento (m.) *apartment*
apetito (m.) *appetite*
apostar *to bet*
  apuesto a que … *to bet that …*
aprender *to learn*

aprender a … *to learn how to …*
Estoy aprendiendo español. *I'm learning Spanish.*
aprobar *to pass*
 aprobar un curso *to pass a course*
 aprobar un examen *to pass a test*
apuesta (f.) *bet*
apuro (m.) *difficult situation*
aquel/aquella (m. sg./f. sg.) *that (far from the speaker and the listener)*
aquél/aquélla (m. sg./f. sg.) *that (one) over there (far from the speaker and the listener)*
aquello (neuter) *that (one, thing) over there (far from the speaker and the listener)*
aquellos/aquellas (m. pl./f. pl.) *those (far from the speaker and the listener)*
aquéllos/aquéllas (m. pl./f. pl.) *those (ones) over there (far from the speaker and the listener)*
aquí *here*
 Aquí está … *Here is …*
 Aquí tiene. *Here you are.*
árbol (m.) *tree*
archivo (m.) *file*
área (m.) *area*
arena (f.) *sand*
Argentina (f.) *Argentina*
argentino/argentina (m./f.) *Argentinian*
armario (m.) *closet, filing cabinet*
arquitecto/arquitecta (m./f.) *architect*
arquitectura (f.) *architecture*
arroz (m.) *rice*
arte (m.) *art*
artesanía (f.) *craft*
artista (m./f.) *artist*
asar *to grill*
 bien asada *well-done*
así *so*
 Así es. *That's right.*
 Así que … *So …*
 por así decir *so to speak*
asignatura (f.) *subject, course*
asistente (m./f.) *assistant*
asistir *to attend, to be present*
astronauta (m./f.) *astronaut*
atardecer (m.) *dusk*
 al atardecer *at dusk*
atención (f.) *attention*
atender *to attend to, to serve, to take care of*

atentamente *carefully*
atleta (m./f.) *athlete*
atlético/atlética (m./f.) *athletic*
atracción (f.) *attraction*
atractivo/atractiva (m./f.) *attractive*
atrás *behind, back*
atún (m.) *tuna*
audífonos (m. pl.) *headphones*
aula (m.) *classroom*
auto (m.) *car*
autobús (m.) *bus*
 recorrido (m.) **por autobús** *tour bus*
automático/automática (m./f.) *automatic*
 contestador (m.) **automático** *answering machine*
automóvil (m.) *car*
autopista (f.) *highway, freeway*
autor/autora (m./f. less common) *author*
autovía (f.) *highway, freeway*
avenida (f.) *avenue*
aventura (f.) *adventure*
 películas (pl.) **de aventuras** *adventure films*
avión (m.) *airplane*
ayer *yesterday*
ayuda (f.) *help*
 Le agradezco su ayuda. *Thank you for your help.*
ayudar *to help*
 ¿Puede ayudarme? *Can you help me?*
ayuntamiento (m.) *city hall*
azúcar (m.) *sugar*
azul (m.) **claro** *the color light blue*
azul (m./f.) *blue*
 azul claro *light blue*
 azul marino *navy blue*
 azul oscuro *dark blue*
 ser de sangre azul *to have blue blood (lit., to be of blue blood)*

B

bailar *to dance*
baile (m.) *dancing*
bajar *to lower, to download*
bajo *under, below*
bajo/baja (m./f.) *short*
 tener la tensión baja *to have low blood pressure*
balcón (m.) *balcony*

balón (m.) *ball*
baloncesto (m.) *basketball*
bañador (m.) *bathing trunks*
banana (f.) *banana*
bañarse *to take a bath, to bathe*
banco (m.) *bank*
banda (f.) *band*
bañera (f.) *bathtub*
baño (m.) *bathroom*
   traje (m.) **de baño** *bathing suit*
banquero/banquera (m./f.) *banker*
bar (m.) *bar*
barato/barata (m./f.) *cheap*
barbería (f.) *barbershop*
barbilla (f.) *chin*
barrio (m.) *neighborhood*
base (f.) *base*
bastante *quite, enough, quite a lot*
bata (f.) *robe*
batidora (f.) *blender*
bebé (m./f.) *baby*
beber *to drink*
bebida (f.) *drink*
bebito/bebita (m./f.) *little baby*
beca (f.) *scholarship*
béisbol (m.) *baseball*
   partido (m.) **de béisbol** *baseball game*
beneficio (m.) *benefit*
besar *to kiss*
biblioteca (f.) *library*
bicicleta (f.) *bicycle*
bien *well*
   Estoy bien. *I'm fine.*
   Que esté bien. *May you be well.*
   Que estés bien. *Take care.*
   ¡Qué bien! *How nice!*
Bienvenido./Bienvenida. (m./f.) *Welcome.* (to a man/to a woman)
billar (m.) *pool, billiards*
billete (m.) *ticket*
biología (f.) *biology*
blanco/blanca (m./f.) *white*
   ir de punta en blanco *to be dressed to the nines* (lit., *to go from the tip in white*)
   vino (m.) **blanco** *white wine*
bloquear *to block*
blusa (f.) *blouse*
bobo/boba (m./f.) *fool, idiot*

boca (f.) *mouth*
boleto (m.) *ticket*
bolígrafo (m.) *pen*
Bolivia (f.) *Bolivia*
boliviano/boliviana (m./f.) *Bolivian*
bolsa (f.) *bag, sack*
bolso (m.) *handbag*
bombachas (f. pl.) *women's underwear*
bonito/bonita (m./f.) *nice, pretty*
bordo (m.) *board*
   a bordo *on board*
   Bienvenidos a bordo. *Welcome aboard.*
borracho/borracha (m./f.) *drunk*
borrar *to erase*
bosque (m.) *forest*
bote (m.) *carton*
botella (f.) *bottle*
botiquín (m.) *medicine cabinet*
bragas (f. pl.) *women's underwear*
Brasil (m.) *Brazil*
brasileño/brasileña (m./f.) *Brazilian* (noun)
brasilero/brasilera (m./f.) *Brazilian* (adjective)
brazo (m.) *arm*
brote (m.) *rash*
buceo (m.) *diving*
buen/bueno/buena (before m. sg. nouns/ m./f.) *good*
   Buenas noches. *Good evening./Good night.*
   Buenas tardes. *Good afternoon.*
   Buenos días. *Good morning.*
   ¡Buen provecho! *Enjoy the meal!*
   ¡Buen trabajo! *Good job!*
   El tiempo es bueno. *The weather is good.*
   Es bueno que … *It's good that …*
   Hace muy buen tiempo. *It's beautiful.*
   Nochebuena (f.) *Christmas Eve*
bufanda (f.) *scarf*
buscar *to look for, to pick up*
buzón (m.) *mailbox*
   buzón de voz *voice mail*

C

caballero (m.) *gentleman*
caballo (m.) *horse*
cabecera (f.) *head*
   pediatra (m./f.) **de cabecera** *regular pediatrician*
cabeza (f.) *head*

pararse de cabeza *to go crazy, to go out of one's mind*
   perder la cabeza *to lose one's head*
   tener dolor de cabeza *to have a headache*
   tener la cabeza fría *to keep a cool head*
cabina (f.) *booth, cabin*
   cabina telefónica *telephone booth*
cable (m.) *cable*
cada (m./f.) *each, every*
cadera (f.) *hip*
caer *to fall*
café (m.) *coffee*
café (m./f.) *coffee-colored*
cafetera (f.) *coffeemaker*
cafetería (f.) *café, coffee shop, cafeteria, diner*
caja (f.) *cash register, box*
cajetilla (f.) *packet*
   cajetilla de cigarrillos *pack of cigarettes*
cajón (m.) *drawer*
calcetines (m. pl.) *socks*
caliente (m./f.) *hot*
calificaciones (f. pl.) *grades*
calle (f.) *street*
   luz (f.) **de la calle** *streetlight*
callejón (m.) *alley*
calor (m.) *heat*
   Hace calor. *It's hot.*
   tener calor *to be hot, to be warm*
calvo/calva (m./f.) *bald*
calzar *to wear (shoes)*
   ¿Qué número calza? *What shoe size do you wear?*
calzoncillos (m. pl.) *men's underpants*
calzoncitos (m. pl.) *women's underwear*
calzones (m. pl.) *men's undergarments*
cama (f.) *bed*
cámara (f.) *camera*
camarera (f.) *waitress*
camarero (m.) *waiter*
camarón (m.) *shrimp*
cambiar *to change, to exchange*
cambio (m.) *change*
caminar *to walk*
camino (m.) *way, path*
camisa (f.) *shirt*
camiseta (f.) *T-shirt, undershirt*
camisilla (f.) *undershirt*
campeón/campeona (m./f.) *champion*

campeonato (m.) *championship*
camping (m.) *camping*
   ir de camping *to go camping*
campo (m.) *field, camp*
Canadá (m.) *Canada*
canadiense (m./f.) *Canadian*
canal (m.) *channel*
cancelar *to cancel*
canción (f.) *song*
candidato/candidata (m./f.) *candidate*
cansado/cansada (m./f.) *tired*
cansancio (m.) *fatigue*
   tener cansancio *to be tired*
cantante (m./f.) *singer*
cantar *to sing*
capacidad (f.) *capacity*
cara (f.) *face*
   dar la cara *to face the circumstances*
   ser caradura *to be shameless*
carbón (m.) *coal*
cárcel (f.) *prison*
carnaval (m.) *carnival*
carne (f.) *meat, beef*
   carne de cerdo (f.) *pork*
carnicería (f.) *butcher shop*
caro/cara (m./f.) *expensive*
carpeta (f.) *file*
carpintero/carpintera (m./f.) *carpenter*
carpio (m.) *carpus*
   síndrome (m.) **del túnel del carpio** *carpal tunnel syndrome*
carrera (f.) *major, university course*
carretera (f.) *highway, freeway*
carril (m.) *lane*
   Siga por el carril de la derecha. *Stay in the right lane.*
carro (m.) *car*
carta (f.) *menu, letter*
   cartas (f. pl.) *playing cards*
cartelera (f.) *billboard, list of plays*
   cartelera de cine *movie listing*
cartera (f.) *wallet, handbag*
cartón (m.) *carton, cardboard*
casa (f.) *house*
casado/casada (m./f.) *married*
casarse *to get married*
   casarse con *to marry (someone)*
casi *almost*

casi nunca *seldom, almost never*
caso (m.) *case*
casualidad (f.) *chance, coincidence*
  por casualidad *by chance*
catedral (f.) *cathedral*
catorce *fourteen*
caza (f.) *hunting*
CD (m.) *CD*
  CD rom (m.) *CD-ROM*
  lector (m.) de CD *CD player*
  lector (m.) de CD rom *CD-ROM drive*
cebolla (f.) *onion*
ceja (f.) *eyebrow*
celeste (m./f.) *sky blue*
celoso/celosa (m./f.) *jealous*
celular (m.) *cell phone*
cena (f.) *dinner*
cenar *to eat dinner*
centralita (f.) *switchboard*
centro (m.) *center*
  centro comercial *shopping mall*
  centro de información *information center*
cerca *close, near*
  cerca de ... *close to/near ...*
cerdo (m.) *pork*
  carne (f.) de cerdo *pork*
cerdo/cerda (m./f.) *pig*
  carne (f.) de cerdo *pork*
cerebro (m.) *brain*
cero *zero*
cerrar *to close*
cerro (m.) *hill*
cerveza (f.) *beer*
cesar *to stop*
  cesar de ... *to stop ... (doing something)*
césped (m.) *lawn, grass*
champaña (m.) *champagne*
champú (m.) *shampoo*
chanchito/chanchita (m./f.) *piglet*
Chao. *Bye.*
chaqueta (f.) *jacket*
charcutería (f.) *delicatessen*
charla (f.) *chat*
  espacio (m.) para charla *chat room*
chat (m.) *chat room*
che *hey (filler word, Argentina)*
cheque (m.) *check*
chica (f.) *girl*

chico (m.) *boy*
Chile (m.) *Chile*
chileno/chilena (m./f.) *Chilean*
chinelas (f. pl.) *slippers*
chino (m.) *Chinese (language)*
chiste (m.) *joke*
  contar un chiste verde *to tell an obscene joke*
    (lit., to tell a green joke)
chocolate (m.) *chocolate*
chuleta (f.) *chop*
  chuleta de cordero *lamb chop*
ciclismo (m.) *biking, cycling*
cielo (m.) *sky*
cien/ciento (before a noun/before a number except
  mil) *one hundred*
  cien personas *one hundred people*
  cien por ciento *one hundred percent*
  ciento tres dólares *one hundred and three*
    dollars
  por ciento *percent*
ciencia (f.) *science*
cierto/cierta (m./f.) *true*
  No es cierto que ... *It is not true that ...*
cigarrillo (m.) *cigarette*
  cajetilla (f.) de cigarrillos *pack of cigarettes*
cinco *five*
  a las cinco *at five (o'clock)*
  cuarenta y cinco *forty-five*
cincuenta *fifty*
cine (m.) *movie*
cinturón (m.) *belt*
  abrocharse el cinturón de seguridad *to*
    buckle up
circo (m.) *circus*
cita (f.) *appointment*
ciudad (f.) *city, town*
claramente *clearly*
claro *clearly*
  ¡Claro que sí! *Of course!*
  Sí, claro. *Yes, of course.*
claro/clara (m./f.) *light*
  azul (m./f.) claro *light blue*
clase (f.) *class, kind*
  toda clase *all kinds*
clásico/clásica (m./f.) *classic*
  música (f.) clásica *classical music*
cliente (m./f.) *customer*
clínica (f.) *clinic*

farmacia (f.) **clínica** *clinical pharmacy*
club (m.) *club*
coca (f.) *coca*
coche (m.) *car*
cocina (f.) *kitchen, stove, cooking*
cocinar *to cook*
código (m.) *code*
codo (m.) *elbow*
coger *to catch, to pick up, to take*
  coger fuerzas (f. pl.) *to regain strength*
  coger un examen *to take a test*
coincidencia (f.) *coincidence*
  ¡Qué coincidencia! *What a coincidence!*
cola (f.) *tail, line*
  hacer una cola *to stand in line*
colección (f.) *collection*
coleccionar *to collect*
colega/colega (m./f.) *colleague*
colegio (m.) *elementary/secondary school*
colgar *to hang*
  colgar el teléfono *to hang up the phone*
colina (f.) *hill*
collar (m.) *necklace*
Colombia (f.) *Colombia*
colombiano/colombiana (m./f.) *Colombian*
colonia (f.) *cologne*
color (m.) *color*
  ¿De qué color es … ? *What color is … ?*
  ver todo color de rosa *to be an optimist, to wear rose colored glasses*
colorado/colorada (m./f.) *red*
  ponerse colorado *to be embarrassed (lit., to turn red)*
columna (f.) *column*
  columna vertebral *backbone, spinal column*
coma (f.) *comma*
combinar *to combine, to match*
  combinar con … *to go with …*
comedia (f.) *comedy*
comedor (m.) *dining room*
comenzar *to start, to begin*
  comenzar a … *to start … (doing something)*
comer *to eat*
comercial (m./f.) *commercial*
  centro (m.) **comercial** *shopping mall*
comida (f.) *food, dinner*
como *as, like*
  como ya sabes *as you already know*

cómo *how* (question)
  ¿Cómo? *What?/Pardon me?*
  ¿Cómo estás (tú)? *How are you?* (infml.)
  ¿Cómo estás de tiempo? *Do you have time?/ How are you doing for time?*
  ¿Cómo está usted? *How are you?* (fml.)
  ¿Cómo se llama usted? *What's your name?* (fml.)
  ¿Cómo te llamas? *What's your name?* (infml.)
  ¿Cómo te trata la vida? *How's life treating you?*
  ¿Cómo va todo? *How is everything going?*
  ¿Sabe cómo … ? *Do you know how to … ?*
cómodo/cómoda (m./f.) *comfortable*
compañía (f.) *company*
completamente *completely*
completar *to complete*
completo/completa (m./f.) *full*
  a tiempo completo *full-time*
compra (f.) *purchase*
  ir de compras *to go shopping*
comprar *to buy, to shop*
  comprar en rebaja *to buy on sale*
comprender *to understand*
computadora (f.) *computer*
comunicar *to communicate*
  Está comunicando. *The line is busy.*
con *with, to*
concierto (m.) *concert*
condimentado/condimentada (m./f.) *spicy*
conducir *to drive*
conectar *to connect*
conexión (f.) *connection*
conferencia (f.) *conference, meeting, lecture*
  sala (f.) **de conferencias** *meeting room*
conjunto (m.) *band (music)*
conocer *to know (people, places), to meet*
  conocer de vista *to know by sight*
  conocer palmo a palmo *to know like the back of one's hand*
  dar a conocer *to make known*
  Gusto en conocerlo/la. *Pleased to meet you.* (to a man/to a woman)
consultar *to look up, to consult*
consultorio (m.) *office*
  consultorio del médico *doctor's office*
contable (m./f.) *accountant*
contar *to count, to tell*

contar un chiste verde *to tell an obscene joke (lit., to tell a green joke)*
contento/contenta (m./f.) *happy*
contestador (m.) (automático) *answering machine*
contestar *to reply to, to answer*
  contestar el teléfono *to answer the phone*
contigo *with you*
continuar *to continue*
  Continúa recto. *Continue straight.*
contra *against*
contrato (m.) *contract*
contribución (f.) *contribution*
copa (f.) *wineglass*
  copa de vino *glass of wine*
copia (f.) *copy*
copiar *to copy*
corazón (m.) *heart*
corbata (f.) *tie*
cordero/cordera (m./f.) *lamb*
  chuleta (f.) de cordero *lamb chop*
coro (m.) *choir*
correo (m.) *post office*
  correo electrónico (correo-e) *e-mail*
  dirección (f.) de correo electrónico *e-mail address*
correr *to run*
cortado/cortada (m./f.) *sour*
cortina (f.) *curtain*
corto/corta (m./f.) *short*
cosa (f.) *thing*
  ¿Cómo van las cosas? *How are things?*
cosquilleo (m.) *tingling feeling*
costar *to cost*
  ¿Cuánto cuesta? *How much does it cost?*
costoso/costosa (m./f.) *expensive*
costura (f.) *sewing*
crédito (m.) *loan, credit*
  tarjeta (f.) de crédito *credit card*
creer *to believe, to think*
  Creo que sí. *I think so.*
  no creer que … *not to believe that …*
  ¿No crees? *Don't you think?*
crema (f.) *creme*
  crema de afeitar *shaving cream*
crío/cría (m./f.) *kid*
cruce (m.) *intersection*
cruzar *to cross*

cuaderno (m.) *notebook*
cuadra (f.) *block*
  Está a dos cuadras de aquí. *It's two blocks from here.*
cuadro (m.) *painting, picture, square*
  a cuadros *plaid*
cual/cuales (sg./pl.) *which* (relative pronoun), *as*
cuál/cuáles (sg./pl.) *which, what* (question)
cualificación (f.) *qualification, skill*
cualificado/cualificada (m./f.) *qualified*
cualquier *any*
cuando *when* (relative adverb)
cuándo *when* (question)
cuanto/cuanta/cuantos/cuantas (m. sg./f. sg./m. pl./f. pl.) *as much, as many*
  en cuanto a … *regarding …*
cuánto/cuánta/cuántos/cuántas (m. sg./f. sg./m. pl./f. pl.) *how much, how many*
  ¿Cuántos años tiene? *How old are you* (sg. fml.)*/is he/is she?*
  ¿Cuánto cuesta? *How much does it cost?*
  ¿Cuánto es? *How much is it?*
cuarenta *forty*
  cuarenta y cinco *forty-five*
cuarto (m.) *quarter, room, bedroom*
  a las seis menos cuarto *at a quarter to six*
  a las seis y cuarto *at a quarter past six*
  término (m.) tres cuartos *medium (cooked meat)*
cuatro *four*
cuatrocientos/cuatrocientas (m./f.) *four hundred*
cuchara (f.) *spoon*
cuchillo (m.) *knife*
cuello (m.) *neck*
cuenco (m.) *bowl*
cuenta (f.) *bill, check, account*
  tener en cuenta *to take into account*
  pagar la cuenta *to check out*
cuero (m.) *leather*
cuerpo (m.) *body*
  cuerpo humano *human body*
cuestionario (m.) *questionnaire*
cuñada (f.) *sister-in-law*
cuñado (m.) *brother-in-law*
currículum (m.) *curriculum*
  currículum vítae *résumé, CV*
curso (m.) *course*

cuyo/cuya/cuyos/cuyas (m. sg./f. sg./m. pl./f. pl.) *whose, of which* (relative pronoun)

D

dar *to give, to show*
  dar a conocer *to make known*
  dar a luz *to give birth*
  dar con *to find (something)*
  dar de narices *to fall flat on one's face*
  dar la cara *to face the circumstances*
  dar la hora *to tell time*
  dar la mano *to shake hands*
  dar la vuelta *to turn around*
  dar (las) gracias *to give thanks*
de *of, from, about*
  de … a … *from … through …*
  ¿De dónde eres? *Where are you from?*
  de la madrugada *in the early morning (before daybreak)*
  de la mañana *in the morning*
  de la noche *in the evening, at night*
  de la tarde *in the afternoon*
  De nada. *You're welcome.*
  ¿De qué color es …? *What color is …?*
debajo *underneath*
  debajo de … *underneath …*
deber *must, to owe*
débil (m./f.) *weak*
década (f.) *decade*
decidir *to decide*
decir *to tell, to say*
  ¿Cómo se dice "…" en …? *How do you say "…" in …?*
  ¿Díga(me)? *Hello? (on the phone)*
  No me digas. *Really?*
  por así decir *so to speak*
  ¿Qué quiere decir eso? *What does that mean?*
decisión (f.) *decision*
dedicar *to dedicate*
dedo (m.) *finger*
  dedo del pie *toe*
dejar *to leave*
  dejar un mensaje después de oír la señal *to leave a message after the tone*
del (de + el) *of the* (m.), *from the* (m.), *about the* (m.)
delante *in front*
  delante de … *in front of …*
delgado/delgada (m./f.) *thin*

delicioso/deliciosa (m./f.) *delicious*
delito (m.) *crime*
demasiado/demasiada (m./f.) *too much, too many*
dentista (m./f.) *dentist*
dentro *inside*
  dentro de … *inside of …*
departamento (m.) *department*
  tienda (f.) por departamentos *department store*
depender *to depend*
  depender de … *to depend on …*
dependiente/dependienta (m./f.) *store clerk*
deporte (m.) *sport*
deportista (m./f.) *person who plays sports*
deportivo/deportiva (m./f.) *athletic*
  zapatillas (f. pl.) deportivas *sneakers, tennis shoes*
derecha (f.) *right side*
  a la derecha *on the right*
  Gira a la derecha. *Turn right.*
derecho *straight*
  Siga derecho. *Go straight.*
derecho (m.) *law, right, duty*
  derechos (pl.) de matrícula *tuition*
derecho/derecha (m./f.) *right-side*
  a mano derecha *on the right-hand side*
desafortunadamente *unfortunately*
desagradable (m./f.) *unpleasant*
desarrollar *to develop*
desastre (m.) *disaster*
desayuno (m.) *breakfast*
descansar *to rest*
desconocer *not to know*
descremado/descremada (m./f.) *skimmed*
  leche (f.) descremada *skim milk*
describir *to describe*
descripción (f.) *description*
descuento (m.) *discount*
  hacer un descuento *to give a discount*
  treinta por ciento de descuento *thirty percent off*
desde *since, from*
desear *to want, to wish*
  desear que … *to wish that …*
  ¿Qué desea? *What would you like?*
desgracia (f.) *misfortune*
  por desgracia *unfortunately*

deshabillé (m.) *robe*
desierto (m.) *desert*
desodorante (m.) *deodorant*
despacho (m.) *office*
despacio *slowly*
  Hable más despacio, por favor. *Speak more slowly, please.*
despedirse *to say good-bye*
despertarse *to wake up, to get up*
después *afterwards*
  después de … *after …*
detalle (m.) *detail*
detergente (m.) *detergent*
  detergente de ropa *laundry detergent*
  detergente de vajilla *dishwashing detergent*
detestar *to detest*
detrás *behind*
  detrás de … *behind …*
día (m.) *day*
  Buenos días. *Good morning.*
  día festivo *holiday*
  dos días a la semana *twice a week*
  este día *this day*
  hoy en día *nowadays*
  Que tenga un buen día. *Have a nice day.*
  todo el día *all day*
  todos los días *every day*
diario (m.) *diary*
  llevar un diario *to keep a diary*
diario/diaria (m./f.) *daily*
diarrea (f.) *diarrhea*
diciembre (m.) *December*
diecinueve *nineteen*
dieciocho *eighteen*
dieciséis *sixteen*
diecisiete *seventeen*
diente (m.) *tooth*
diez *ten*
  a las ocho y diez *at eight ten (8:10)*
  diez mil *ten thousand*
  diez y seis *sixteen*
  diez y siete *seventeen*
  diez y ocho *eighteen*
  diez y nueve *nineteen*
diferencia (f.) *difference*
diferente (m./f.) *different*
difícil (m./f.) *difficult*
digital (m./f.) *digital*

línea (f.) de suscriptor/abonado digital (DSL) *DSL*
diligentemente *diligently*
dinero (m.) *money*
Dios (m.) *God*
  ¡Por Dios! *For God's sake!*
diploma (m.) *diploma*
dirección (f.) *address, direction*
  dirección de correo electrónico *e-mail address*
dirigir *to direct*
disco (m.) *disk, record*
  disco de vinilo *vinyl record, LP*
disculpa (f.) *excuse, apology*
disculpar *to excuse*
  Disculpa./Disculpe. *Excuse me.* (infml./fml.)
discutir *to discuss*
diseño (m.) *design*
Disneylandia *Disneyland*
disponible (m./f.) *available*
diversión (f.) *amusement*
  parque (m.) de diversiones *amusement park*
divertido/divertida (m./f.) *fun*
divertirse *to have fun*
divorciado/divorciada (m./f.) *divorced*
divorciarse *to get a divorce*
  divorciarse de … *to divorce (someone)*
doblar *to turn*
doce *twelve*
doctor/doctora (m./f.) *doctor*
documental (m.) *documentary*
documento (m.) *document, file*
  documento adjunto *attachment*
dólar (m.) *dollar*
dolor (m.) *pain*
  tener dolor de cabeza *to have a headache*
  tener dolor de garganta *to have a sore throat*
dominar *to dominate, to master*
  Domino el francés. *I speak French fluently.*
domingo (m.) *Sunday*
don (m.) *Mr.*
doña (f.) *Mrs.*
donde *where* (relative adverb)
dónde *where* (question)
  ¿De dónde eres? *Where are you from?*
dorado/dorada (m./f.) *gold (color)*
dormir *to sleep*
dormitorio (m.) *bedroom*

dos *two*
  dos días a la semana *twice a week*
doscientos/doscientas (m./f.) *two hundred*
dotado/dotada (m./f.) *talented*
drama (m.) *drama*
dramático/dramática (m./f.) *dramatic*
  obra (f.) **dramática** *drama*
ducha (f.) *shower*
ducharse *to take a shower/bath*
dudar *to doubt*
  dudar que ... *to doubt that ...*
dulce (m.) *sweet, pastry*
dulce (m./f.) *sweet*
durante *during*
duro/dura (m./f.) *hard*
  ser caradura *to be shameless*
DVD (m.) *DVD*
  lector (m.) **de DVD** *DVD player*

E

economía (f.) *economics*
económico/económica (m./f.) *economical, low-cost*
  precio (m.) **económico** *reasonable price*
Ecuador (m.) *Ecuador*
ecuatoriano/ecuatoriana (m./f.) *Ecuadorian*
edad (f.) *age*
edificio (m.) *building*
efectivamente *actually*
efectivo (m.) *cash*
  pagar en efectivo *to pay cash*
eficientemente *efficiently*
ejercicio (m.) *exercise*
el *the* (m. sg.)
  el de ella *hers*
  el de ellas *theirs* (f. pl.)
  el de ellos *theirs* (m. pl./mixed group)
  el de él *his*
  el de usted *yours* (sg. fml.)
  el de ustedes *yours* (pl.)
él *he*
  el de él (m. sg.) *his*
  la de él (f. sg.) *his*
eléctrico/eléctrica (m./f.) *electric, electrical*
electricista/electricista (m./f.) *electrician*
electrodoméstico (m.) *electrical appliance*
  tienda (f.) **de electrodomésticos** *electronics store*

electrónico/electrónica (m./f.) *electronic*
  correo (m.) **electrónico** *e-mail*
  dirección (f.) **de correo electrónico** *e-mail address*
elefante (m.) *elephant*
elegante (m./f.) *elegant*
elegir *to choose*
eliminar *to delete, to eliminate*
ella *she*
  el de ella (m. sg.) *hers*
  la de ella (f. sg.) *hers*
ellas *they* (f. pl.)
  el de ellas (m. sg.) *theirs* (f. pl.)
  la de ellas (f. sg.) *theirs* (f. pl.)
ellos *they* (m. pl./mixed group)
  el de ellos (m. sg.) *theirs* (m. pl./mixed group)
  la de ellos (m. sg.) *theirs* (m. pl./mixed group)
embarazada (f.) *pregnant*
embotellamiento (m.) *traffic jam*
emocionante (m./f.) *exciting*
empatado/empatada (m./f.) *tied*
  quedar empatados *to be tied*
empatar *to draw, to tie*
empezar *to begin*
empleado/empleada (m./f.) *employee*
empleo (m.) *job, employment*
en *in, at, by (means), on*
enamorado/enamorada (m./f.) *in love*
encantar *to enchant*
  Encantado./Encantada. *Pleased to meet you.* (said by a man/said by a woman)
  Me encanta/encantan ... (sg./pl.) *I really like ...*
  ¡Me encantaría! *I'd love to!*
encanto (m.) *charm*
encima *above*
  encima de ... *above ...*
  y encima ... *and on top of that ...*
encontrar *to meet up with, to find*
  encontrarse con ... *to meet ... (somebody)*
enero (m.) *January*
enfadarse *to get angry*
  enfadarse de que ... *to be angry that ...*
enfermedad (f.) *illness, disease*
enfermo/enferma (m./f.) *sick*
enfrente *opposite*
  enfrente de ... *across from ... , in front of ...*
enhorabuena (f.) *congratulations*

enorme (m./f.) *huge*
ensalada (f.) *salad*
entender *to understand*
enterizo/enteriza (m./f.) *one-piece*
entero/entera (m./f.) *whole*
  leche (f.) entera *whole milk*
entonces *then*
  Hasta entonces. *Until then.*
entrada (f.) *entrance, ticket, appetizer*
entrante (m./f.) *coming*
  mes (m.) entrante *next month*
entrar *to enter*
entre *between*
  entre ... y ... *between ... and ...*
entregar *to submit*
entrenador/entrenadora (m./f.) *coach*
entretenimiento (m.) *entertainment*
entrevista (f.) *interview*
  programa (m.) de entrevistas *talk show*
entrevistar *to interview*
enviar *to send*
equipo (m.) *team*
equitación (f.) *horseback riding*
equivocado/equivocada (m./f.) *wrong*
  número (m.) equivocado *wrong number*
escaleras (f. pl.) *stairs*
escaparate (m.) *display window*
  ir de escaparates *to go window-shopping*
escoba (f.) *broom*
escoger *to choose*
escondidas (f. pl.) *hide-and-seek*
escotado/escotada (m./f.) *low-cut*
escribir *to write*
escritor/escritora (m./f.) *writer*
escritorio (m.) *desk, study*
escuchar *to listen to*
escuela (f.) *school*
escultura (f.) *sculpture*
ese/esa (m. sg./f. sg.) *that (near the listener)*
ése/ésa (m. sg./f. sg.) *that (one) (near the listener)*
eso (neuter) *that (one, thing) (near the listener)*
  a eso de *about, around*
  a eso de las nueve *at about nine o'clock*
  por eso *for this reason*
esos/esas (m. pl./f. pl.) *those (near the listener)*
ésos/ésas (m. pl./f. pl.) *those (ones) (near the listener)*
espacio (m.) *space*

espacio para charla *chat room*
espalda (f.) *back*
España (f.) *Spain*
español (m.) *Spanish (language)*
  Estoy aprendiendo español. *I'm learning Spanish.*
  Hablo un poco de español. *I speak a little Spanish.*
español/española (m./f.) *Spanish*
espantoso/espantosa (m./f.) *scary*
especialidad (f.) *specialty, major*
especialización (f.) *specialization, master's degree*
especializarse *to specialize*
  especializarse en ... *to major in ...*
espectador/espectadora (m./f.) *spectator*
espejo (m.) *mirror*
espera (f.) *wait*
  poner en espera *to put on hold*
esperar *to hope, to wait*
  esperar que ... *to hope that ...*
  Espere, por favor. *Hold on, please.*
  ¡Yo espero que sí! *I hope so!*
espeso/espesa (m./f.) *thick*
espía (m./f.) *spy*
esposa (f.) *wife*
esposo (m.) *husband*
esquiar *to ski*
esquina (f.) *corner*
  a la vuelta de la esquina *around the corner*
estación (f.) *station*
  estación de ferrocarril *train station*
  estación de tren *train station*
estación (f.) *season*
estadio (m.) *stadium*
estado (m.) *state*
  los Estados Unidos *the United States*
estadounidense (m./f.) *American*
estampado/estampada (m./f.) *with a pattern, patterned*
estampilla (f.) *postage stamp*
estanque (m.) *pond*
estante (m.) *shelf, bookshelf*
estar *to be*
  Aquí está ... *Here is ...*
  ¿Cómo estás (tú)? *How are you?* (infml.)
  ¿Cómo estás de tiempo? *Do you have time?/ How are you doing for time?*

¿Cómo está usted? *How are you?* (fml.)
Está granizando. *It's hailing.*
Está lloviendo. *It's raining.*
Está nevando. *It's snowing.*
Está nublado. *It's cloudy.*
estar en buenas manos *to be in good hands*
estar mal *to be not doing well*
Estoy aprendiendo español. *I'm learning Spanish.*
Estoy bien. *I'm fine.*
No está mal. *It's not bad.*
Que esté bien. *May you be well.*
Que estés bien. *Take care.*
este (m.) *east*
este/esta (m. sg./f. sg.) *this (near the speaker)*
  esta noche (f.) *this evening, tonight*
éste/ésta (m. sg./f. sg.) *this (one) (near the speaker)*
estilo (m.) *style*
esto (neuter) *this (one, thing) (near the speaker)*
estómago (m.) *stomach*
  tener mal de estómago *to have an upset stomach*
estos/estas (m. pl./f. pl.) *these (near the speaker)*
éstos/éstas (m. pl./f. pl.) *these (ones) (near the speaker)*
estrecho/estrecha (m./f.) *narrow*
estrella (f.) *star*
estrenar *to use for the first time*
estresante (m./f.) *stressing, stressful*
estudiante/estudiante (m./f.) *student*
estudiar *to study*
estudio (m.) *study, office*
  estudios (pl.) *studies*
estupendo/estupenda (m./f.) *fine, wonderful, marvelous*
  ¡Estupendo! *Great!*
etiqueta (f.) *tag, label*
  etiqueta con el precio *price tag*
ex *ex-*
exacto/exacta (m./f.) *exact*
  Exacto. *Exactly.*
examen (m.) *test*
  aprobar un examen *to pass a test*
  hacer un examen, presentarse a un examen *to take a test*
  hacerse un examen de sangre *to take a blood test*

suspender un examen *to fail a test*
exceder *to exceed*
excelente (m./f.) *excellent*
excepción (f.) *exception*
excursionismo (m.) *hiking*
  hacer excursionismo *to go hiking*
exigente (m./f.) *demanding*
exigir *to demand*
éxito (m.) *success*
experiencia (f.) *experience*
explicación (f.) *explanation*
exterior (m.) *outside*
extra (m./f.) *extra*
  horas (f. pl.) extras *extra hours, overtime*
extranjero/extranjera (m./f.) *foreign, foreigner*
extraño/extraña (m./f.) *strange*
  persona (f.) extraña *strange person*
extraordinario/extraordinaria (m./f.) *extraordinary*
extrovertido/extrovertida (m./f.) *extroverted*

F

fábrica (f.) *factory*
fácil (m./f.) *easy*
fácilmente *easily*
facultad (f.) *department (at college/university)*
falda (f.) *skirt*
faltar *to miss, to be lacking, to be necessary*
fama (f.) *fame*
familia (f.) *family*
familiar (m./f.) *(of) family, familiar*
famoso/famosa (m./f.) *famous*
fantástico/fantástica (m./f.) *fantastic*
farmacéutico/farmacéutico (m./f.) *pharmacist*
farmacia (f.) *drugstore, pharmacy*
  farmacia clínica *clinical pharmacy*
farola (f.) *lamppost*
favor (m.) *favor*
  Hágame el favor de … *Do me the favor of …*
  Por favor. *Please.*
favorito/favorita (m./f.) *favorite*
fax (m.) *fax machine*
febrero (m.) *February*
fecha (f.) *date*
felicitar *to congratulate*
  ¡Felicitaciones! *Congratulations!*
feliz (m./f.) *happy*
felizmente *happily*

feo/fea (m./f.) *ugly*
ferrocarril (m.) *railroad, train*
  estación (f.) de ferrocarril *train station*
festivo/festiva (m./f.) *festive*
  día (m.) festivo *holiday*
fiebre (f.) *fever*
  tener fiebre *to have a fever*
fiesta (f.) *party, holiday*
fijo/fija (m./f.) *fixed, permanent*
  trabajo (m.) fijo *steady job*
fila (f.) *line*
  hacer una fila *to stand in line*
filatelia (f.) *stamp collecting*
filosofía (f.) *philosophy*
fin (m.) *end*
  fin de semana *weekend*
  por fin *finally, at last*
final (m.) *end*
finanzas (f. pl.) *finance*
firma (f.) *signature*
física (f.) *physics*
flor (f.) *flower*
folleto (m.) *brochure*
fontanero/fontanera (m./f.) *plumber*
forma (f.) *way, manner*
fósil (m.) *fossil*
foto (f.) *picture, photograph*
  hacer una foto *to take a picture*
fotografía (f.) *photography*
francés (m.) *French (language)*
francés/francesa (m./f.) *French*
frasco (m.) *jar, bottle*
frase (f.) *phrase*
frecuencia (f.) *frequency*
  con frecuencia *frequently, often*
frecuente (m./f.) *frequent*
frecuentemente *frequently*
fregadero (m.) *(kitchen) sink*
freno (m.) *brake (automobile)*
  poner el pie en el freno *to hit the brakes*
frente (f.) *forehead*
fríjol (m.) *bean*
frío (m.) *cold temperature/sensation*
  Hace frío. *It's cold.*
  tener frío *to be cold*
frío/fría (m./f.) *cold*
  tener la cabeza fría *to keep a cool head*
frito/frita (m./f.) *fried*

fruta (f.) *fruit*
fuera *outside*
  fuera de … *outside of …*
fuerte (m./f.) *strong*
fuerza (f.) *strength*
  coger fuerzas (f. pl.) *to regain strength*
fumar *to smoke*
funcionar *to work, to function*
fútbol (m.) *soccer*
  fútbol americano *football*
futuro (m.) *future*

G

gabardina (f.) *raincoat*
gafas (f. pl.) *eyeglasses*
  gafas de sol *sunglasses*
galería (f.) *gallery*
galleta (f.) *cookie*
gamba (f.) *shrimp*
gamuza (f.) *suede*
gana (f.) *wish, desire*
  tener ganas de … *to feel like …*
ganar *to earn, to win*
  ¡Ojalá que ganen! *I hope they win!*
ganga (f.) *bargain*
garaje (m.) *garage*
garganta (f.) *throat*
  tener dolor de garganta *to have a sore throat*
gasolinera (f.) *gas station*
gasto (m.) *expense*
gato (m.) *cat*
gel (m.) *gel*
generalmente *generally*
generoso/generosa (m./f.) *generous*
gente (f.) *people*
geografía (f.) *geography*
gerente (m.) *manager*
gimnasia (f.) *gymnastics*
gimnasio (m.) *gymnasium*
girar *to turn*
  Gira a la derecha. *Turn right.*
  Gira a la izquierda. *Turn left.*
gol (m.) *goal*
  anotar/hacer/marcar un gol *to score a goal*
gordo/gorda (m./f.) *fat, big*
gracia (f.) *grace, appeal*
  dar (las) gracias *to give thanks*
  gracias (pl.) *thanks*

Gracias. *Thank you.*
Muchas gracias. *Thanks a lot.*
gracioso/graciosa (m./f.) *funny*
grado (m.) *degree*
graduarse *to graduate*
gráfico/gráfica (m./f.) *graphic*
gramo (m.) *gram*
gran/grande (before sg. nouns/all other cases) *big, large, great*
granizar *to hail*
Está granizando. *It's hailing.*
granjero/granjera (m./f.) *farmer*
gratis *free*
grave (m./f.) *serious*
gris (m.) *the color gray*
gris (m./f.) *gray*
gritar *to shout, to scream*
grito (m.) *cry, scream*
último grito *the very latest*
guantes (m. pl.) *gloves*
guardar *to save, to keep*
guayaba (f.) *guava*
guía (f.) *(guide) book*
guía telefónica *phone book*
guitarra (f.) *guitar*
tocar la guitarra *to play the guitar*
gustar *to please*
gustar que ... *to like (it) that ...*
Me gusta/gustan ... (sg./pl.) *I like ...*
Me gustaría ... *I'd like ...*
gusto (m.) *pleasure, taste*
Gusto en conocerlo/la. *Pleased to meet you.* (to a man/to a woman)
Mucho gusto. *It's a pleasure.*

H

haber *to have*
¿Cómo te ha ido? *How have you been?*
Hay ... *There is .../There are ...*
Hay que ... *It is necessary to ...*
No hay nada que ... *There's nothing that ...*
No hay nadie que ... *There's no one who/ that ...*
No hay ningún ... que ... *There's no ... that/ who ...*
¿Qué hay? *What's up?/What's going on?*
habitación (f.) *room, bedroom*
hablar *to speak, to talk*

hablar con .... *to speak to ...*
¿Hablas inglés? *Do you speak English?* (infml.)
¿Habla usted inglés? *Do you speak English?* (fml.)
Hable más despacio, por favor. *Speak more slowly, please.*
Hablo un poco de español. *I speak a little Spanish.*
hacer *to do, to make*
Hace calor. *It's hot.*
Hace frío. *It's cold.*
Hace muy buen tiempo. *It's beautiful.*
hacer a la medida *to custom sew*
hacer deporte *to play sports*
hacer una cola/fila *to stand in line*
hacer un descuento *to give a discount*
hacer excursionismo *to go hiking*
hacer senderismo *to go hiking*
hacer una foto *to take a picture*
hacer una llamada internacional/local/ nacional *to make an international/local/ national call*
hacerse un examen de sangre *to take a blood test*
Hace sol. *It's sunny.*
Hace viento. *It's windy.*
Hágame el favor de ... *Do me the favor of ...*
Se me hace tarde. *I'm late.*
hacha (f.) *axe*
hacia *toward*
hambre (f.) *hunger*
tener hambre *to be hungry*
hasta *until, even*
Hasta entonces. *Till then.*
Hasta luego. *I'll see you later.*
Hasta mañana. *Until tomorrow./See you tomorrow.*
Hasta más tarde. *Until later.*
Hasta pronto. *See you soon.*
hecho/hecha (m./f.) *made, done*
heladería (f.) *ice cream parlor*
helado (m.) *ice cream*
heredar *to inherit*
hermana (f.) *sister*
hermano (m.) *brother*
hermanos (pl.) *brothers, brothers and sisters, siblings*
hielo (m.) *ice*

hierba (f.) *herb*
higiénico/higiénica (m./f.) *hygienic*
  papel (m.) higiénico *toilet paper*
hija (f.) *daughter*
hijastra (f.) *stepdaughter*
hijastro (m.) *stepson*
hijo (m.) *son*
  hijos (pl.) *sons, children (sons and daughters)*
hincha (m./f.) *fan, supporter*
hincharse *to swell*
historia (f.) *history*
historial (m.) *background, record*
  historial de trabajo *résumé*
hockey (m.) *hockey*
hoja (f.) *sheet (of paper)*
  hoja de vida *résumé*
Hola. *Hello.*
hombre (m.) *man*
  hombre de negocios *businessman*
hombro (m.) *shoulder*
homeopatía (f.) *homeopathy*
honesto/honesta (m./f.) *honest*
honorarios (m. pl.) *fees*
hora (f.) *time, hour*
  ¿A qué hora es? *At what time is it?*
  dar la hora *to tell time*
  horas (f. pl.) extras *extra hours, overtime*
  ¿Qué hora es? *What time is it?*
  ¿Qué horas son? *What time is it?*
  ¿Qué hora tiene? *What time do you have?*
horario (m.) *schedule*
horno (m.) *oven*
horror (m.) *horror*
hospital (m.) *hospital*
hostal (m.) *youth hostel*
hotel (m.) *hotel*
hoy *today*
  hoy en día *nowadays*
hueso (m.) *bone*
huevo (m.) *egg*
humano/humana (m./f.) *human*
  cuerpo (m.) humano *human body*
huracán (m.) *hurricane*

I

ida (f.) *outbound journey*
idea (f.) *idea*
ideal (m./f.) *ideal*

idioma (m.) *language*
iglesia (f.) *church*
igual (m./f.) *equal*
  … es igual a … *… equals (=) …*
igualmente *also, likewise*
  Igualmente. *The same to you.*
imaginar *to imagine*
impedir *to prevent*
importante (m./f.) *important*
importar *to matter*
  No importa. *It doesn't matter.*
imposible (m./f.) *impossible*
  Es imposible que … *It is impossible that …*
impresionante (m./f.) *impressive*
impresora (f.) *printer*
impuesto (m.) *tax*
  planilla (f.) de impuestos *tax return*
incentivo (m.) *incentive*
incluir *to include*
  ¿Está incluido el servicio? *Is service included?*
incómodo/incómoda (m./f.) *uncomfortable*
infantil (m./f.) *children's*
  sicología (f.) infantil *child psychology*
información (f.) *information*
  centro (m.) de información *information center*
informal (m./f.) *casual*
informe (m.) *report*
ingeniería (f.) *engineering*
  ingeniería mecánica *mechanical engineering*
ingeniero/ingeniera (m./f.) *engineer*
Inglaterra (f.) *England*
inglés (m.) *English (language)*
  ¿Hablas inglés? *Do you speak English?* (infml.)
  ¿Habla usted inglés? *Do you speak English?* (fml.)
inglés/inglesa (m./f.) *English*
ingrediente (m.) *ingredient*
ingreso (m.) *earnings*
inmediatamente *immediately*
inmediato/inmediata (m./f.) *immediate*
  de inmediato *immediately*
inodoro (m.) *toilet*
insistir *to insist*
  insistir en que … *to insist that …*
instantáneo/instantánea (m./f.) *instantaneous*
  mensaje (m.) instantáneo *instant message*

inteligente (m./f.) *intelligent, smart*
intercambiar *to exchange*
interés (m.) *interest*
  tener interés en … *to be interested in …*
  visitar los lugares de interés *to go sightseeing*
interesante (m./f.) *interesting*
interesar *to interest*
  Me interesa/interesan … (sg./pl.) *I'm
    interested in …*
intermedio/intermedia (m./f.) *intermediate*
internacional (m./f.) *international*
  llamada (f.) internacional *international call*
Internet *internet*
  por Internet *online*
intersección (f.) *intersection*
investigación (f.) *research, investigation*
  trabajo (m.) de investigación *research paper*
invierno (m.) *winter*
invitación (f.) *invitation*
invitado/invitada (m./f.) *guest*
invitar *to invite*
ir *to go*
  ¿Cómo te ha ido? *How have you been?*
  ¿Cómo van las cosas? *How are things?*
  ir a … *to go to (a place), to be going to (do)*
  ir a pie/caminar *to walk*
  ir de camping *to go camping*
  ir de compras *to go shopping*
  ir de escaparates *to go window-shopping*
  ir de punta en blanco *to be dressed to the
    nines (lit., to go from the tip in white)*
ira (f.) *anger*
  estar rojo de la ira *to be very angry (lit., to be
    red with fury)*
italiano (m.) *Italian (language)*
italiano/italiana (m./f.) *Italian*
izquierda (f.) *left side*
  a la izquierda *on the left*
  Gira a la izquierda. *Turn left.*
izquierdo/izquierda (m./f.) *left*
  a mano izquierda *on the left-hand side*

J

jabón (m.) *soap*
jamón (m.) *ham*
jardín (m.) *garden*
jazz (m.) *jazz*
jeans (m. pl.) *jeans*

jefe/jefa (m./f.) *boss*
jersey (m.) *sweater*
jornada (f.) *working day*
jornal (m.) *wage*
jota (f.) *the letter j*
  no saber ni jota de … *to not have a clue
    about …*
joven (m./f.) *young*
jubilado/jubilada (m./f.) *retired, retired person*
juego (m.) *game*
jueves (m.) *Thursday*
juez (m.) *judge*
jugador/jugadora (m./f.) *player*
jugar *to play*
jugo (m.) *juice*
julio (m.) *July*
junio (m.) *June*
junto/junta (m./f.) *together*
juzgado (m.) *court*

K

kilo (m.) *kilo, kilogram*
kilómetro (m.) *kilometer*

L

la *the (f. sg.); it (f.), her, you (f. sg. fml.)* (direct
  object pronoun)
  la de ella *hers*
  la de ellas *theirs (f. pl.)*
  la de ellos *theirs (m. pl./mixed group)*
  la de él *his*
  la de usted *yours (sg. fml.)*
  la de ustedes *yours (pl.)*
labio (m.) *lip*
lado (m.) *side*
  al lado de … *next to …*
ladrón (m./f.) *thief*
lago (m.) *lake*
lámpara (f.) *lamp*
lana (f.) *wool*
langosta (f.) *lobster*
lápiz (m.) *pencil*
largo/larga (m./f.) *long*
las *the (f. pl.); them (f.), you (f. pl.)* (direct object
  pronoun)
lástima (f.) *pity*
  Es una lástima que … *It's a pity that …*
lata (f.) *can*

lavabo (m.) *sink, wash basin*
lavadora (f.) *washing machine*
lavaplatos (m.) *dishwasher*
lavar *to wash*
  lavar a mano *to hand wash*
  lavar en seco *to dry-clean*
  lavar la ropa *to do the laundry*
  lavar los platos *to do the dishes*
lavarse *to wash oneself*
le *(to/for) him, her, it, you* (fml. sg.) (indirect object pronoun)
lección (f.) *lesson*
leche (f.) *milk*
  leche en polvo *powdered milk*
lechería (f.) *dairy store*
lechuga (f.) *lettuce*
lector (m.) *reader*
  lector de CD *CD player*
  lector de CD rom *CD-ROM drive*
  lector de DVD *DVD player*
lectura (f.) *reading*
leer *to read*
lejía (f.) *bleach*
lejos *far*
  lejos de … *far from …*
lengua (f.) *tongue, language*
lentamente *slowly*
lento/lenta (m./f.) *slow*
les *(to/for) them, you* (fml. pl.) (indirect object pronoun)
lesión (f.) *injury*
levantar *to raise, to lift*
levantarse *to get up, to rise*
  Me levanto. *I get up.*
libra (f.) *pound*
  media libra *half pound*
libre (m./f.) *free*
librería (f.) *bookstore*
libro (m.) *book*
  libro de texto *textbook*
licenciatura (f.) *bachelor's degree*
ligero/ligera (m./f.) *light, thin*
límite (m.) *limit*
limón (m.) *lemon*
limonada (f.) *lemonade*
limpio/limpia (m./f.) *clean*
línea (f.) *line*
  línea de suscriptor/abonado digital

  (DSL) *DSL*
lino (m.) *linen*
lista (f.) *list*
listo/lista (m./f.) *ready*
  ¿Listos? *Ready?*
literatura (f.) *literature*
litro (m.) *liter*
llamada (f.) *phone call*
  hacer una llamada internacional/local/
    nacional *to make an international/local/*
    national call
llamar *to call*
  llamar por teléfono *to make a phone call*
  llamar por teléfono a … *to call … on the*
    phone
  ¿Quién lo llama? *Who's calling?*
llamarse *to be called*
  ¿Cómo se llama usted? *What's your*
    name? (fml.)
  ¿Cómo te llamas? *What's your name?* (infml.)
  Me llamo … *My name is …*
llave (f.) *key*
llegar *to arrive*
  llegar a … *to get to …, to arrive at …*
llenar *to fill*
llevar *to wear, to carry, to take, to keep*
  llevar un diario *to keep a diary*
llorar *to cry*
llover *to rain*
  Está lloviendo. *It's raining.*
lluvia (f.) *rain*
lo *it* (m.), *him, you* (m. sg. fml.) (direct object pronoun)
  Lo siento. *I'm sorry.*
local (m./f.) *local*
  llamada (f.) local *local call*
Londres *London*
los *the* (m. pl.); *them* (m.), *you* (m. pl.) (direct object pronoun)
Los Ángeles *Los Angeles*
lotería (f.) *lottery*
luego *later, then*
  Hasta luego. *I'll see you later.*
lugar (m.) *place*
  visitar los lugares de interés *to go sightseeing*
luna (f.) *moon*
lunar (m.) *mole, beauty mark*
  de lunares *polka-dotted*

lunes (m.) *Monday*
luz (f.) *light*
  apagar las luces *to turn off the lights*
  dar a luz *to give birth*
  luz de la calle *streetlight*

M

madera (f.) *wood*
  de madera *wooden*
madrastra (f.) *stepmother*
madre (f.) *mother*
madrugada (f.) *late night, early morning (from midnight till daybreak)*
  de la madrugada *in the early morning*
  Es la una y diez de la madrugada. *It's ten after one in the morning.*
maestro/maestra (m./f.) *teacher*
mágico/mágica (m./f.) *magical*
magnífico/magnífica (m./f.) *magnificent, great*
mal *bad(ly), poorly*
  estar mal *to be not doing well*
  No está mal. *It's not bad.*
mal (m.) *illness*
  estar mal del estómago *to have an upset stomach*
maleta (f.) *suitcase*
malo/mala (m./f.) *bad*
mamá (f.) *mom*
mami (f.) *mom*
mañana (f.) *morning, tomorrow*
  a las nueve de la mañana *at nine a.m.*
  de la mañana *in the morning*
  esta mañana *this morning*
  Hasta mañana. *Until tomorrow./See you tomorrow.*
manejar *handle*
mano (f.) *hand*
  a la mano *at hand*
  a mano derecha *on the right-hand side*
  a mano izquierda *on the left-hand side*
  dar la mano *to shake hands*
  estar en buenas manos *to be in good hands*
  lavar a mano *to hand wash*
manojo (m.) *handful, bunch*
mantequilla (f.) *butter*
manzana (f.) *apple, block*
mapa (m.) *map*
mar (m.) *sea, ocean*

maravilla (f.) *wonder, miracle*
marcador (m.) *scoreboard*
marcar *to mark, to dial*
  marcar un gol *to make a goal*
  marcar un número de teléfono *to dial a phone number*
marchar *to go, to leave*
mareado/mareada (m./f.) *dizzy*
mareo (m.) *sickness*
  tener mareo *to be dizzy*
marido (m.) *husband*
marino/marina (m./f.) *marine*
  azul (m./f.) **marino** *navy blue*
marrón (m./f.) *brown*
martes (m.) *Tuesday*
martini (m.) *martini*
mártir (m./f.) *martyr*
marzo (m.) *March*
mas *but*
más *more, plus (+)*
  alguien más *somebody else*
  el/la/los/las (m. sg./f. sg./m. pl./f. pl.) **más … de …** *the most … in/of …*
  Hasta más tarde. *Until later.*
  más o menos *more or less, so-so, just okay*
  más … que … *more …/-er than …*
  más tarde *later*
matemáticas (f. pl.) *mathematics*
materia (f.) *school subject*
material (m.) *material*
matrícula (f.) *registration*
  derechos (m. pl.) **de matrícula** *tuition*
matricularse *to register*
matrimonio (m.) *marriage*
mayo (m.) *May*
mayor (m./f.) *older, bigger*
  el/la/los/las (m. sg./f. sg./m. pl./f. pl.) **mayor** *the oldest, the biggest*
mazorca (f.) *corncob*
me *me* (direct object pronoun); *(to/for) me* (indirect object pronoun); *myself*
  Me aburre/aburren … (sg./pl.) *I'm bored by …*
  Me encanta/encantan … (sg./pl.) *I really like …*
  Me gusta/gustan … (sg./pl.) *I like …*
  Me gustaría … *I'd like …*
  Me interesa/interesan … (sg./pl.) *I'm interested in …*
  Me levanto. *I get up.*

Me llamo … *My name is …*
¿Me permite … ? *May I please … ?* (fml.)
¿Me permites … ? *May I please … ?* (infml.)
mecánico/mecánica (m./f.) *mechanical*
  ingeniería (f.) mecánica *mechanical*
    engineering
mediano/mediana (m./f.) *medium*
medianoche (f.) *midnight*
  a medianoche *at midnight*
medias (f. pl.) *stockings, socks*
medicamento (m.) *medication*
  tomar un medicamento *to take medication*
medicina (f.) *medicine*
médico/médica (m./f.) *doctor*
  consultorio (m.) del médico *doctor's office*
medida (f.) *measurement*
  hacer a la medida *to custom sew*
medio/media (m./f.) *half, midway*
  a las cinco y media *at five thirty*
  medianoche (f.) *midnight*
  medio tiempo (m.) *halftime*
  término (m.) medio *medium-rare*
mediodía (m.) *noon*
  a mediodía *at noon*
  Son las doce del mediodía. *It's twelve noon.*
medir *to measure*
mejilla (f.) *cheek*
mejor (m./f.) *better*
  el/la/los/las (m. sg./f. sg./m. pl./f. pl.) mejor *the best*
  Es mejor que … *It's better that …*
memoria (f.) *memory*
menor (m./f.) *younger, smaller*
  el/la/los/las (m. sg./f. sg./m. pl./f. pl.) menor *the youngest, the smallest*
menos *less, minus (-)*
  a las seis menos cuarto *at a quarter to six*
  el/la/los/las (m. sg./f. sg./m. pl./f. pl.) menos … de … *the least … in/of …*
  Es la una menos cinco. *It's five to one. (12:55)*
  más o menos *more or less, so-so, just okay*
  menos … que … *less … than …*
mensaje (m.) *message*
  dejar un mensaje después de oír la señal *to leave a message after the tone*
  mensaje instantáneo *instant message*
mente (f.) *mind*
mentir *to lie*

mercadillo (m.) *flea market*
mercado (m.) *market*
merienda (f.) *snack time*
mermelada (f.) *jam*
mes (m.) *month*
  este mes *this month*
  mes entrante *next month*
  mes pasado *last month*
  mes que viene *next month*
mesa (f.) *table*
mesera (f.) *waitress*
mesero (m.) *waiter*
metro (m.) *metro, subway*
mexicano/mexicana (m./f.) *Mexican*
México (m.) *Mexico*
mezquita (f.) *mosque*
mí *me* (after a preposition)
mi/mis (sg./pl.) *my*
microondas (m.) *microwave*
miedo (m.) *fear*
  tener miedo *to be scared/afraid*
  tener miedo de que … *to be scared/afraid that …*
miel (f.) *honey*
mientras *while*
  mientras tanto *meanwhile*
miércoles (m.) *Wednesday*
mil *one thousand*
  cien mil *hundred thousand*
  diez mil *ten thousand*
  veinte mil *twenty thousand*
millón *one million*
  un millón de casas *one million houses*
minuto (m.) *minute*
mío/mía/míos/mías (m. sg./f. sg./m. pl./f. pl.) *mine*
mirar *to watch, to look at*
  mirar la televisón *to watch television*
  Mire … *Hmm …/Look …*
mismo/misma (m./f.) *same*
  ahora mismo *right now*
mixto/mixta (m./f.) *mixed*
moda (f.) *fashion*
  de moda *in fashion, in style*
módem (m.) *modem*
moderno/moderna (m./f.) *modern*
molestarse *to be bothered*
  molestarse de que … *to be bothered that …*

momento (m.) *moment*
  en este momento *at this moment, right now*
  Un momento. *Hold on./One moment.*
monitor (m.) *monitor*
montaña (f.) *mountain*
montar *to ride*
monumento (m.) *monument*
morado/morada (m./f.) *purple*
moreno/morena (m./f.) *dark-haired, dark-skinned*
morir *to die*
Moscú *Moscow*
mostrador (m.) *counter*
mostrar *to show*
mover *to move*
móvil (m.) *mobile phone*
muchacha (f.) *girl*
muchacho (m.) *boy*
mucho *a lot, much, very*
mucho/mucha (m./f.) *a lot of*
  Mucho gusto. *It's a pleasure.*
muchos/muchas (m. pl./f. pl.) *many, a lot of*
  Muchas gracias. *Thanks a lot.*
muebles (m. pl.) *furniture*
muela (f.) *molar*
muerto/muerta (m./f.) *dead person, dead*
mujer (f.) *woman, wife*
  mujer de negocios *businesswoman*
  mujer policía *policewoman*
muletilla (f.) *filler word/phrase*
multa (f.) *fine*
mundial (m./f.) *worldwide, worldly*
  campeonato (m.) **mundial** *world championship*
mundo (m.) *world*
muñeca (f.) *wrist*
músculo (m.) *muscle*
museo (m.) *museum*
música (f.) *music*
  música clásica *classical music*
musical (m.) *musical*
músico (m./f.) *musician*
muy *very*

N

nacional (m./f.) *national*
  llamada (f.) **nacional** *national call*
nacionalidad (f.) *nationality*

nada *nothing*
  De nada. *You're welcome.*
  nada más *nothing else*
  No hay nada que … *There's nothing that …*
  No, para nada. *No, not at all.*
nadar *to swim*
nadie *nobody, no one*
  No hay nadie que … *There's no one who/that …*
naipes (m. pl.) *(playing) cards*
naranja (f.) *orange (fruit)*
nariz (f.) *nose*
  dar de narices *to fall flat on one's face*
natación (f.) *swimming*
natural (m./f.) *natural*
naturaleza (f.) *nature*
náusea (f.) *nausea, sickness*
  tener náusea(s) *to be nauseated, to have nausea*
navaja (f.) *pocket-knife*
  navaja de afeitar *razor*
necesario/necesaria (m./f.) *necessary*
  Es necesario que … *It's necessary that …*
necesitar *to need*
negar *to deny*
  negar que … *to deny that …*
negocio (m.) *business*
  hombre (m.) **de negocios** *businessman*
  mujer (f.) **de negocios** *businesswoman*
negro/negra (m./f.) *black*
  estar negro de la risa *to laugh very hard (lit., to turn black with laughter)*
  ver todo negro *to be a pessimist (lit., to see everything as black)*
nervio (m.) *nerve*
nevar *to snow*
  Está nevando. *It's snowing.*
nevera (f.) *refrigerator*
ni *nor*
  ni … ni *neither … nor*
niebla (f.) *fog*
  niebla tóxica/con humo *smog*
nieta (f.) *granddaughter*
nieto (m.) *grandson*
  nietos (pl.) *grandsons, grandchildren*
nieve (f.) *snow*
niña (f.) *young girl, female child*
ningún/ninguno/ninguna (before m. sg.

nouns/m. sg./f. sg.) *no, none*
No hay ningún … que … *There's no … that/
who …*
niño (m.) *young boy, male child*
no *not, no*
No, para nada. *No, not at all.*
noche (f.) *evening, night*
a las siete de la noche *at seven p.m.*
Buenas noches. *Good evening./Good night.*
de la noche *at night, in the evening*
esta noche *tonight*
medianoche *midnight*
Nochebuena *Christmas Eve*
por la noche *at night*
nombre (m.) *name*
normal (m./f.) *normal*
normalmente *normally*
norte (m.) *north*
nos *us* (direct object pronoun); *(to/for) us* (indirect
object pronoun); *ourselves*
nosotras *we* (f. pl.)
nosotros *we* (m. pl./mixed group)
nota (f.) *note, grade*
sacar buenas/malas notas *to get good/bad
grades*
tomar nota *to take note*
noticia (f.) *a piece of news*
noticias (pl.) *news*
novecientos/novecientas (m./f.) *nine hundred*
novela (f.) *novel*
novela rosa *romance novel*
noventa *ninety*
novia (f.) *girlfriend, fiancée*
noviembre (m.) *November*
novio (m.) *boyfriend, fiancé*
nube (f.) *cloud*
nublado/nublada (m./f.) *cloudy*
Está nublado. *It's cloudy.*
nuera (f.) *daughter-in-law*
nuestro/nuestra/nuestros/nuestras (m. sg./f.
sg./m. pl./f. pl.) *our*
nuestro/nuestra/nuestros/nuestras (m. sg./f.
sg./m. pl./f. pl.) *ours*
Nueva York *New York*
nuevamente *once again*
nueve *nine*
nuevo/nueva (m./f.) *new*
número (m.) *number*

número de teléfono *telephone number*
nunca *never*
casi nunca *seldom, almost never*

O

o *or*
más o menos *more or less, so-so, just okay*
o … o *either … or*
objetivo (m.) *objective, aim*
objeto (m.) *object*
obra (f.) *play (theater)*
obra dramática *drama*
obrero/obrera (m./f.) *construction worker*
occidente (m.) *west*
océano (m.) *ocean*
ochenta *eighty*
ocho *eight*
a las ocho y diez *at eight ten (8:10)*
ochocientos/ochocientas (m./f.) *eight hundred*
octubre (m.) *October*
ocupado/ocupada (m./f.) *busy*
oeste (m.) *west*
oferta (f.) *offer*
oficina (f.) *office*
oficinista (m./f.) *office worker*
ofrecer *to offer*
oír *to hear*
Ojalá que … *I hope/wish …*
ojo (m.) *eye*
ojo por ojo *an eye for an eye*
oler *to smell*
olvidar *to forget*
once *eleven*
onza (f.) *ounce*
ópera (f.) *opera*
operadora (f.) *operator*
operarse *to have an operation*
opuesto/opuesta (m./f.) *opposite*
oración (f.) *prayer*
ordenador (m.) *computer*
oreja (f.) *ear*
oriente (m.) *east*
os *all of you* (infml.) (direct object pronoun);
(to/for) you (infml. pl.)*(indirect object pronoun);
yourselves* (infml.)
oscuro/oscura (m./f.) *dark*
azul (m./f.) **oscuro** *dark blue*
verde (m./f.) **oscuro** *dark green*

otoño (m.) *fall*
otro/otra (m./f.) *another*

P

paciencia (f.) *patience*
  tener paciencia *to be patient*
padrastro (m.) *stepfather*
padre (m.) *father*
  padres (pl.) *fathers, parents*
paga (f.) *wage*
pagar *to pay*
  pagar en efectivo *to pay cash*
  pagar la cuenta *to check out, to pay the bill/ check*
página (f.) *page*
  páginas (pl.) amarillas *yellow pages*
  página web *webpage*
pago (m.) *payment*
país (m.) *country*
palabra (f.) *word*
palacio (m.) *palace*
palmo (m.) *palm*
  conocer palmo a palmo *to know like the back of one's hand*
palo (m.) *stick*
pan (m.) *bread*
panadería (f.) *bakery*
panameño/panameña (m./f.) *Panamanian*
pantalla (f.) *screen*
pantalones (m. pl.) *pants*
pantis (m. pl.) *women's underwear*
pantuflas (f. pl.) *slippers*
pantymedias (f. pl.) *stockings*
papa (f.) *potato*
papá (m.) *dad*
papi (m.) *dad*
papaya (f.) *papaya*
papel (m.) *paper*
  papel higiénico *toilet paper*
paquete (m.) *package*
para *for, towards, in order to, intended for, by/ until a certain time*
  espacio (m.) para charla *chat room*
  No, para nada. *No, not at all.*
parada (f.) *stop, bus stop*
parado/parada (m./f.) *unemployed*
paraguas (m.) *umbrella*
Paraguay (m.) *Paraguay*

parar *to stop, to leave*
  pararse de cabeza *to go crazy, to go out of one's mind*
parcial (m./f.) *partial*
  a tiempo parcial *part-time*
pardo/parda (m./f.) *grayish brown*
parecer *to look like, to seem*
  ¿Qué te parece ... ? *What do you think of ... ?*
  ¿Qué te parece si ... ? *How about if ... ?*
pared (f.) *wall*
pariente (m./f.) *relative*
París *Paris*
parque (m.) *park*
parqueadero (m.) *parking lot*
parrilla (f.) *grill*
  a la parrilla *grilled*
parte (f.) *part, side*
  ¿De parte de quién? *Who's calling?*
  por otra parte *on the other hand*
  por una parte *on the one hand*
particular (m./f.) *particular*
partido (m.) *(sport) game*
  partido de béisbol *baseball game*
partir *to leave, to set off*
  partir de ... *to start from ...*
párvulo/párvula (m./f.) *young child*
pasado/pasada (m./f.) *spoiled*
pasado/pasada (m./f.) *past*
  año (m.) pasado *last year*
  mes (m.) pasado *last month*
  semana (f.) pasada *last week*
pasaje (m.) *ticket*
pasaporte (m.) *passport*
pasar *to pass, to forward, to go by, to happen, to spend*
  Le paso. *I'm putting you through. (on the phone)*
  pasar el día *to spend the day*
  ¿Qué pasa? *How's it going?*
pasatiempos (m.) *hobby*
Pascua (f.) *Easter*
pastelería (f.) *bakery (for pastries, etc.)*
pastilla (f.) *pill*
patata (f.) *potato*
patio (m.) *backyard*
peaje (m.) *toll*
peatón (m.) *pedestrian*
pecho (m.) *breast, chest*

pediatra (m./f.) *pediatrician*
pediatría (f.) *pediatrics*
pedir *to order, to ask for*
  pedir que ... *to request that ...*
película (f.) *movie, film*
  películas (pl.) de aventuras *adventure films*
  películas de horror *horror films*
  películas de suspenso *suspense films*
  películas románticas *romantic films*
pelo (m.) *hair*
pelota (f.) *ball*
peluquería (f.) *hair salon*
pena (f.) *pain, pity*
  ¡Qué pena! *That's too bad!*
pendientes (m. pl.) *earrings*
penicilina (f.) *penicillin*
pensar *to think*
  no pensar que ... *not to think that ...*
pensión (f.) *pension*
peor (m./f.) *worse*
  el/la/los/las (m. sg./f. sg./m. pl./f. pl.) peor
    the worst
pepino (m.) *cucumber*
pequeño/pequeña (m./f.) *small*
pera (f.) *pear*
percibir *to perceive*
perder *to lose, to miss*
  perder la cabeza *to lose one's head*
Perdón. *Excuse me.*
perezoso/perezosa (m./f.) *lazy*
  ser perezoso *to be lazy*
perfecto/perfecta (m./f.) *perfect*
perfume (m.) *perfume*
periódico (m.) *newspaper*
periodista (m./f.) *journalist*
período (m.) *period*
  período de prueba *probationary period*
permitir *to allow*
  ¿Me permite ... ? *May I please ... ?* (fml.)
  ¿Me permites ... ? *May I please ... ?* (infml.)
pero *but*
perro (m.) *dog*
persona (f.) *person*
  persona extranjero *stranger*
personal (m.) *staff*
Perú (m.) *Peru*
peruano/peruana (m./f.) *Peruvian*
pesar *to weigh*

pescadería (f.) *fish shop, fish market*
pescado (m.) *fish*
pésimo/pésima (m./f.) *terrible*
peso (m.) *peso*
pestañas (f. pl.) *eyelashes*
piano (m.) *piano*
picante (m./f.) *spicy*
pie (m.) *foot*
  dedo (m.) del pie *toe*
  ir a pie *to walk*
  poner el pie en el freno *to hit the brakes*
  tener los pies en la tierra *to have both feet on*
    the ground
piel (f.) *skin*
pierna (f.) *leg*
pieza (f.) *piece*
  de dos piezas *two-piece*
pijama (m.) *pajamas*
pimienta (f.) *pepper (spice)*
pimiento (m.) *pepper (vegetable)*
pinta (f.) *spot, appearance*
pintor/pintora (m./f.) *painter*
pintura (f.) *painting*
piscina (f.) *swimming pool*
piso (m.) *floor, apartment*
placer (m.) *pleasure*
plan (m.) *plan*
plancha (f.) *iron*
planchar *to iron*
  tabla (f.) de planchar *ironing board*
planilla (f.) *form*
  planilla de impuestos *tax return*
plano (m.) *map*
plano/plana (m./f.) *flat*
planta (f.) *plant*
plantilla (f.) *staff*
plástico (m.) *plastic*
plátano (m.) *banana*
plateado/plateada (m./f.) *silver (color)*
plato (m.) *plate, dish*
  lavar los platos *to do the dishes*
  plato del día *special of the day*
  plato principal *main dish*
playa (f.) *beach*
plaza (f.) *plaza, square*
  plaza de mercado *outdoor market*
pluma (f.) *pen*
pobre (m./f.) *poor, poor person*

los pobres *the poor*
poco *little*
  Hablo un poco de español. *I speak a little Spanish.*
  un poco *a little*
pocos/pocas (m. pl./f. pl.) *few*
poder *can, to be able to, to have permission to*
  ¿Podría ... ? *Could you ... ?*
podrido/podrida (m./f.) *bad, rotten*
policía (m./f.) *police officer*
  mujer (f.) policía *policewoman*
poliéster (m.) *polyester*
pollo (m.) *chicken*
polvo (m.) *dust, powder*
  leche (f.) en polvo *powdered milk*
poner *to put, to place*
  poner el pie en el freno *to hit the brakes*
  poner en espera *to put on hold*
ponerse *to become, to turn, to put something on*
  ponerse colorado *to be embarrassed (lit., to turn red)*
por *for, by, around, at, because of, due to, in place of, in exchange for, through*
  por casualidad *by chance*
  por desgracia *unfortunately*
  ¡Por Dios! *For God's sake!*
  por eso *for this reason*
  Por favor. *Please.*
  por fin *finally, at last*
  por la noche *at night*
  por la radio *on the radio*
  por lo tanto *therefore*
  por lo visto *apparently*
  por otra parte *on the other hand*
  por qué *why*
  por supuesto *of course*
  por teléfono *on the phone*
  por una parte *on the one hand*
porque *because*
portero (m.) *goalkeeper*
portugués/portuguesa (m./f.) *Portuguese*
poseer *to own, to hold*
posible (m./f.) *possible*
  Es posible que ... *It is possible that ...*
  lo antes posible *as soon as possible*
postre (m.) *dessert*
practicar *to practice, to play (sports)*
precio (m.) *price*

etiqueta (f.) con el precio *price tag*
  precio económico *reasonable price*
precisamente *precisely*
preferible (m./f.) *preferable*
  Es preferible que ... *It's preferable that ...*
preferir *to prefer*
  preferir que ... *to prefer that ...*
pregunta (f.) *question*
preguntar *to ask*
premio (m.) *prize*
prenda (f.) *garment*
preocuparse *to worry*
  No se preocupe. *Don't worry.*
  preocuparse de que ... *to worry that ...*
preparado/preparada (m./f.) *ready, prepared*
  ¿Preparados? *Ready?*
presentación (f.) *presentation*
presentar *to introduce*
  Te presento a ... *Let me introduce you to ...*
presidente/presidenta (m./f.) *president*
presión (f.) *pressure*
prestigioso/prestigiosa (m./f.) *prestigious*
primavera (f.) *spring*
primer/primero/primera (before m. sg. nouns/ m./f.) *first*
primo/prima (m./f.) *cousin*
  primos (pl.) *cousins*
principal (m./f.) *main*
  plato (m.) principal *main dish*
prisa (f.) *hurry*
  aprisa *quickly*
  tener prisa *to be in a hurry*
probador (m.) *dressing room*
probar *to try, to taste*
probarse *to try on (clothes)*
problema (m.) *problem*
producir *to produce*
producto (m.) *product*
profesión (f.) *profession*
profesional (m./f.) *professional*
profesionalmente *professionally*
profesor/profesora (m./f.) *professor*
profesorado (m.) *faculty*
programa (m.) *program*
  programa de entrevistas *talk show*
  programa de televisión *television program*
prohibir *to forbid, to prohibit*
  prohibir que ... *to forbid that/to ...*

prometer *to promise*
prometido/prometida (m./f.) *fiancé(e)*
pronto *soon*
propina (f.) *tip*
proteger *to protect*
provecho (m.) *benefit*
  ¡Buen provecho! *Enjoy the meal!*
próximo/próxima (m./f.) *near, next*
  próxima semana (f.) *next week*
proyecto (m.) *project*
prueba (f.) *proof, test, probation*
  período (m.) **de prueba** *probationary period*
pueblo (m.) *town*
puente (m.) *bridge, long weekend*
puerta (f.) *door*
  abrir la puerta *to open the door*
pues *so, since, therefore, well, then*
  Pues, aquí estamos. *Here we are.*
  Pues bien. *Fine.*
  Pues, nada. *Not much.*
puesto (m.) *(job) position, post*
pulmones (m. pl.) *lungs*
pulsera (f.) *bracelet*
punta (f.) *tip, end*
  ir de punta en blanco *to be dressed to the nines (lit., to go from the tip in white)*
punto (m.) *point*
  en punto *exactly*
  Son las tres en punto. *It's three o'clock sharp.*
puntual (m./f.) *punctual*
púrpura (m./f.) *purple*

Q

que *which, that* (relative pronoun, conjunction)
qué *what* (question)
  ¿A qué hora es? *At what time is it?*
  ¿De qué color es …? *What color is …?*
  por qué *why*
  ¡Qué …! *How …!*
  ¡Qué bien! *How nice!*
  ¿Qué hay? *What's up?/What's going on?*
  ¿Qué hora es? *What time is it?*
  ¿Qué horas son? *What time is it?*
  ¿Qué pasa? *How's it going?*
  ¡Qué pena! *That's too bad!*
  ¿Qué quiere decir eso? *What does that mean?*
  ¿Qué tal? *What's happening?*
  ¿Qué tal si …? *How about if …?*
  ¿Qué te parece si …? *How about if …?*
  ¡Yo qué sé! *How do I know!?/How should I know!?*
quedar *to remain, to retain, to fit*
  quedar empatados *to be tied*
quemado/quemada (m./f.) *burnt*
querer *to want, to love*
  querer que … *to want that/to …*
  ¿Qué quiere decir eso? *What does that mean?*
  Quisiera … *I'd like …*
  Te quiero. *I love you.*
queso (m.) *cheese*
quien/quienes (sg./pl.) *who, whom* (relative pronoun)
quién/quiénes (sg./pl.) *who, whom* (question)
  ¿De parte de quién? *Who's calling?*
  ¿De quién …? *Whose …?*
  ¿Quién lo llama? *Who's calling?*
química (f.) *chemistry*
quince *fifteen*
quinientos/quinientas (m./f.) *five hundred*

R

racimo (m.) *bunch (of grapes)*
  racimo de uvas *bunch of grapes*
radio (f.) *radio*
  por la radio *on the radio*
rampa (f.) *ramp*
rápidamente *fast, quickly*
rápido *fast, quickly*
rápido/rápida (m./f.) *fast, quick*
ratón (m.) *mouse*
raya (f.) *stripe*
  a rayas *striped*
razón (f.) *reason*
  tener razón *to be right*
realismo (m.) *realism*
realista (m./f.) *realistic*
realmente *actually*
rebaja (f.) *discount*
  comprar en rebaja *to buy on sale*
rebajado/rebajada (m./f.) *reduced*
rebanada (f.) *slice*
recepción (f.) *reception desk*
recepcionista (m./f.) *receptionist*
receso (m.) *recess*
receta (f.) *recipe*
recibir *to receive*

recoger *to pick up*
recomendar *to recommend*
  recomendar que ... *to recommend that ...*
reconocer *to recognize*
recordar *to remember*
recorrido (m.) *route*
  recorrido por autobús *tour bus trip*
recreo (m.) *recreation*
recto *straight*
  Continúa recto. *Continue straight.*
redondo/redonda (m./f.) *round*
reducir *to reduce*
referencia (f.) *reference*
refresco (m.) *soft drink, soda*
regalar *to give (a gift)*
regalo (m.) *gift*
región (f.) *region*
regional (m./f.) *regional*
registrarse *to check in*
regresar *to return*
reír *to laugh*
relación (f.) *relationship*
relámpago (m.) *lightening*
relleno (m.) *stuffing, filling*
  frase (f.) de relleno *filler phrase*
reloj (m.) *watch, clock*
repetir *to repeat*
  Repita, por favor *Repeat, please.*
representante (m.) *representative*
reserva (f.) *reservation*
reservación (f.) *reservation*
resolver *to resolve*
responder *to answer*
responsable (m./f.) *responsible*
respuesta (f.) *answer*
restaurante (m.) *restaurant*
resto (m.) *rest*
resultado (m.) *result*
retransmitir *to forward*
retrasado/retrasada (m./f.) *slow, behind*
retrasar *to delay, to postpone*
retribución (f.) *repayment*
reunión (f.) *meeting*
reunir *to gather, to meet*
revista (f.) *magazine*
rico/rica (m./f.) *rich*
río (m.) *river*
risa (f.) *laughter*

estar negro de la risa *to laugh very hard (lit., to turn black with laughter)*
roca (f.) *rock*
rodilla (f.) *knee*
rojo/roja (m./f.) *red*
  estar rojo de la ira *to be very angry (lit., to be red with fury)*
romántico/romántica (m./f.) *romantic*
ropa (f.) *clothing*
  detergente (m.) de ropa *laundry detergent*
  lavar la ropa *to do the laundry*
  tienda (f.) de ropa *clothing store*
rosa (f.) *rose*
  novela (f.) rosa *romance novel*
  ver todo color de rosa *to be an optimist, to wear rose colored glasses (lit., to see everything pink)*
rosado/rosada (m./f.) *pink*
rubio/rubia (m./f.) *blonde*
rural (m /f.) *rural*
ruso (m.) *Russian (language)*

S

sábado (m.) *Saturday*
saber (intransitive verb) *to taste*
saber (transitive verb) *to know (facts, information), to learn*
  no saber ni jota de ... *to not have a clue about ...*
  ¿Quién sabe? *Who knows?*
  ¿Sabe cómo ...? *Do you know how to ...?*
  ¡Yo qué sé! *How do I know!?/How should I know!?*
saborear *to taste*
sacar *to take out, to get*
  sacar buenas notas *to get good grades*
  sacar malas notas *to get bad grades*
saco (m.) *jacket*
sal (f.) *salt*
sala (f.) *living room*
  sala de conferencias *meeting room, conference room, lecture hall*
salado/salada (m./f.) *salty*
salario (m.) *salary*
salida (f.) *exit*
salir *to leave, to go out*
  salir de viaje *to go on a trip*
salsa (f.) *sauce, salsa*

saltar *to skip*
  saltarse el semáforo *to go through a light*
saludable (m./f.) *healthy*
saludo (m.) *greeting*
  ¡Saludos! *Hello!*
sandalias (f. pl.) *sandals*
sangre (f.) *blood*
  hacerse un examen de sangre *to take a blood test*
  ser de sangre azul *to have blue blood (lit., to be of blue blood)*
se *himself, herself, itself, yourself* (fml.), *themselves, yourselves* (fml.); *(to/for) him, her, it, you* (fml. sg./pl.), *them* (indirect object pronoun, used in place of le/les when preceding lo/la/los/las); *you, people, one* (impersonal pronoun)
secadora (f.) *dryer*
sección (f.) *section*
seco/seca (m./f.) *dry*
  lavar en seco *to dry-clean*
secretaria (m./f.) *secretary*
secreto (m.) *secret*
sed (f.) *thirst*
  tener sed *to be thirsty*
seda (f.) *silk*
seguir *to follow*
  Siga derecho. *Go straight.*
  Siga por el carril de la derecha. *Stay in the right lane.*
segundo/segunda (m./f.) *second*
  segundo año *second year*
seguridad (f.) *safety, security*
  abrocharse el cinturón de seguridad *to buckle up*
seguro (m.) *insurance*
seguro/segura (m./f.) *sure, safe*
  Seguro/Segura que sí. *I'm sure.*
seis *six*
seiscientos/seiscientas (m./f.) *six hundred*
semáforo (m.) *traffic light*
  saltarse el semáforo *to go through a light*
semana (f.) *week*
  dos días a la semana *twice a week*
  esta semana *this week*
  fin (m.) de semana *weekend*
  próxima semana *next week*
  semana pasada *last week*
  semana que viene *next week*

  todas las semanas *every week*
semanal (m./f.) *weekly*
semestre (m.) *semester*
señal (f.) *signal*
  dejar un mensaje después de oír la señal *to leave a message after the tone*
senderismo (m.) *hiking*
  hacer senderismo *to go hiking*
seno (m.) *breast*
señor (m.) *Mr.*
señora (f.) *Mrs.*
sensatamente *sensibly*
sensiblemente *perceptibly*
sentar *to seat*
  estar sentado *to be seated*
sentarse *to sit down*
sentido (m.) *sense, direction*
  de sentido único *one-way*
sentir *to feel*
  Lo siento. *I'm sorry.*
  sentir que … *to regret that …*
sentirse *to feel*
septiembre (m.) *September*
ser *to be*
  Es la una. *It's one o'clock.*
  Son las tres. *It's three o'clock.*
  Son las tres en punto. *It's three o'clock sharp.*
  ser caradura *to be shameless*
serie (f.) *series*
serio/seria (m./f.) *serious*
serpiente (f.) *snake*
servicio (m.) *service*
  ¿Está incluido el servicio? *Is service included?*
servilleta (f.) *napkin*
servir *to serve*
  ¿En qué puedo servirle? *How may I help you?*
sesenta *sixty*
sesión (f.) *session*
setecientos/setecientas (m./f.) *seven hundred*
setenta *seventy*
si *if*
  ¿Qué tal si …? *How about if …?*
  ¿Qué te parece si …? *How about if …?*
sí *yes*
  ¡Claro que sí! *Of course!*
  Creo que sí. *I think so.*
  Seguro/segura que sí. *I'm sure.*

¡Yo espero que sí! *I hope so!*
sicología (f.) *psychology*
siempre *always*
siesta (f.) *nap*
siete *seven*
siglo (m.) *century*
  este siglo *this century*
significar *to mean*
silenciosamente *quietly*
silla (f.) *chair, seat*
simpático/simpática (m./f.) *friendly*
simplemente *simply, only*
sin *without*
sindicato (m.) *union*
síndrome (m.) *syndrome*
  síndrome del túnel del carpio *carpal tunnel*
    syndrome
síntoma (m.) *symptom*
sistema (m.) *system*
  sistema de sonido *sound system*
sitio (m.) *place*
  sitio web *website*
situación (f.) *situation*
sobre *on top of, over, above, about*
  sobre todo *especially*
sobrecocido/sobrecocida (m./f.) *overcooked*
sobremesa (f.) *after-dinner conversation*
sobrina (f.) *niece*
sobrino (m.) *nephew*
sofá (m.) *sofa, couch*
sol (m.) *sun*
  gafas (f. pl.) de sol *sunglasses*
  Hace sol. *It's sunny.*
solamente *only*
soledad (f.) *solitude*
solicitar *to apply for, to request*
solicitud (f.) *application*
sólo *merely, solely, only*
solo/sola (m./f.) *sole, only, alone*
soltero/soltera (m./f.) *single*
solución (f.) *solution*
sombrero (m.) *hat*
sonar *to sound, to ring*
soñar *to dream*
  ¡Ni lo sueñes! *Don't even dream about it!*
  soñar con ... *to dream about ...*
sonido (m.) *sound*
  sistema (m.) de sonido *sound system*

sonido (m.) *sound*
sonreír *to smile*
sopa (f.) *soup*
sorprenderse *to be surprised*
  sorprenderse de que ... *to be surprised*
    that ...
sorpresa (f.) *surprise*
sótano (m.) *basement*
su/sus (sg./pl.) *his, her, its, their, your* (pl./sg. fml.)
suave (m./f.) *soft*
subasta (f.) *auction*
subterráneo (m.) *subway*
suburbano/suburbana (m./f.) *suburban*
suceso (m.) *event, happening*
sucio/sucia (m./f.) *dirty*
Sudamérica *South America*
suegra (f.) *mother-in-law*
suegro (m.) *father-in-law*
sueldo (m.) *pay*
suelo (m.) *floor*
suelto/suelta (m./f.) *loose, flowing*
sueño (m.) *sleepiness, sleep*
  tener sueño *to be sleepy*
suerte (f.) *luck*
suéter (m.) *sweater*
suficiente (m./f.) *enough*
sufrir *to suffer*
sugerir *to suggest*
  sugerir que ... *to suggest that ...*
supermercado (m.) *supermarket*
supuesto (m.) *supposition*
  por supuesto *of course*
sur (m.) *south*
suscriptor/suscriptora (m./f.) *subscriber*
  línea (f.) de suscriptor digital (DSL) *DSL*
suspender *to fail, to suspend*
  suspender un examen *to fail a test*
suspenso (m.) *suspense*
  películas (f. pl.) de suspenso *suspense films*
suyo/suya/suyos/suyas (m. sg./f. sg./m. pl./f.
  pl.) *his, hers, theirs, yours*

T

tabla (f.) *table, board*
  tabla de planchar *ironing board*
tacón (m.) *heel*
tajada (f.) *slice*
tal *such*

¿Qué tal? *How's it going?*
¿Qué tal si … ? *How about if … ?*
tal vez *perhaps*
talla (f.) *size*
tamaño (m.) *size*
también *also, too*
tampoco *neither, not either*
tan *so (very)*
tan … como *as … as* (comparison)
tanto *in such a manner*
  mientras tanto *meanwhile*
  por lo tanto *therefore*
tanto/tanta (m./f.) *as much, as many*
  tanto/tanta/tantos/tantas (m. sg./f. sg./m. pl./f. pl.) … como *as … as* (comparison)
taquilla (f.) *box office*
tarde *late*
  Hasta más tarde. *Until later.*
  más tarde *later*
  Se me hace tarde. *I'm late.*
tarde (f.) *afternoon*
  a las cuatro de la tarde *at four p.m.*
  Buenas tardes. *Good afternoon.*
  de la tarde *in the afternoon*
  esta tarde *this afternoon*
tarea (f.) *homework*
tarjeta (f.) *card*
  tarjeta de crédito *credit card*
taxi (m.) *taxi*
taxista (m./f.) *taxi driver*
taza (f.) *cup*
tazón (m.) *bowl*
te *you* (infml. sg.) (direct object pronoun); *(to/for) you* (infml. sg.) (indirect object pronoun); *yourself* (infml.)
  Te presento a … *Let me introduce you to …*
té (m.) *tea*
teatro (m.) *theater*
techo (m.) *ceiling*
teclado (m.) *keyboard*
tecnología (f.) *technology*
tejanos (m. pl.) *jeans*
telefónico/telefónica (m./f.) *(of) telephone, telephonic*
  cabina (f.) telefónica *telephone booth*
  guía (f.) telefónica *phone book*
teléfono (m.) *telephone*
  colgar el teléfono *to hang up the phone*

contestar el teléfono *to answer the phone*
llamar por teléfono *to make a phone call*
llamar por teléfono a … *to call … on the phone*
marcar un número de teléfono *to dial a phone number*
número (m.) de teléfono *telephone number*
televisión (f.) *television*
mirar la televisón *to watch television*
programa (m.) de televisión *television program*
televisor (m.) *television (set)*
temer *to fear, to be afraid of*
temperatura (f.) *temperature*
templo (m.) *temple*
temprano *early* (adverb)
temprano/temprana (m./f.) *early*
tendón (m.) *tendon*
tenedor (m.) *fork*
tener *to have*
  Aquí tiene. *Here you are.*
  ¿Cuántos años tiene? *How old are you* (sg. fml.)*/is he/is she?*
  Que tenga un buen día. *Have a nice day.*
  tener … años *to be … years old*
  tener calor *to be hot, to be warm*
  tener cansancio *to be tired*
  tener dolor de cabeza *to have a headache*
  tener dolor de garganta *to have a sore throat*
  tener fiebre *to have a fever*
  tener frío *to be cold*
  tener ganas de … *to feel like …*
  tener hambre *to be hungry*
  tener interés en … *to be interested in …*
  tener la cabeza fría *to keep a cool head*
  tener la tensión alta/baja *to have high/low blood pressure*
  tener los pies en la tierra *to have both feet on the ground*
  tener mareo *to be dizzy*
  tener miedo *to be scared*
  tener náusea(s) *to be nauseated, to have nausea*
  tener paciencia *to be patient*
  tener prisa *to be in a hurry*
  tener que … *to have to …*
  tener razón *to be right*
  tener sed *to be thirsty*

Essential Spanish

tener sueño *to be sleepy*
tener tos *to have a cough*
tenis (m.) *tennis*
tensión (f.) *tension*
tener la tensión alta/baja *to have high/low blood pressure*
tomar la tensión *to take the blood pressure*
tercero/tercer/tercera (m. sg./m. sg. before a m. noun/f.) *third*
tercer año *third year*
terminar *to finish*
término (m.) *term, period, point*
término medio *medium-rare*
término tres cuartos *medium*
tesis (f.) *dissertation*
tetera (f.) *teakettle*
texto (m.) *text*
libro (m.) de texto *textbook*
ti *you* (infml. sg.) (after a preposition)
tía (f.) *aunt, woman*
tiempo (m.) *time, weather*
a tiempo *on time, in time*
a tiempo completo *full-time*
a tiempo parcial *part-time*
El tiempo es bueno. *The weather is good.*
¿Cómo estás de tiempo? *Do you have time?/ How are you doing for time?*
Hace muy buen tiempo. *It's beautiful.*
medio tiempo *halftime*
tienda (f.) *store, convenience store*
tienda de antigüedades *antique store*
tienda de electrodomésticos *appliances store*
tienda de ropa *clothing store*
tienda por departamentos *department store*
Tienes que … *You have to …*
tierra (f.) *land*
tener los pies en la tierra *to have both feet on the ground*
tímido/tímida (m./f.) *shy*
tinto/tinta (m./f.) *dark red*
vino (m.) tinto *red wine*
tío (m.) *uncle, man*
típico/típica (m./f.) *typical*
tipo (m.) *type*
tiquete (m.) *ticket*
título (m.) *degree, diploma*
toalla (f.) *towel*
tobillo (m.) *ankle*

tocar *to touch, to play an instrument*
tocar el piano *to play the piano*
tocar la guitarra *to play the guitar*
todavía *still, yet*
todo (m.) *everything*
sobre todo *especially*
todo/toda (m./f.) *all, every*
todas las semanas *every week*
todo el día *all day*
todos los días *every day*
tomar *to take, to have (food and drink)*
tomar la tensión *to take the blood pressure*
tomar un medicamento *to take medication*
tomate (m.) *tomato*
tono (m.) *tone, dial tone*
tormenta (f.) *storm*
torta (f.) *cake*
tos (f.) *cough*
tener tos *to have a cough*
tostada (f.) *toast*
totalmente *absolutely*
tóxico/tóxica (m./f.) *toxic*
niebla (f.) tóxica *smog*
trabajador/trabajadora (m./f.) *hardworking*
trabajar *to work*
¿En qué trabaja? *What do you do for a living?*
trabajo (m.) *job, work*
¡Buen trabajo! *Good job!*
historial (m.) de trabajo *résumé*
trabajo de investigación *research paper*
trabajo de verano *summer job*
trabajo fijo *steady job*
traducir *to translate*
traer *to bring, to get, to take*
tráfico (m.) *traffic*
traje (m.) *suit*
traje de baño *bathing suit*
tranquilo/tranquila (m./f.) *quiet, calm*
trasladar *to transfer*
tratamiento (m.) *treatment*
tratar *to treat*
¿Cómo te trata la vida? *How's life treating you?*
tratar *to try*
tratar de … *to try … (to do something)*
trece *thirteen*
treinta *thirty*
tren (m.) *train*

estación (f.) de tren *train station*
tres *three*
trescientos/trescientas (m./f.) *three hundred*
triste (m./f.) *sad*
  Es triste que … *It's sad that …*
tristemente *sadly*
trotar *to jog*
trueno (m.) *thunder*
tú *you* (sg. infml.) (subject pronoun)
tu/tus (sg./pl.) *your* (sg. infml.)
túnel (m.) *tunnel*
  síndrome (m.) del túnel del carpio *carpal tunnel syndrome*
turismo (m.) *tourism*
turista (m./f.) *tourist*
tuyo/tuya/tuyos/tuyas (m. sg./f. sg./m. pl./f. pl.) *yours* (infml.)

U

último/última (m./f.) *last*
  último grito (m.) *the very latest*
un *a* (m.)
una *a* (f.), *one (o'clock)*
  Es la una. *It's one o'clock.*
It's one o'clock.
uña (f.) *nail, claw*
unas *some* (f. pl.)
único/única (m./f.) *only, unique, single*
  de sentido (m.) único *one-way*
unido/unida (m./f.) *united*
  los Estados Unidos *the United States*
universidad (f.) *university*
uno *one*
unos *some* (m. pl.)
urbano/urbana (m./f.) *urban*
urgentemente *urgently*
Uruguay (m.) *Uruguay*
uruguayo/uruguaya (m./f.) *Uruguayan*
usar *to use, to take*
usted *you* (sg. fml.) (subject pronoun)
  el de usted (m. sg.) *yours* (sg. fml.)
  la de usted (f. sg.) *yours* (sg. fml.)
ustedes *you* (pl.) (subject pronoun)
  el de ustedes (m. sg.) *yours* (pl.) (referring to a masculine singular object)
  la de ustedes (f. sg.) *yours* (pl.) (referring to a feminine singular object)
uvas (f. pl.) *grapes*

racimo (m.) de uvas *bunch of grapes*

V

vacaciones (f. pl.) *vacation*
  de vacaciones *on vacation*
vajilla (f.) *tableware*
  detergente (m.) de vajilla *dishwashing detergent*
vale (m.) *coupon, voucher*
  ¿Cuánto vale? *How much is it?*
Vamos … *Let's go …*
vaqueros (m. pl.) *jeans*
variedad (f.) *variety*
varios/varias (m./f.) *several*
vaso (m.) *glass*
vecino/vecina (m./f.) *neighbor*
vegetal (m.) *vegetable*
veinte *twenty*
veinticinco *twenty-five*
veinticuatro *twenty-four*
veintidós *twenty-two*
veintinueve *twenty-nine*
veintiocho *twenty-eight*
veintiséis *twenty-six*
veintisiete *twenty-seven*
veintitrés *twenty-three*
veintiuno *twenty-one*
velocidad (f.) *speed*
vendaje (m.) *bandage*
vendedor/vendedora (m./f.) *salesman/ saleswoman*
vender *to sell*
venezolano/venezolana (m./f.) *Venezuelan*
Venezuela (f.) *Venezuela*
venir *to come, to fit (somebody)*
  año (m.) que viene *next year*
  mes (m.) que viene *next month*
  Me viene bien. *It suits me fine.*
  semana (f.) que viene *next week*
venta (f.) *sale*
ventana (f.) *window*
ver *to see*
  A ver … *Let's see …*
  Nos vemos. *See you. (lit., We see each other.)*
  por lo visto *apparently*
  ver todo negro *to be a pessimist (lit., to see everything as black)*
verano (m.) *summer*

trabajo (m.) de verano *summer job*
verdad (f.) *truth*
  Es verdad. *That's right.*
  No es verdad que ... *It is not true that ...*
  ¿verdad? *right?*
verde (m./f.) *green*
  contar un chiste verde *to tell a dirty joke (lit.,*
    to tell a green joke)
  verde oscuro *dark green*
verdura (f.) *vegetable*
vertebral (m./f.) *vertebral*
  columna (f.) vertebral *backbone, spinal*
    column
vestíbulo (m.) *hall*
vestido (m.) *dress*
  vestido de noche *evening dress*
vestir *to dress (someone)*
vestirse *to get dressed*
veterinario/veterinaria (m./f.) *veterinarian*
vez (f.) *time*
  a veces *sometimes*
  dos veces por semana *twice a week*
  una vez *once*
  tal vez *perhaps*
vía (f.) *lane*
viajar *to travel*
viaje (m.) *travel, trip*
  Buen viaje. *Have a good trip.*
  salir de viaje *to go on a trip*
vida (f.) *life*
  ¿Cómo te trata la vida? *How's life treating*
    you?
  hoja (f.) de vida *résumé*
viejo/vieja (m./f.) *old*
viento (m.) *wind*
  Hace viento. *It's windy.*
viento (m.) *wind*
viernes (m.) *Friday*
vincularse *to form links*
  vincularse con ... *to form links with ...*
vinilo (m.) *vinyl*
  disco (m.) de vinilo *vinyl record*
vino (m.) *wine*
  vino blanco *white wine*
  vino tinto *red wine*
violeta (m./f.) *violet (color)*
violín (m.) *violin*
visita guiada (f.) *guided tour*

visitante (m./f.) *visitor*
visitar *to visit*
  visitar los lugares de interés *to go sightseeing*
vista (f.) *view*
  conocer de vista *to know by sight*
vitorear *to cheer*
vivir *to live*
volar *to fly*
volver *to turn, to return*
vosotras *you* (f. pl. infml.) (subject pronoun)
  (used in Spain)
vosotros *you* (m. pl. infml./mixed group infml.)
  (subject pronoun) (used in Spain)
voz (f.) *voice*
  buzón (m.) de voz *voice mail*
vuelo (m.) *flight*
vuelta (f.) *turn*
  a la vuelta de la esquina *around the corner*
vuestro/vuestra/vuestros/vuestras (m. sg./f.
  sg./m. pl./f. pl.) *your/yours* (pl. infml.) (used in
  Spain)

W

web (f.) *web (internet)*
  página (f.) web *webpage*
  sitio (m.) web *website*

Y

y *and*
  a las ocho y diez *at eight ten (8:10)*
  a las cinco y media *at a half past five*
  treinta y uno *thirty-one*
ya *already, now, right*
  Ya está. *That's it.*
yerno (m.) *son-in-law*
yo *I*

Z

zanahoria (f.) *carrot*
zapatería (f.) *shoe store*
zapatillas (f. pl.) *slippers*
  zapatillas deportivas *sneakers, tennis shoes*
zapatos (m. pl.) *shoes*
zumo (m.) *juice*

English-Spanish

A

a *un/una* (m./f.)
  a lot *mucho*
  a lot of *mucho/mucha* (m./f.), *muchos/muchas* (m. pl./f. pl.)
abdomen *abdomen* (m.)
about *de, sobre, a eso de*
  about the (m.) *del (de + el)*
  at about nine o'clock *a eso de las nueve*
  dream about … *soñar con …*
  How about if …? *¿Qué tal si …?/¿Qué te parece si …?*
  not have a clue about … (to) *no saber ni jota de …*
above *encima, sobre*
  above … *encima de …*
absolute *absoluto/absoluta* (m./f.)
absolutely *absolutamente, totalmente*
  absolutely not *en absoluto*
absurd *absurdo/absurda* (m./f.)
academic *académico/académica* (m./f.)
academy *academia* (f.)
accept (to) *aceptar*
accident *accidente* (m.)
account *cuenta* (f.)
accountant *contable* (m./f.)
across from … *enfrente de …*
actor *actor* (m.)
actress *actriz* (f.)
actually *efectivamente, realmente*
acupuncture *acupuntura* (f.)
address *dirección* (f.)
adult *adulto/adulta* (m./f.)
adventure *aventura* (f.)
  adventure films *películas* (pl.) *de aventuras*
advise (to) *aconsejar*
  advise that/to … (to) *aconsejar que …*
after … *después de …*
  after-dinner conversation *sobremesa* (f.)
  It's ten after one in the morning. *Es la una y diez de la madrugada.*
afternoon *tarde* (f.)
  Good afternoon. *Buenas tardes.*
  in the afternoon *de la tarde*
  this afternoon *esta tarde*

afterwards *después*
against *contra*
age *edad* (f.)
agency *agencia* (f.)
agent *agente* (m./f.)
agitated *agitado/agitada* (m./f.)
agreement *acuerdo* (m.)
aim *objetivo* (m.)
airline *aerolínea* (f.)
airplane *avión* (m.)
airport *aeropuerto* (m.)
algebra *álgebra* (f.)
all *todo/toda* (m./f.)
  all day *todo el día*
  All right. *De acuerdo.*
  No, not at all. *No, para nada.*
allergic *alérgico/alérgica* (m./f.)
allergy *alergia* (f.)
alley *callejón* (m.)
allow (to) *permitir*
almost *casi*
  almost never *casi nunca*
alone *solo/sola* (m./f.)
already *ya*
  as you already know *como ya sabes*
also *igualmente, también*
always *siempre*
a.m. *de la mañana, de la madrugada*
  at nine a.m. *a las nueve de la mañana*
American *americano/americana* (m./f.), *estadounidense* (m./f.)
amusement *diversión* (f.)
  amusement park *parque* (m.) *de diversiones*
and *y*
  and on top of that … *y encima …*
anger *ira* (f.)
ankle *tobillo* (m.)
another *otro/otra* (m./f.)
answer *respuesta* (f.)
answer (to) *responder, contestar*
  answer the phone (to) *contestar el teléfono*
answering machine *contestador* (m.) *(automático)*
antique *antigüedad* (f.)
antiques *antigüedades* (f. pl.)
  antique store *tienda* (f.) *de antigüedades*
any *cualquier*
Anything else? *¿Algo más?*

apartment *apartamento* (m.), *piso* (m.)
apology *disculpa* (f.)
apparently *por lo visto*
appeal *gracia* (f.)
appearance *pinta* (f.)
appetite *apetito* (m.)
appetizer *entrada* (f.)
apple *manzana* (f.)
application *solicitud* (f.)
apply for (to) *solicitar*
appointment *cita* (f.)
April *abril* (m.)
architect *arquitecto/arquitecta* (m./f.)
architecture *arquitectura* (f.)
area *área* (m.)
Argentina *Argentina* (f.)
Argentinian *argentino/argentina* (m./f.)
arm *brazo* (m.)
around *por, a eso de*
  around the corner *a la vuelta de la esquina*
  around town *por la ciudad*
arrive (to) *llegar*
  arrive at … (to) *llegar a …*
art *arte* (m.)
artist *artista* (m./f.)
as *como, cual/cuales* (sg./pl.)
  as … as *tan … como (comparisons), tanto/
  tanta/tantos/tantas* (m. sg./f. sg./m. pl./f. pl.) …
  como (comparisons)
  as many/much *cuanto/cuanta/cuantos/
  cuantas* (m. sg./f. sg./m. pl./f. pl.), *tanto/tanta*
  (m./f.)
  as soon as possible *lo antes posible*
  as you already know *como ya sabes*
ask (to) *preguntar*
ask for (to) *pedir*
assistant *asistente* (m./f.)
astronaut *astronauta* (m./f.)
at *a, en, por*
  arrive at … (to) *llegar a …*
  at a quarter to six *a las seis menos cuarto*
  at about nine o'clock *a eso de las nueve*
  at dawn *al amanecer*
  at dusk *al atardecer*
  at five (o'clock) *a las cinco*
  at hand *a la mano*
  at last *por fin*
  at midnight *a medianoche*

  at night *por la noche*
  at noon *a mediodía*
  at the (m.) *al (a + el)*
  at the present time *actualmente*
  at this moment *en este momento*
  At what time is it? *¿A qué hora es?*
  look at (to) *mirar*
  No, not at all. *No, para nada.*
athlete *atleta* (m./f.)
athletic *atlético/atlética* (m./f.), *deportivo/
  deportiva* (m./f.)
attach (to) *adjuntar*
  attach a file (to) *adjuntar un documento/
  archivo*
attachment *anexo* (m.), *archivo* (m.), *documento*
  (m.) *adjunto*
attend (to) *asistir*
  attend to (to) *atender*
attention *atención* (f.)
attraction *atracción* (f.)
attractive *atractivo/atractiva* (m./f.)
auction *subasta* (f.)
August *agosto* (m.)
aunt *tía* (f.)
author *autor* (m.)
automatic *automático/automático* (m./f.)
available *disponible* (m./f.)
avenue *avenida* (f.)
avocado *aguacate* (m.)
axe *hacha* (f.)

B

baby *bebé* (m./f.)
  little baby *bebito/bebita* (m./f.)
bachelor's degree *licenciatura* (f.)
back *espalda* (f.), *atrás*
  know like the back of one's hand (to) *conocer
  palmo a palmo*
backbone *columna* (f.) *vertebral*
background *historial* (m.)
backyard *patio* (m.)
bad *malo/mala* (m./f.), *podrido/podrida* (m./f.)
  It's not bad. *No está mal.*
bad(ly) *mal*
bag *bolsa* (f.)
baggy *ancho/ancha* (m./f.)
bakery *panadería* (f.), *pastelería* (f.) (for pastries,
  etc.)

balcony *balcón* (m.)
bald *calvo/calva* (m./f.)
ball *balón* (m.), *pelota* (f.)
banana *plátano* (m.), *banana* (f.)
band *banda* (f.), *conjunto* (m.) *(music)*
bandage *vendaje* (m.)
bank *banco* (m.)
banker *banquero/banquera* (m./f.)
bar *bar* (m.)
barbershop *barbería* (f.)
bargain *ganga* (f.)
base *base* (f.)
baseball *béisbol* (m.)
  baseball game *partido* (m.) *de béisbol*
basement *sótano* (m.)
basketball *baloncesto* (m.)
bathe (to) *bañarse*
bathing suit *traje* (m.) *de baño*
bathing trunks *bañador* (m.)
bathroom *baño* (m.)
bathtub *bañera* (f.)
be (to) *estar, ser*
  be … years old (to) *tener … años*
  be a pessimist (to) *ver todo negro* (lit., *to see*
   everything as black)
  be able to (to) *poder*
  be afraid (to) *tener miedo*
  be afraid of (to) *temer*
  be afraid that … (to) *tener miedo de que …*
  be an optimist (to) *ver todo color de rosa* (lit.,
   to see everything pink)
  be angry that … (to) *enfadarse de que …*
  be bored (to) *aburrirse*
  be bothered (to) *molestarse*
  be bothered that … (to) *molestarse de que …*
  be called (to) *llamarse*
  be cold (to) *tener frío*
  be dizzy (to) *tener mareo*
  be dressed to the nines (to) *ir de punta en*
   blanco (lit., *to go from the tip in white*)
  be embarrassed (to) *ponerse colorado* (lit., *to*
   turn red)
  be glad (to) *alegrarse*
  be glad that … (to) *alegrarse de que …*
  be going to (do) (to) *ir a …*
  be hot (to) *tener calor*
  be hungry (to) *tener hambre*
  be in a hurry (to) *tener prisa, tener cansancio*

  be in good hands (to) *estar en buenas manos*
  be interested in … (to) *tener interés en …*
  be lacking (to) *faltar*
  be lazy (to) *ser perezoso*
  be nauseated (to) *tener náusea(s)*
  be necessary (to) *faltar*
  be not doing well (to) *estar mal*
  be patient (to) *tener paciencia*
  be present (to) *asistir*
  be right (to) *tener razón*
  be scared (to) *tener miedo*
  be scared that … (to) *tener miedo de que …*
  be seated (to) *estar sentado*
  be shameless (to) *ser caradura*
  be sleepy (to) *tener sueño*
  be surprised (to) *sorprenderse*
  be surprised that … (to) *sorprenderse de*
   que …
  be thankful (to) *agradecer*
  be thirsty (to) *tener sed*
  be tied (to) *quedar empatados*
  be tired (to) *tener consancio*
  be very angry (to) *estar rojo de la ira* (lit., *to*
   be red with fury)
  be warm (to) *tener calor*
  May you be well. *Que esté bien.*
beach *playa* (f.)
bean *fríjol* (m.)
beauty mark *lunar* (m.)
because *porque*
  because of *por*
become (to) *ponerse*
bed *cama* (f.)
bedroom *dormitorio* (m.), *alcoba* (f.), *cuarto* (m.)
beef *carne* (f.)
beer *cerveza* (f.)
before *antes*
  before … *antes de …*
begin (to) *empezar, comenzar*
behind *detrás, atrás, retrasado/retrasada* (m./f.)
  behind … *detrás de …*
believe (to) *creer*
  not believe that … (to) *no creer que …*
below *bajo*
belt *cinturón* (m.)
benefit *beneficio* (m.), *provecho* (m.)
best (the) *el/la/los/las* (m. sg./f. sg./m. pl./f. pl.)
  mejor

bet *apuesta* (f.)
bet (to) *apostar*
  bet that ... (to) *apuesto a que ...*
better *mejor* (m./f.)
  It's better that ... *Es mejor que ...*
between *entre*
  between ... and ... *entre ... y ...*
bicycle *bicicleta* (f.)
big *gran/grande* (before sg. nouns/all other cases), *gordo/gorda* (m./f.)
  bigger *mayor* (m./f.)
  biggest (the) *el/la/los/las* (m. sg./f. sg./m. pl./f. pl.) *mayor*
biking *ciclismo* (m.)
bill *cuenta* (f.)
billboard *cartelera* (f.)
billiards *billar* (m.)
biology *biología* (f.)
bitter *amargo/amarga* (m./f.)
black *negro/negra* (m./f.)
bleach *lejía* (f.)
blender *batidora* (f.)
block *cuadra* (f.), *manzana* (f.)
  It's two blocks from here. *Está a dos cuadras de aquí.*
block (to) *bloquear*
blonde *rubio/rubia* (m./f.)
blood *sangre* (f.)
  have blue blood (to) *ser de sangre azul* (lit., to be of blue blood)
  have high/low blood pressure (to) *tener la tensión alta/baja*
  take a blood test (to) *hacerse un examen de sangre*
  take the blood pressure (to) *tomar la tensión*
blouse *blusa* (f.)
blue *azul* (m./f.)
  color light blue (the) *azul* (m.) *claro*
  dark blue *azul oscuro*
  have blue blood (to) *ser de sangre azul* (lit., to be of blue blood)
  light blue *azul claro*
  navy blue *azul marino*
  sky blue *celeste* (m./f.)
board *bordo* (m.), *tabla* (f.)
  ironing board *tabla de planchar*
  on board *a bordo*
  Welcome aboard. *Bienvenidos a bordo.*

body *cuerpo* (m.)
Bolivia *Bolivia* (f.)
Bolivian *boliviano/boliviana* (m./f.)
bone *hueso* (m.)
book *libro* (m.)
bookshelf *estante* (m.)
bookstore *librería* (f.)
booth *cabina* (f.)
bore (to) *aburrir*
  I'm bored by ... *Me aburre/aburren ...* (sg./pl.)
bored *aburrido/aburrida* (m./f.)
  be bored (to) *aburrirse*
boring *aburrido/aburrida* (m./f.)
boss *jefe/jefa* (m./f.)
bottle *botella* (f.), *frasco* (m.)
bowl *cuenco* (m.), *tazón* (m.)
box *caja* (f.)
box office *taquilla* (f.)
boy *chico* (m.), *muchacho* (m.)
boyfriend *novio* (m.)
bracelet *pulsera* (f.)
brain *cerebro* (m.)
brake (automobile) *freno* (m.)
  hit the brakes (to) *poner el pie en el freno*
Brazil *Brasil* (m.)
Brazilian *brasilero/brasilera* (m./f.) (adjective), *brasileño/brasileña* (m./f.) (noun)
bread *pan* (m.)
breakfast *desayuno* (m.)
breast *seno* (m.), *pecho* (m.)
bridge *puente* (m.)
bring (to) *traer*
brochure *folleto* (m.)
broom *escoba* (f.)
brother *hermano* (m.)
  brothers, brothers and sisters *hermanos* (pl.)
brother-in-law *cuñado* (m.)
brown *marrón* (m./f.)
  grayish brown *pardo/parda* (m./f.)
buckle up (to) *abrocharse el cinturón de seguridad*
building *edificio* (m.)
bunch *manojo* (m.)
  bunch of grapes *racimo* (m.) *de uvas*
burnt *quemado/quemada* (m./f.)
bus *autobús* (m.)
  tour bus *recorrido* (m.) *por autobús*
bus stop *parada* (f.)

Glossary

business *negocio* (m.)
  businessman *hombre* (m.) *de negocios*
  businesswoman *mujer* (f.) *de negocios*
busy *ocupado/ocupada* (m./f.)
  The line is busy. *Está comunicando.*
but *pero, mas*
butcher shop *carnicería* (f.)
butter *mantequilla* (f.)
buy (to) *comprar*
  buy on sale (to) *comprar en rebaja*
by *por, en*
  by chance *por casualidad*
  by (a certain time) *para*
  go by (to) *pasar*
  I'm bored by … *Me aburre/aburren …* (sg./pl.)
  know by sight (to) *conocer de vista*
Bye. *Chao.*

C

cabin *cabina* (f.)
cable *cable* (m.)
café *cafetería* (f.)
cafeteria *cafetería* (f.)
cake *torta* (f.)
call (to) *llamar*
  be called (to) *llamarse*
  call … on the phone (to) *llamar por teléfono a …*
  make a phone call (to) *llamar por teléfono*
  Who's calling? *¿Quién lo llama?*
calm *tranquilo/tranquila* (m./f.)
camera *cámara* (f.)
camp *campo* (m.)
camping *cámping* (m.)
  go camping (to) *ir de cámping*
can *lata* (f.)
can *poder*
  Could you … ? *¿Podría … ?*
Canada *Canadá* (m.)
Canadian *canadiense* (m./f.)
cancel (to) *cancelar*
candidate *candidato/candidata* (m./f.)
capacity *capacidad* (f.)
car *auto* (m.), *automóvil* (m.), *carro* (m.), *coche* (m.)
card *tarjeta* (f.)
  playing cards *naipes* (m. pl.), *cartas* (f. pl.)
cardboard *cartón* (m.)
carefully *atentamente*

carnival *carnaval* (m.)
carpal tunnel syndrome *síndrome* (m.) *del túnel del carpio*
carpenter *carpintero/carpintera* (m./f.)
carpet *alfombra* (f.)
carpus *carpio* (m.)
carrot *zanahoria* (f.)
carry (to) *llevar*
carton *bote* (m.), *cartón* (m.)
case *caso* (m.)
cash *efectivo* (m.)
  pay cash (to) *pagar en efectivo*
cash register *caja* (f.)
casual *informal* (m./f.)
cat *gato* (m.)
catch (to) *coger*
cathedral *catedral* (f.)
CD *CD* (m.)
  CD player *lector* (m.) *de CD*
  CD-ROM *CD rom* (m.)
  CD-ROM drive *lector* (m.) *de CD rom*
ceiling *techo* (m.)
cell phone *celular* (m.)
center *centro* (m.)
century *siglo* (m.)
  this century *este siglo*
chair *silla* (f.)
champagne *champaña/champán* (f./m.)
champion *campeón/campeona* (m./f.)
championship *campeonato* (m.)
chance *casualidad* (f.)
  by chance *por casualidad*
change *cambio* (m.)
change (to) *cambiar*
channel *canal* (m.)
charm *encanto* (m.)
chat *charla* (f.)
  chat room *espacio* (m.) *para charla, chat* (m.)
cheap *barato/barata* (m./f.)
check *cheque* (m.), *cuenta* (f.)
check in (to) *registrarse*
check out (to) *pagar la cuenta*
cheek *mejilla* (f.)
cheer (to) *vitorear*
cheese *queso* (m.)
chemistry *química* (f.)
chess *ajedrez* (m.)
chest *pecho* (m.)

chicken *pollo* (m.)
child (male/female) *niño/niña* (m./f.)
  child psychology *sicología* (f.) *infantil*
  children (sons and daughters) *hijos* (pl.)
  children's *infantil* (m./f.)
  young child *párvulo/párvula* (m./f.)
Chile *Chile* (m.)
Chilean *chileno/chilena* (m./f.)
chin *barbilla* (f.)
Chinese (language) *chino* (m.)
chocolate *chocolate* (m.)
choir *coro* (m.)
choose (to) *elegir, escoger*
chop *chuleta* (f.)
  lamb chop *chuleta de cordero*
Christmas Eve *Nochebuena*
church *iglesia* (f.)
cigarette *cigarrillo* (m.)
  pack of cigarettes *cajetilla* (f.) *de cigarrillos*
circus *circo* (m.)
city *ciudad* (f.)
city hall *ayuntamiento* (m.)
class *clase* (f.)
classic *clásico/clásica* (m./f.)
  classical music *música* (f.) *clásica*
classroom *aula* (m.)
claw *uña* (f.)
clean *limpio/limpia* (m./f.)
clearly *claramente, claro*
clinic *clínica* (f.)
  clinical pharmacy *farmacia* (f.) *clínica*
clock *reloj* (m.)
close *cerca*
  close to … *cerca de …*
close (to) *cerrar*
closet *armario* (m.)
clothing *ropa* (f.)
  clothing store *tienda* (f.) *de ropa*
cloud *nube* (f.)
cloudy *nublado/nublada* (m./f.)
  It's cloudy. *Está nublado.*
club *club* (m.)
coach *entrenador/entrenadora* (m./f.)
coal *carbón* (m.)
coca *coca* (f.)
code *código* (m.)
coffee *café* (m.)
  coffee shop *cafetería* (f.)

coffee-colored *café* (m./f.)
coffeemaker *cafetera* (f.)
coincidence *coincidencia* (f.)
  What a coincidence! *¡Qué coincidencia!*
coincidence *casualidad* (f.)
cold *frío/fría* (m./f.)
cold temperature/sensation *frío* (m.)
  be cold (to) *tener frío*
  It's cold. *Hace frío.*
colleague *colega/colega* (m./f.)
collect (to) *coleccionar*
collection *colección* (f.)
cologne *colonia* (f.)
Colombia *Colombia* (f.)
Colombian *colombiano/colombiana* (m./f.)
color *color* (m.)
  color gray (the) *gris* (m.)
  color light blue (the) *azul* (m.) *claro*
  wear rose-colored glasses (to) *ver todo color de rosa* (lit., to see everything pink)
  What color is …? *¿De qué color es …?*
column *columna* (f.)
combine (to) *combinar*
come (to) *venir*
comedy *comedia* (f.)
comfortable *cómodo/cómoda* (m./f.)
coming *entrante* (m./f.)
comma *coma* (f.)
commercial *comercial* (m./f.)
communicate (to) *comunicar*
company *compañía* (f.)
complete (to) *completar*
completely *completamente*
computer *computadora* (f.), *ordenador* (m.)
concert *concierto* (m.)
conference *conferencia* (f.)
  conference room *sala de conferencias*
congratulate (to) *felicitar*
congratulations *enhorabuena* (f.)
  Congratulations! *¡Felicitaciones!*
connect (to) *conectar*
connection *conexión* (f.)
construction worker *obrero/obrera* (m./f.)
consult (to) *consultar*
continue (to) *continuar*
  Continue straight. *Continúa recto.*
contract *contrato* (m.)
contribution *contribución* (f.)

convenience store *tienda* (f.)
cook (to) *cocinar*
cookie *galleta* (f.)
cooking *cocina* (f.)
copy *copia* (f.)
copy (to) *copiar*
corncob *mazorca* (f.)
corner *esquina* (f.)
  around the corner *a la vuelta de la esquina*
cost (to) *costar*
  How much does it cost? *¿Cuánto cuesta?*
cotton *algodón* (m.)
couch *sofá* (m.)
cough *tos* (f.)
  have a cough (to) *tener tos*
count (to) *contar*
counter *mostrador* (m.)
country *país* (m.)
coupon *vale* (m.)
course *curso* (m.), *asignatura* (f.)
court *juzgado* (m.)
cousin *primo/prima* (m./f.)
  cousins *primos* (pl.)
craft *artesanía* (f.)
credit *crédito* (m.)
  credit card *tarjeta* (f.) *de crédito*
creme *crema* (f.)
crime *delito* (m.)
cross (to) *cruzar*
cry *grito* (m.)
cry (to) *llorar*
cucumber *pepino* (m.)
cup *taza* (f.)
cupboard *aparador* (m.)
curriculum *currículum* (m.)
  CV *currículum vítae*
curtain *cortina* (f.)
custom sew (to) *hacer a la medida*
customer *cliente* (m./f.)
cycling *ciclismo* (m.)

D

dad *papá* (m.), *papi* (m.)
daily *diario/diaria* (m./f.)
dairy store *lechería* (f.)
dance (to) *bailar*
dancing *baile* (m.)
dark *oscuro/oscura* (m./f.)

dark blue *azul* (m./f.) *oscuro*
dark green *verde* (m./f.) *oscuro*
dark-skinned *moreno/morena* (m./f.)
date *fecha* (f.)
daughter *hija* (f.)
daughter-in-law *nuera* (f.)
dawn *amanecer* (m.)
  at dawn *al amanecer*
day *día* (m.)
  all day *todo el día*
  every day *todos los días*
  Have a nice day. *Que tenga un buen día.*
  special of the day *plato del día*
  spend the day (to) *pasar el día*
  this day *este día*
  working day *jornada* (f.)
dead person, dead *muerto/muerta* (m./f.)
decade *década* (f.)
December *diciembre* (m.)
decide (to) *decidir*
decision *decisión* (f.)
dedicate (to) *dedicar*
degree *grado* (m.), *título* (m.)
delay (to) *retrasar*
delete (to) *eliminar*
delicatessen *charcutería* (f.)
delicious *delicioso/deliciosa* (m./f.)
demand (to) *exigir*
demanding *exigente* (m./f.)
dentist *dentista* (m./f.)
deny (to) *negar*
  deny that … (to) *negar que …*
deodorant *desodorante* (m.)
department *departamento* (m.), *facultad* (f.) (at a college/university)
  department store *tienda* (f.) *por departamentos*
depend (to) *depender*
  depend on … (to) *depender de …*
describe (to) *describir*
description *descripción* (f.)
desert *desierto* (m.)
design *diseño* (m.)
desire *gana* (f.)
desk *escritorio* (m.)
dessert *postre* (m.)
detail *detalle* (m.)
detergent *detergente* (m.)

dishwashing detergent *detergente de vajilla*
laundry detergent *detergente de ropa*
detest (to) *detestar*
develop (to) *desarrollar*
dial (to) *marcar*
  dial a phone number (to) *marcar un número de teléfono*
dial tone *tono* (m.)
diarrhea *diarrea* (f.)
diary *diario* (m.)
  keep a diary (to) *llevar un diario*
die (to) *morir*
difference *diferencia* (f.)
different *diferente* (m./f.)
difficult *difícil* (m./f.)
  difficult situation *apuro* (m.)
digital *digital* (m./f.)
diligently *diligentemente*
diner *cafetería* (f.)
dining room *comedor* (m.)
dinner *cena* (f.), *comida* (f.)
diploma *diploma* (m.), *título* (m.)
direct (to) *dirigir*
direction *dirección* (f.), *sentido* (m.)
dirty *sucio/sucia* (m./f.)
disaster *desastre* (m.)
discount *descuento* (m.), *rebaja* (f.)
  give a discount (to) *hacer un descuento*
discuss (to) *discutir*
disease *enfermedad* (f.)
dish *plato* (m.)
  do the dishes (to) *lavar los platos*
  main dish *plato principal*
dishwasher *lavaplatos* (m.)
dishwashing detergent *detergente* (m.) *de vajilla*
disk *disco* (m.)
Disneyland *Disneylandia*
display window *escaparate* (m.)
dissertation *tesis* (f.)
diving *buceo* (m.)
divorce (someone) (to) *divorciarse de ...*
  get a divorce (to) *divorciarse*
divorced *divorciado/divorciada* (m./f.)
dizzy *mareado/mareada* (m./f.)
  be dizzy (to) *tener mareo*
do (to) *hacer*
  be not doing well (to) *estar mal*

Do me the favor of ... *Hágame el favor de ...*
  do the dishes (to) *lavar los platos*
  do the laundry (to) *lavar la ropa*
doctor *doctor/doctora* (m./f.), *médico/médica* (m./f.)
  doctor's office *consultorio* (m.) *del médico*
document *documento* (m.)
documentary *documental* (m.)
dog *perro* (m.)
dollar *dólar* (m.)
dominate (to) *dominar*
done *hecho/hecha* (m./f.)
door *puerta* (f.)
doubt (to) *dudar*
  doubt that ... (to) *dudar que ...*
download (to) *bajar*
drama *drama* (m.), *obra* (f.) *dramática*
dramatic *dramático/dramática* (m./f.)
draw (to) *empatar*
drawer *cajón* (m.)
dream (to) *soñar*
  Don't even dream about it! *¡Ni lo sueñes!*
  dream about ... *soñar con ...*
dress *vestido* (m.)
  be dressed to the nines (to) *ir de punta en blanco* (lit., to go from the tip in white)
  evening dress *vestido de noche*
dress (someone) (to) *vestir*
dressing room *probador* (m.)
drink *bebida* (f.)
drink (to) *beber*
drive (to) *conducir*
drugstore *farmacia* (f.)
drunk *borracho/borracha* (m./f.)
dry *seco/seca* (m./f.)
dry-clean (to) *lavar en seco*
dryer *secadora* (f.)
DSL *línea* (f.) *de suscriptor/abonado digital* (DSL)
due to *por*
during *durante*
dusk *atardecer* (m.)
  at dusk *al atardecer*
dust *polvo* (m.)
duty *derecho* (m.)
DVD *DVD* (m.)
  DVD player *lector* (m.) *de DVD*

E

each *cada* (m./f.)

ear *oreja* (f.)

early *temprano/temprana* (m./f.)
  early morning (from midnight till
    daybreak) *madrugada* (f.)

early (adverb) *temprano*

earn (to) *ganar*

earnings *ingreso* (m.)

earrings *pendientes* (m. pl.)

easily *fácilmente*

east *este* (m.), *oriente* (m.)

Easter *Pascua* (f.)

easy *fácil* (m./f.)

eat (to) *comer*
  eat dinner (to) *cenar*

economical *económico/económica* (m./f.)

economics *economía* (f.)

Ecuador *Ecuador* (m.)

Ecuadorian *ecuatoriano/ecuatoriana* (m./f.)

efficiently *eficientemente*

egg *huevo* (m.)

eight *ocho*
  at eight ten (8:10) *a las ocho y diez*
  eight hundred *ochocientos/ochocientas* (m./f.)
  twenty-eight *veintiocho*

eighteen *dieciocho, diez y ocho*

eighty *ochenta*

elbow *codo* (m.)

electric *eléctrico/eléctrica* (m./f.)

electrical *eléctrico/eléctrica* (m./f.)
  electrical appliance *electrodoméstico* (m.)

electrician *electricista/electricista* (m./f.)

electronic *electrónico/electrónica* (m./f.)
  electronics store *tienda* (f.) *de
    electrodomésticos*

elegant *elegante* (m./f.)

elementary school *colegio* (m.)

elephant *elefante* (m.)

eleven *once*

eliminate (to) *eliminar*

e-mail *correo* (m.) *electrónico, correo-e* (m.)
  e-mail address *dirección* (f.) *de correo
    electrónico*
  e-mail attachment *anexo* (m.) *al correo
    electrónico*

employee *empleado/empleada* (m./f.)

employment *empleo* (m.)

enchant (to) *encantar*

enclosed *adjunto/adjunta* (m./f.)

end *fin* (m.), *final* (m.), *punta* (f.)

engineer *ingeniero/ingeniera* (m./f.)

engineering *ingeniería* (f.)
  mechanical engineering *ingeniería mecánica*

England *Inglaterra* (f.)

English *inglés/inglesa* (m./f.)

English (language) *inglés* (m.)
  Do you speak English? (infml.) *¿Hablas inglés?*
  Do you speak English? (fml.) *¿Habla usted
    inglés?*

Enjoy the meal! *¡Buen provecho!*

enough *suficiente* (m./f.), *bastante*

enter (to) *entrar*

entertainment *entretenimiento* (m.)

entrance *entrada* (f.)

equal *igual* (m./f.)
  … equals (=) … *… es igual a …*

erase (to) *borrar*

especially *sobre todo*

even *hasta*

evening *noche* (f.)
  evening dress *vestido* (m.) *de noche*
  Good evening. *Buenas noches.*
  in the evening *de la noche*
  this evening *esta noche* (f.)

event *suceso* (m.)

every *todo/toda* (m./f.), *cada* (m./f.)
  every day *todos los días*
  every week *todas las semanas*

everything *todo* (m.)
  How is everything going? *¿Cómo va todo?*

ex- *ex*

exact *exacto/exacta* (m./f.), *en punto*
  Exactly. *Exacto.*

exceed (to) *exceder*

excellent *excelente* (m./f.)

exception *excepción* (f.)

exchange (to) *cambiar, intercambiar*
  in exchange for *por*

exciting *emocionante* (m./f.)

excuse *disculpa* (f.)

excuse (to) *disculpar*
  Excuse me. *Disculpa./Disculpe.* (infml./fml.)/
    Perdón.

exercise *ejercicio* (m.)

exit *salida* (f.)
expense *gasto* (m.)
expensive *caro/cara* (m./f.), *costoso/costosa* (m./f.)
experience *experiencia* (f.)
explanation *explicación* (f.)
extra *extra* (m./f.)
  extra hours *horas* (f. pl.) *extras*
extraordinary *extraordinario/extraordinaria*
  (m./f.)
extroverted *extrovertido/extrovertida* (m./f.)
eye *ojo* (m.)
  an eye for an eye *ojo por ojo*
eyebrow *ceja* (f.)
eyeglasses *gafas* (f. pl.)
  wear rose-colored glasses (to) *ver todo color*
  de rosa (lit., to see everything pink)
eyelashes *pestañas* (f. pl.)

F

face *cara* (f.)
  face the circumstances (to) *dar la cara*
factory *fábrica* (f.)
faculty *profesorado* (m.)
fail (to) *suspender*
  fail a test (to) *suspender un examen*
fall *otoño* (m.)
fall (to) *caer*
  fall flat on one's face (to) *dar de narices*
fame *fama* (f.)
familiar *familiar* (m./f.)
family *familia* (f.)
  (of) family *familiar* (m./f.)
famous *famoso/famosa* (m./f.)
fan *aficionado/aficionada* (m./f.), *hincha* (m./f.)
fantastic *fantástico/fantástica* (m./f.)
far *lejos*
  far from ... *lejos de* ...
farmer *granjero/granjera* (m./f.)
fashion *moda* (f.)
  in fashion *de moda*
fast (adjective) *rápido/rápida* (m./f.)
fast (adverb) *rápidamente, rápido*
fasten (to) *abrochar*
fat *gordo/gorda* (m./f.)
father *padre* (m.)
father-in-law *suegro* (m.)
fatigue *consancio* (m.)
favor *favor* (m.)

  Do me the favor of ... *Hágame el favor de* ...
favorite *favorito/favorita* (m./f.)
fax machine *fax* (m.)
fear *miedo* (m.)
fear (to) *temer*
February *febrero* (m.)
feel (to) *sentir, sentirse*
  feel like ... (to) *tener ganas de* ...
fees *honorarios* (m. pl.)
festive *festivo/festiva* (m./f.)
fever *fiebre* (f.)
  have a fever (to) *tener fiebre*
few *pocos/pocas* (m. pl./f. pl.)
fiancé(e) *prometido/prometida* (m./f.)
field *campo* (m.)
fifteen *quince*
fifty *cincuenta*
file *archivo* (m.), *carpeta* (f.), *documento* (m.)
filing cabinet *armario* (m.)
fill (to) *llenar*
filler phrase *frase* (f.) *de relleno*
  filler word/phrase *muletilla* (f.)
filling *relleno* (m.)
film *película* (f.)
  adventure films *películas* (pl.) *de aventuras*
  horror films *películas de horror*
  romantic films *películas románticas*
  suspense films *películas de suspenso*
finally *por fin*
finance *finanzas* (f. pl.)
find (to) *encontrar*
  find (something) (to) *dar con*
fine (adjective) *estupendo/estupenda* (m./f.)
  Fine. *Pues bien.*
  I'm fine. *Estoy bien.*
fine (noun) *multa* (f.)
finger *dedo* (m.)
finish (to) *acabar, terminar*
first *primer/primero/primera* (before m. sg.
  nouns/m./f.)
fish *pescado* (m.)
  fish shop/market *pescadería* (f.)
fit (to) *quedar*
  fit (somebody) (to) *venir*
  It suits me fine. *Me viene bien.*
five *cinco*
  at a half past five *a las cinco y media*
  at five (o'clock) *a las cinco*

five hundred *quinientos/quinientas* (m./f.)
forty-five *cuarenta y cinco*
It's five to one. (12:55) *Es la una menos cinco.*
twenty-five *veinticinco*
fixed *fijo/fija* (m./f.)
flat *plano/plana* (m./f.)
flea market *mercadillo* (m.)
flight *vuelo* (m.)
floor *suelo* (m.), *piso* (m.)
flower *flor* (f.)
flowing *suelto/suelta* (m./f.)
fly (to) *volar*
fog *niebla* (f.)
follow (to) *seguir*
food *comida* (f.)
fool *bobo/boba* (m./f.)
foot *pie* (m.)
  have both feet on the ground (to) *tener los pies en la tierra*
football *fútbol americano*
for *por, para*
  For God's sake! *¡Por Dios!*
  for this reason *por eso*
forbid (to) *prohibir*
  forbid that/to … (to) *prohibir que …*
forehead *frente* (f.)
foreign *extranjero/extranjera* (m./f.)
forest *bosque* (m.)
forget (to) *olvidar*
fork *tenedor* (m.)
form *planilla* (f.)
  form links (to) *vincularse*
  form links with … (to) *vincularse con …*
forty *cuarenta*
  forty-five *cuarenta y cinco*
forward (to) *retransmitir, pasar*
fossil *fósil* (m.)
four *cuatro*
  at four p.m. *a las cuatro de la tarde*
  four hundred *cuatrocientos/cuatrocientas* (m./f.)
  twenty-four *veinticuatro*
fourteen *catorce*
free *gratis, libre* (m./f.)
freeway *autopista* (f.), *autovía* (f.), *carretera* (f.)
French *francés/francesa* (m./f.)
French (language) *francés* (m.)
  I speak French fluently. *Domino el francés.*

frequency *frecuencia* (f.)
frequent *frecuente* (m./f.)
frequently *frecuentemente, con frecuencia*
Friday *viernes* (m.)
fried *frito/frita* (m./f.)
friend *amigo/amiga* (m./f.)
friendly *simpático/simpática* (m./f.)
from *de, desde*
  across from … *enfrente de …*
  far from … *lejos de …*
  from the (m.) *del (de + el)*
  from … through … *de … a …*
  It's two blocks from here. *Está a dos cuadras de aquí.*
  start from … (to) *partir de …*
  Where are you from? *¿De dónde eres?*
fruit *fruta* (f.)
full *completo/completa* (m./f.)
  full-time *a tiempo completo*
fun *divertido/divertida* (m./f.)
  have fun (to) *divertirse*
function (to) *funcionar*
funny *gracioso/graciosa* (m./f.)
furnished *amueblado/amueblada* (m./f.)
furniture *muebles* (m. pl.)
future *futuro* (m.)

G

gallery *galería* (f.)
game *juego* (m.), *partido* (m.) *(sport)*
garage *garaje* (m.)
garden *jardín* (m.)
garment *prenda* (f.)
gas station *gasolinera* (f.)
gather (to) *reunir*
gel *gel* (m.)
generally *generalmente*
generous *generoso/generosa* (m./f.)
gentleman *caballero* (m.)
geography *geografía* (f.)
German *alemán/alemana* (m./f.)
German (language) *alemán* (m.)
get (to) *sacar, traer*
  get a divorce (to) *divorciarse*
  get angry (to) *enfadarse*
  get dressed (to) *vestirse*
  get good/bad grades (to) *sacar buenas/malas notas*

get married (to) *casarse*
get to … (to) *llegar a …*
get up (to) *levantarse, despertarse*
  I get up. *Me levanto.*
gift *regalo* (m.)
girl *chica* (f.), *muchacha* (f.)
girlfriend *novia* (f.)
give (to) *dar*
  give (a gift) (to) *regalar*
  give a discount (to) *hacer un descuento*
  give birth (to) *dar a luz*
  give thanks (to) *dar (las) gracias*
glass *vaso* (m.)
gloves *guantes* (m. pl.)
go (to) *ir, marchar*
  be going to (do) (to), go to (a place) (to) *ir a …*
  go by (to) *pasar*
  go camping (to) *ir de cámping*
  go crazy (to), go out of one's mind (to) *pararse de cabeza*
  go hiking (to) *hacer excursionismo, hacer senderismo*
  go on a trip (to) *salir de viaje*
  go out (to) *salir*
  go shopping (to) *ir de compras*
  go sightseeing (to) *visitar los lugares de interés*
  Go straight. *Siga derecho.*
  go through a light (to) *saltarse el semáforo*
  go to bed (to) *acostarse*
  go window-shopping (to) *ir de escaparates*
  go with … (to) *combinar con …*
  How's it going? *¿Qué pasa?*
  What's going on? *¿Qué hay?*
goal *gol* (m.)
  score a goal (to) *anotar/hacer/marcar un gol*
goalkeeper *portero* (m.)
God *Dios* (m.)
  For God's sake! *¡Por Dios!*
gold (color) *dorado/dorada* (m./f.)
good *buen/bueno/buena* (before m. sg. nouns/m./f.)
  be in good hands (to) *estar en buenas manos*
  Good afternoon. *Buenas tardes.*
  Good evening./Good night. *Buenas noches.*
  Good job! *¡Buen trabajo!*
  Good morning. *Buenos días.*
  Have a good trip. *Buen viaje.*

  It's good that … *Es bueno que …*
  The weather is good. *El tiempo es bueno.*
Good-bye. *Adiós.*
  say good-bye (to) *despedirse*
grace *gracia* (f.)
grade *nota* (f.)
  grades *calificaciones* (f. pl.)
  get good/bad grades (to) *sacar buenas/malas notas*
graduate (to) *graduarse*
gram *gramo* (m.)
grandchildren *nietos* (pl.)
granddaughter *nieta* (f.)
grandfather *abuelo* (m.)
grandmother *abuela* (f.)
grandparents *abuelos* (pl.)
grandson *nieto* (m.)
grapes *uvas* (f. pl.)
  bunch of grapes *racimo* (m.) *de uvas*
graphic *gráfico/gráfica* (m./f.)
grass *césped* (m.)
gray *gris* (m./f.)
  gray (the color) *gris* (m.)
great *gran/grande* (before sg. nouns/all other cases), *magnífico/magnífica* (m./f.)
  Great! *¡Estupendo!*
green *verde* (m./f.)
  dark green *verde oscuro*
greeting *saludo* (m.)
grill *parrilla* (f.)
  grilled *a la parrilla*
grill (to) *asar*
guava *guayaba* (f.)
guest *invitado/invitada* (m./f.)
guidebook *guía* (f.)
guided tour *visita guiada* (f.)
guitar *guitarra* (f.)
  play the guitar (to) *tocar la guitarra*
gymnasium *gimnasio* (m.)
gymnastics *gimnasia* (f.)

H

hail (to) *granizar*
  It's hailing. *Está granizando.*
hair *pelo* (m.)
hair salon *peluquería* (f.)
half *medio/media* (m./f.)
  at a half past five *a las cinco y media*

halftime *medio tiempo* (m.)
hall *vestíbulo* (m.)
ham *jamón* (m.)
hand *mano* (f.)
  at hand *a la mano*
  be in good hands (to) *estar en buenas manos*
  hand wash (to) *lavar a mano*
  know like the back of one's hand (to) *conocer palmo a palmo*
  on the left-hand side *a mano izquierda*
  on the one hand *por una parte*
  on the other hand *por otra parte*
  on the right-hand side *a mano derecha*
  shake hands (to) *dar la mano*
handbag *bolso* (m.), *cartera* (f.)
handful *manojo* (m.)
handle *manejar*
hang (to) *colgar*
  hang up the phone (to) *colgar el teléfono*
happen (to) *pasar*
  What's happening? *¿Qué tal?*
happening *suceso* (m.)
happily *felizmente*
happy *alegre* (m./f.), *contento/contenta* (m./f.), *feliz* (m./f.)
hard *duro/dura* (m./f.)
hardworking *trabajador* (m./f.)
hat *sombrero* (m.)
have (to) *tener, haber, tomar (food and drink)*
  Do you have time? *¿Cómo estás de tiempo?*
  have a cough (to) *tener tos*
  have a fever (to) *tener fiebre*
  Have a good trip. *Buen viaje.*
  have a headache (to) *tener dolor de cabeza*
  Have a nice day. *Que tenga un buen día.*
  have a sore throat (to) *tener dolor de garganta*
  have an operation (to) *operarse*
  have an upset stomach (to) *estar mal del estómago*
  have blue blood (to) *ser de sangre azul (lit., to be of blue blood)*
  have both feet on the ground (to) *tener los pies en la tierra*
  have fun (to) *divertirse*
  have high/low blood pressure (to) *tener la tensión alta/baja*
  have just … (done something) (to) *acabar de …*

have lunch (to) *almorzar*
have nausea (to) *tener náusea(s)*
have permission to (to) *poder*
have to … (to) *tener que …*
How have you been? *¿Cómo te ha ido?*
not have a clue about … (to) *no saber ni jota de …*
What time do you have? *¿Qué hora tiene?*
You have to … *Tienes que …*
he *él*
head *cabeza* (f.), *cabecera* (f.)
  have a headache (to) *tener dolor de cabeza*
  keep a cool head (to) *tener la cabeza fría*
  lose one's head (to) *perder la cabeza*
headphones *audífonos* (m. pl.)
healthy *saludable* (m./f.)
hear (to) *oír*
heart *corazón* (m.)
heat *calor* (m.)
heel *tacón* (m.)
height *alto* (m.)
Hello. *Hola.*
  Hello! *¡Saludos!*
  Hello? (on the phone) *¿Aló?/¿Dígame?*
help *ayuda* (f.)
  How may I help you? *¿En qué puedo servirle?*
  Thank you for your help. *Le agradezco su ayuda.*
help (to) *ayudar*
  Can you help me? *¿Puede ayudarme?*
her (before a noun) *su/sus* (sg./pl.)
  her (direct object pronoun) *la*
  (to/for) her (indirect object pronoun) *le, se (used in place of le when preceding lo/la/los/las)*
herb *hierba* (f.)
here *aquí*
  Here is … *Aquí está …*
  Here you are. *Aquí tiene.*
  Here we are. *Pues, aquí estamos.*
  It's two blocks from here. *Está a dos cuadras de aquí.*
hers *suyo/suya/suyos/suyas* (m. sg./f. sg./m. pl./f. pl.), *el de ella* (m. sg.), *la de ella* (f. sg.)
herself *se*
hey (filler word) *che (Argentina), oye*
hide-and-seek *escondidas* (f. pl.)
high *alto/alta* (m./f.)
  have high blood pressure (to) *tener la tensión*

alta

highway *autopista* (f.), *autovía* (f.), *carretera* (f.)

hiking *excursionismo* (m.), *senderismo* (m.)
  go hiking (to) *hacer excursionismo, hacer senderismo*

hill *cerro* (m.), *colina* (f.)

him (direct object pronoun) *lo*
  (to/for) him (indirect object pronoun) *le, se* (used in place of le when preceding lo/la/los/las)

himself *se*

hip *cadera* (f.)

his *suyo/suya/suyos/suyas* (m. sg./f. sg./m. pl./f. pl.), *el de él* (m. sg.), *la de él* (f. sg.)
  his (before a noun) *su/sus* (sg./pl.)

history *historia* (f.)

Hmm ... *Mire ...*

hobby *afición* (f.), *pasatiempos* (m.)

hockey *hockey* (m.)

hold (to) *poseer*
  Hold on. *Un momento.*
  Hold on, please. *Espere, por favor.*
  put on hold (to) *poner en espera*

holiday *fiesta* (f.), *día* (m.) *festivo*

homeopathy *homeopatía* (f.)

homework *tarea* (f.)

honest *honesto/honesta* (m./f.)

honey *miel* (f.)

hope (to) *esperar*
  hope that ... (to) *esperar que ...*
  I hope ... *Ojalá que ...*
  I hope so! *¡Yo espero que sí!*

horror *horror* (m.)
  horror films *películas* (f. pl.) *de horror*

horse *caballo* (m.)

horseback riding *equitación* (f.)

hospital *hospital* (m.)

hot *caliente* (m./f.)
  be hot (to) *tener calor*
  It's hot. *Hace calor.*

hotel *hotel* (m.)

hour *hora* (f.)
  extra hours *horas* (pl.) *extras*

house *casa* (f.)

how *cómo*
  Do you know how to ... ? *¿Sabe cómo ... ?*
  How ... ! *¡Qué ... !*
  How about if ... ? *¿Qué tal si ... ?/¿Qué te*

parece si ... ?
  How are things? *¿Cómo van las cosas?*
  How are you doing for time? *¿Cómo estás de tiempo?*
  How are you? *¿Cómo está usted?* (fml.)/*¿Cómo estás (tú)?* (infml.)
  How do I know!?/How should I know!? *¡Yo qué sé!*
  How do you say " ... " in ... ? *¿Cómo se dice " ... " en ... ?*
  How have you been? *¿Cómo te ha ido?*
  How is everything going? *¿Cómo va todo?*
  how many *cuántos/cuántas* (m. pl./f. pl.)
  How may I help you? *¿En qué puedo servirle?*
  how much *cuánto/cuánta* (m./f.)
  How much does it cost? *¿Cuánto cuesta?*
  How much is it? *¿Cuánto es?/¿Cuánto vale?*
  How nice! *¡Qué bien!*
  How old are you (sg. fml.)/is he/is she? *¿Cuántos años tiene?*
  How's it going? *¿Qué pasa?*
  How's life treating you? *¿Cómo te trata la vida?*
  learn how to ... (to) *aprender a ...*

huge *enorme* (m./f.)

human *humano/humana* (m./f.)
  human body *cuerpo* (m.) *humano*

hundred *cien/ciento* (before a noun/before a number except mil)
  eight hundred *ochocientos/ochocientas* (m./f.)
  five hundred *quinientos/quinientas* (m./f.)
  four hundred *cuatrocientos/cuatrocientas* (m./f.)
  hundred thousand *cien mil*
  nine hundred *novecientos/novecientas* (m./f.)
  one hundred and three dollars *ciento tres dólares*
  one hundred people *cien personas*
  one hundred percent *cien por ciento*
  seven hundred *setecientos/setecientas* (m./f.)
  six hundred *seiscientos/seiscientas* (m./f.)
  three hundred *trescientos/trescientas* (m./f.)
  two hundred *doscientos/doscientas* (m./f.)

hunger *hambre* (f.)

hunting *caza* (f.)

hurricane *huracán* (m.)

hurry *prisa* (f.)
  be in a hurry (to) *tener prisa*

husband *esposo* (m.), *marido* (m.)
hygienic *higiénico/higiénica* (m./f.)

I

I *yo*
ice *hielo* (m.)
ice cream *helado* (m.)
  ice cream parlor *heladería* (f.)
idea *idea* (f.)
ideal *ideal* (m./f.)
idiot *bobo/boba* (m./f.)
if *si*
  How about if … ? *¿Qué tal si … ?/¿Qué te parece si … ?*
illness *enfermedad* (f.), *mal* (m.)
imagine (to) *imaginar*
immediate *inmediato/inmediata* (m./f.)
immediately *inmediatamente, de inmediato*
important *importante* (m./f.)
impossible *imposible* (m./f.)
  It is impossible that … *Es imposible que …*
impressive *impresionante* (m./f.)
in *en*
  be in a hurry (to) *tener prisa*
  be in good hands (to) *estar en buenas manos*
  be interested in … (to) *tener interés en …*
  check in (to) *registrarse*
  in exchange for *por*
  in fashion *de moda*
  in front *delante*
  in front of … *delante de …/enfrente de …*
  in love *enamorado/enamorada* (m./f.)
  in order to *para*
  in place of *por*
  in style *de moda*
  in the afternoon *de la tarde*
  in the early morning *de la madrugada*
  in the evening *de la noche*
  in the morning *de la mañana*
incentive *incentivo* (m.)
include (to) *incluir*
  Is service included? *¿Está incluido el servicio?*
information *información* (f.)
  information center *centro* (m.) *de información*
ingredient *ingrediente* (m.)
inherit (to) *heredar*
injury *lesión* (f.)

inside *dentro*
  inside of … *dentro de …*
insist (to) *insistir*
  insist that … (to) *insistir en que …*
instantaneous *instantáneo/instantánea* (m./f.)
instant message *mensaje* (m.) *instantáneo*
insurance *seguro* (m.)
intelligent *inteligente* (m./f.)
intended for *para*
interest *interés* (m.)
interest (to) *interesar*
  be interested in … (to) *tener interés en …*
  I'm interested in … (to) *Me interesa/interesan …* (sg./pl.)
interesting *interesante* (m./f.)
intermediate *intermedio/intermedia* (m./f.)
international *internacional* (m./f.)
  international call *llamada* (f.) *internacional*
internet *Internet*
intersection *cruce* (m.), *intersección* (f.)
interview *entrevista* (f.)
interview (to) *entrevistar*
introduce (to) *presentar*
  Let me introduce you to … *Te presento a …*
investigation *investigación* (f.)
invitation *invitación* (f.)
invite (to) *invitar*
iron *plancha* (f.)
iron (to) *planchar*
  ironing board *tabla* (f.) *de planchar*
it (direct object pronoun) *lo/la* (m./f.)
  (to/for) it (indirect object pronoun) *le, se* (used in place of *le* when preceding *lo/la/los/las*)
  That's it. *Ya está.*
It is … *Es …/Está …*
  It's a pity that … *Es una lástima que …*
  It's a pleasure. *Mucho gusto.*
  It's beautiful. (weather) *Hace muy buen tiempo.*
  It's better that … *Es mejor que …*
  It's cloudy. *Está nublado.*
  It's cold. *Hace frío.*
  It's five to one. (12:55) *Es la una menos cinco.*
  It's good that … *Es bueno que …*
  It's hailing. *Está granizando.*
  It's hot. *Hace calor.*
  It's impossible that … *Es imposible que …*
  It's necessary that … *Es necesario que …*

It's necessary to ... *Hay que ...*
It's not bad. *No está mal.*
It's not true that ... *No es cierto que ...*
It's one o'clock. *Es la una.*
It's possible that ... *Es posible que ...*
It's preferable that ... *Es preferible que ...*
It's raining. *Está lloviendo.*
It's sad that ... *Es triste que ...*
It's snowing. *Está nevando.*
It's sunny. *Hace sol.*
It's ten after one in the morning. *Es la una y diez de la madrugada.*
It's three o'clock sharp. *Son las tres en punto.*
It's three o'clock. *Son las tres.*
It's twelve noon. *Son las doce del mediodía.*
It's two blocks from here. *Está a dos cuadras de aquí.*
It's windy. *Hace viento.*
Italian *italiano/italiana* (m./f.)
Italian (language) *italiano* (m.)
its *su/sus* (sg./pl.)
itself *se*

J

jacket *americana* (f.), *chaqueta* (f.), *saco* (m.)
jam *mermelada* (f.)
January *enero* (m.)
jar *frasco* (m.)
jazz *jazz* (m.)
jealous *celoso/celosa* (m./f.)
jeans *jeans* (m. pl.), *tejanos* (m. pl.), *vaqueros* (m. pl.)
job *trabajo* (m.), *empleo* (m.)
  Good job! *¡Buen trabajo!*
  summer job *trabajo de verano*
  steady job *trabajo fijo*
jog (to) *trotar*
joke *chiste* (m.)
  tell a dirty joke (to) (lit., to tell a green joke) *contar un chiste verde*
journalist *periodista* (m./f.)
judge *juez* (m.)
juice *jugo* (m.), *zumo* (m.)
July *julio* (m.)
June *junio* (m.)

K

keep (to) *llevar, guardar*
  keep a cool head (to) *tener la cabeza fría*

keep a diary (to) *llevar un diario*
key *llave* (f.)
keyboard *teclado* (m.)
kid *crío/cría* (m./f.)
kilo, kilogram *kilo* (m.)
kilometer *kilómetro* (m.)
kind *clase* (f.)
  all kinds *toda clase*
kiss (to) *besar*
kitchen *cocina* (f.)
knee *rodilla* (f.)
knife *cuchillo* (m.)
know (to) *saber (facts, information), conocer (people, places)*
  as you already know *como ya sabes*
  Do you know how to ... ? *¿Sabe cómo ...?*
  How do I know!?/How should I know!? *¡Yo qué sé!*
  know by sight (to) *conocer de vista*
  know like the back of one's hand (to) *conocer palmo a palmo*
  make known (to) *dar a conocer*
  not have a clue about ... (to) *no saber ni jota de ...*
  not know (to) *desconocer*
  Who knows? *¿Quién sabe?*

L

label *etiqueta* (f.)
lake *lago* (m.)
lamb *cordero/cordera* (m./f.)
  lamb chop *chuleta* (f.) *de cordero*
lamp *lámpara* (f.)
lamppost *farola* (f.)
land *tierra* (f.)
lane *carril* (m.), *vía* (f.)
  Stay in the right lane. *Siga por el carril de la derecha.*
language *idioma* (m.), *lengua* (f.)
large *gran/grande* (before sg. nouns/all other cases)
last *último/última* (m./f.)
  at last *por fin*
  last month *mes* (m.) *pasado*
  last night *anoche*
  last week *semana* (f.) *pasada*
  last year *año* (m.) *pasado*
late *tarde*

I'll see you later. *Hasta luego.*
I'm late. *Se me hace tarde.*
late night (from midnight) *madrugada* (f.)
later *más tarde, luego*
Until later. *Hasta más tarde.*
very latest (the) *último grito* (m.)
laugh (to) *reír*
  laugh very hard (to) (lit., to turn black with laughter) *estar negro de la risa*
laughter *risa* (f.)
laundry detergent *detergente* (m.) *de ropa*
law *derecho* (m.)
lawn *césped* (m.)
lawyer *abogado/abogada* (m./f.)
lazy *perezoso/perezosa* (m./f.)
  be lazy (to) *ser perezoso*
learn (to) *aprender, saber*
  learn how to … (to) *aprender a …*
  I'm learning Spanish. *Estoy aprendiendo español.*
least … in/of … (the) *el/la/los/las* (m. sg./f. sg./m. pl./f. pl.) *menos … de …*
leather *cuero* (m.)
leave (to) *dejar, marchar, parar, partir, salir*
  leave a message after the tone (to) *dejar un mensaje después de oír la señal*
lecture *conferencia* (f.)
  lecture hall *sala* (f.) *de conferencias*
left side *izquierda* (f.)
  on the left *a la izquierda*
  Turn left. *Gira a la izquierda.*
left-hand *izquierdo/izquierda* (m./f.)
  on the left-hand side *a mano izquierda*
leg *pierna* (f.)
lemon *limón* (m.)
lemonade *limonada* (f.)
less *menos*
  least … in/of … (the) *el/la/los/las* (m. sg./f. sg./m. pl./f. pl.) *menos … de …*
  less … than … *menos … que …*
  more or less *más o menos*
lesson *lección* (f.)
Let's go … *Vamos …*
Let's see … *A ver …*
letter *cartas* (f. pl.)
lettuce *lechuga* (f.)
library *biblioteca* (f.)
lie (to) *mentir*

life *vida* (f.)
  How's life treating you? *¿Cómo te trata la vida?*
lift (to) *levantar*
light *luz* (f.)
  turn off the lights (to) *apagar las luces*
light *claro/clara* (m./f.), *ligero/ligera* (m./f.)
  light blue *azul* (m./f.) *claro*
lightening *relámpago* (m.)
like *como*
like (to) *(se) gustar*
  I like … *Me gusta/gustan …* (sg./pl.)
  I really like … *Me encanta/encantan …* (sg./pl.)
  I'd like … *Me gustaría …*
  like (it) that … (to) *gustar que …*
  What would you like? *¿Qué desea?*
likewise *igualmente*
limit *límite* (m.)
line *cola* (f.), *fila* (f.), *línea* (f.)
  stand in line (to) *hacer una cola/fila*
  The line is busy. *Está comunicando.*
linen *lino* (m.)
lip *labio* (m.)
list *lista* (f.)
  list of plays *cartelera* (f.)
listen to (to) *escuchar*
liter *litro* (m.)
literature *literatura* (f.)
little *poco*
  a little *un poco*
  I speak a little Spanish. *Hablo un poco de español.*
live (to) *vivir*
  What do you do for a living? *¿En qué trabaja?*
living room *sala* (f.)
loan *crédito* (m.), *préstamo* (m.)
lobster *langosta* (f.)
local *local* (m./f.)
  local call *llamada* (f.) *local*
London *Londres*
long *largo/larga* (m./f.)
  long weekend *puente* (m.)
look at (to) *mirar*
look for (to) *buscar*
look like (to) *parecer*
look up (to) *consultar*
loose *suelto/suelta* (m./f.)
Los Angeles *Los Ángeles*

lose (to) *perder*
  lose one's head (to) *perder la cabeza*
lottery *lotería* (f.)
love (to) *querer, amar*
  I love you. *Te quiero.*
  I'd love to! *¡Me encantaría!*
  in love *enamorado/enamorada* (m./f.)
low-cost *económico/económica* (m./f.)
low-cut *escotado/escotada* (m./f.)
lower (to) *bajar*
LP *disco de vinilo* (m.)
luck *suerte* (f.)
lunch *almuerzo* (m.)
  have lunch (to) *almorzar*
lungs *pulmones* (m. pl.)

M

made *hecho/hecha* (m./f.)
magazine *revista* (f.)
magical *mágico/mágica* (m./f.)
magnificent *magnífico/magnífica* (m./f.)
mailbox *buzón* (m.)
main *principal* (m./f.)
  main dish *plato* (m.) *principal*
major *carrera* (f.), *especialidad* (f.)
major in … (to) *especializarse en …*
  make (to) *hacer*
  make an international/local/national call
    (to) *hacer una llamada internacional/local/
    nacional*
  make known (to) *dar a conocer*
man *hombre* (m.), *tío* (m., colloquial)
manager *gerente* (m.)
manner *forma* (f.)
many *muchos/muchas* (m. pl./f. pl.)
  how many *cuántos/cuántas* (m. pl./f. pl.)
map *mapa* (m.), *plano* (m.)
March *marzo* (m.)
marine *marino/marina* (m./f.)
mark (to) *marcar*
market *mercado* (m.)
  flea market *mercadillo*
marriage *matrimonio* (m.)
married *casado/casada* (m./f.)
marry (someone) (to) *casarse con*
  get married (to) *casarse*
martini *martini* (m.)
martyr *mártir* (m./f.)

marvelous *estupendo/estupenda* (m./f.)
master (to) *dominar*
master's degree *maestría* (f.), *especialización* (f.)
match (to) *combinar*
material *material* (m.)
mathematics *matemáticas* (f. pl.)
matter (to) *importar*
  It doesn't matter. *No importa.*
May *mayo* (m.)
May I please … ? (fml.) *¿Me permite … ?*
  (fml.)/*¿Me permites … ?* (infml.)
  May you be well. *Que esté bien.*
mayor *alcalde* (m.)
me (after a proposition) *mí*
  me (direct object pronoun) *me*
  (to/for) me (indirect object pronoun) *me*
mean (to) *significar*
  What does that mean? *¿Qué quiere decir eso?*
meanwhile *mientras tanto*
measure (to) *medir*
measurement *medida* (f.)
meat *carne* (f.)
mechanical *mecánico/mecánica* (m./f.)
  mechanical engineering *ingeniería* (f.)
    mecánica
medication *medicamento* (m.)
  take medication (to) *tomar un medicamento*
medicine *medicina* (f.)
  medicine cabinet *botiquín* (m.)
medium *mediano/mediana* (m./f.), *término* (m.)
  tres cuartos (cooked meat)
  medium-rare *término* (m.) *medio*
meet (to) *conocer, reunirse*
  meet (somebody) (to) *conocer (a alguien),
    encontrarse con*
  meet up with (to) *encontrar*
  Pleased to meet you. *Gusto en conocerlo/la.*
meeting *reunión* (f.), *conferencia* (f.)
  meeting room *sala* (f.) *de conferencias*
memory *memoria* (f.)
menu *carta* (f.)
merely *sólo*
message *mensaje* (m.)
  instant message *mensaje instantáneo*
  leave a message after the tone (to) *dejar un
    mensaje después de oír la señal*
metro *metro* (m.)
Mexican *mexicano/mexicana* (m./f.)

Mexico *México* (m.)

microwave *microondas* (m.)

midnight *medianoche* (f.), *media noche* (f.)

  at midnight *a medianoche*

midway *medio/media* (m./f.)

milk *leche* (f.)

  powdered milk *leche en polvo*

  skim milk *leche descremada*

million *millón*

  one million houses *un millón de casas*

mind *mente* (f.)

  go out of one's mind (to) *pararse de cabeza*

mine *mío/mía/míos/mías* (m. sg./f. sg./m. pl./f. pl.)

minus (-) *menos*

minute *minuto* (m.)

miracle *maravilla* (f.)

mirror *espejo* (m.)

misfortune *desgracia* (f.)

miss (to) *perder, faltar*

mixed *mixto/mixta* (m./f.)

mobile phone *móvil* (m.)

modem *módem* (m.)

modern *moderno/moderna* (m./f.)

molar *muela* (f.)

mole *lunar* (m.)

mom *mamá* (f.), *mami* (f.)

moment *momento* (m.)

  at this moment *en este momento*

  One moment. *Un momento.*

Monday *lunes* (m.)

money *dinero* (m.)

monitor *monitor* (m.)

month *mes* (m.)

  last month *mes pasado*

  next month *mes entrante, mes que viene*

  this month *este mes*

monument *monumento* (m.)

moon *luna* (f.)

more *más*

  more or less *más o menos*

  more …/-er than … *más … que …*

moreover *además*

morning *mañana* (f.)

  early morning (from midnight till
    daybreak) *madrugada* (f.)

  Good morning. *Buenos días.*

  in the early morning *de la madrugada*

  in the morning *de la mañana*

  It's ten after one in the morning. *Es la una y diez de la madrugada.*

  this morning *esta mañana*

Moscow *Moscú*

mosque *mezquita* (f.)

most … in/of … (the) *el/la/los/las* (m. sg./f. sg./m. pl./f. pl.) *más … de …*

mother *madre* (f.)

mother-in-law *suegra* (f.)

mountain *montaña* (f.)

mouse *ratón* (m.)

mouth *boca* (f.)

move (to) *mover*

movie *película* (f.)

  movie listing *cartelera de cine*

  movie theater *cine* (m.)

Mr. *señor* (m.), *don* (m.)

Mrs. *señora* (f.), *doña* (f.)

much *mucho*

  how much *cuánto/cuánta* (m./f.)

municipal building *ayuntamiento* (m.), *alcaldía* (f.)

muscle *músculo* (m.)

museum *museo* (m.)

music *música* (f.)

  classical music *música clásica*

musical *musical* (m.)

musician *músico* (m.)

must *deber*

my *mi/mis* (sg./pl.)

myself *me*

N

nail *uña* (f.)

name *nombre* (m.)

  My name is … *Me llamo …*

  What's your name? *¿Cómo se llama usted?* (fml.)/*¿Cómo te llamas?* (infml.)

nap *siesta* (f.)

napkin *servilleta* (f.)

narrow *angosto/angosta* (m./f.), *estrecho/estrecha* (m./f.)

national *nacional* (m./f.)

  national call *llamada* (f.) *nacional*

nationality *nacionalidad* (f.)

natural *natural* (m./f.)

nature *naturaleza* (f.)

nausea *náusea* (f.)

be nauseated/have nausea (to) *tener náusea(s)*
navy blue *azul* (m./f.) *marino*
near *cerca, próximo/próxima* (m./f.)
  near ... *cerca de ...*
necessary *necesario/necesaria* (m./f.)
  be necessary (to) *faltar*
  It's necessary that ... *Es necesario que ...*
  It's necessary to ... *Hay que ...*
neck *cuello* (m.)
necklace *collar* (m.)
need (to) *necesitar*
needle *aguja* (f.)
neighbor *vecino/vecina* (m./f.)
neighborhood *barrio* (m.)
neither *tampoco*
  neither ... nor *ni ... ni*
nephew *sobrino* (m.)
nerve *nervio* (m.)
never *nunca*
  almost never *casi nunca*
new *nuevo/nueva* (m./f.)
news *noticias* (pl.)
  a piece of news *noticia* (f.)
newspaper *periódico* (m.)
New York *Nueva York*
next *próximo/próxima* (m./f.)
  next month *mes* (m.) *que viene*
  next to ... *al lado de ...*
  next week *próxima semana* (f.), *semana* (f.) *que viene*
  next year *año* (m.) *que viene*
nice *bonito/bonita* (m./f.)
  Have a nice day. *Que tenga un buen día.*
  How nice! *¡Qué bien!*
niece *sobrina* (f.)
night *noche* (f.)
  at night *de la noche*
  Good night. *Buenas noches.*
  last night *anoche*
  late night (from midnight) *madrugada* (f.)
nine *nueve*
  at about nine o'clock *a eso de las nueve*
  at nine a.m. *a las nueve de la mañana*
  be dressed to the nines (to) *ir de punta en blanco* (lit., to go from the tip in white)
  nine hundred *novecientos/novecientas* (m./f.)
  twenty-nine *veintinueve*

nineteen *diecinueve, diez y nueve*
ninety *noventa*
no *no, ningún/ninguno/ninguna* (before m. sg. nouns/m. sg./f. sg.)
  no one *nadie*
  No, not at all. *No, para nada.*
  There's no ... that/who ... *No hay ningún ... que ...*
  There's no one who/that ... *No hay nadie que ...*
nobody *nadie*
  There's no one who/that ... *No hay nadie que ...*
none *ningún/ninguno/ninguna* (before m. sg. nouns/m. sg./f. sg.)
noon *mediodía* (m.)
  at noon *a mediodía*
  It's twelve noon. *Son las doce del mediodía.*
nor *ni*
  neither ... nor *ni ... ni*
normal *normal* (m./f.)
normally *normalmente*
north *norte* (m.)
nose *nariz* (f.)
not *no*
  absolutely not *en absoluto*
  be not doing well (to) *estar mal*
  It's not bad. *No está mal.*
  No, not at all. *No, para nada.*
  not either *tampoco*
note *nota* (f.)
  take note (to) *tomar nota*
notebook *cuaderno* (m.)
nothing *nada*
  nothing else *nada más*
  There's nothing that ... *No hay nada que ...*
novel *novela* (f.)
  romance novel *novela rosa*
November *noviembre* (m.)
now *ahora, ya*
  right now *ahora mismo*
nowadays *hoy en día*
number *número* (m.)
  telephone number *número de teléfono*

object *objeto* (m.)
objective *objetivo* (m.)

ocean *océano* (m.), *mar* (m.)

October *octubre* (m.)

of *de*

  because of *por*

  in place of *por*

  of course *por supuesto*

  Of course! *¡Claro que sí!*

  of the (m.) *del (de + el)*

  of which (relative pronoun) *cuyo/cuya/cuyos/ cuyas* (m. sg./f. sg./m. pl./f. pl.)

  on top of *sobre*

  outside of … *fuera de …*

  Yes, of course. *Sí, claro.*

offer *oferta* (f.)

offer (to) *ofrecer*

office *oficina* (f.), *despacho* (m.), *estudio* (m.), *consultorio* (m.)

  doctor's office *consultorio del médico*

  office worker *oficinista* (m./f.)

often *con frecuencia*

oil *aceite* (m.)

(just) okay *más o menos*

old *viejo/vieja* (m./f.), *antiguo/antigua* (m./f.)

  be … years old (to) *tener … años*

  How old are you (sg. fml.)/is he/is she? *¿Cuántos años tiene?*

  older *mayor* (m./f.)

  oldest (the) *el/la/los/las* (m. sg./f. sg./m. pl./f. pl.) *mayor*

on *en*

  buy on sale (to) *comprar en rebaja*

  depend on … (to) *depender de …*

  go on a trip (to) *salir de viaje*

  Hold on, please. *Espere, por favor.*

  Hold on. *Un momento.*

  on board *a bordo*

  on the left *a la izquierda*

  on the left-hand side *a mano izquierda*

  on the one hand *por una parte*

  on the other hand *por otra parte*

  on the phone *por teléfono*

  on the radio *por la radio*

  on the right *a la derecha*

  on the right-hand side *a mano derecha*

  on the sidewalk *por el andén*

  on time *a tiempo*

  on top of *sobre*

  on vacation *de vacaciones*

  put on hold (to) *poner en espera*

  put something on (to) *ponerse*

  try on (clothes) (to) *probarse*

once again *nuevamente*

one *uno*

  It's five to one. (12:55) *Es la una menos cinco.*

  It's one o'clock. *Es la una.*

  no one *nadie*

  on the one hand *por una parte*

  one (o'clock) *una*

  One moment. *Un momento.*

  once *una vez*

  once again *nuevamente*

  one-piece *enterizo/enteriza* (m./f.)

  one-way *de sentido* (m.) *único*

  thirty-one *treinta y uno*

  twenty-one *veintiuno*

one (impersonal pronoun) *se*

onion *cebolla* (f.)

online *por Internet, en línea*

only (adjective) *único/única* (m./f.), *solo/sola* (m./f.)

only (adverb) *solamente, sólo, simplemente*

open (to) *abrir*

  open the door (to) *abrir la puerta*

opera *ópera* (f.)

operator *operadora* (f.)

opposite *opuesto/opuesta* (m./f.)

or *o*

  either … or *o … o*

  more or less *más o menos*

orange (color) *anaranjado/anaranjada* (m./f.)

orange (fruit) *naranja* (f.)

order (to) *pedir*

  in order to *para*

ounce *onza* (f.)

our *nuestro/nuestra/nuestros/nuestras* (m. sg./f. sg./m. pl./f. pl.)

ours *nuestro/nuestra/nuestros/nuestras* (m. sg./f. sg./m. pl./f. pl.)

ourselves *nos*

outbound journey *ida* (f.)

outdoor market *plaza de mercado*

outside (adverb) *afuera, fuera*

  outside of … *fuera de …*

outside (noun) *exterior* (m.)

outskirts *afueras* (f. pl.)

oven *horno* (m.)

over *sobre*
overcoat *abrigo* (m.)
overcooked *sobrecocido/sobrecocida* (m./f.)
overtime *horas* (f. pl.) *extras*
owe (to) *deber*
own (to) *poseer*

P

package *paquete* (m.)
packet *cajetilla* (f.)
  pack of cigarettes *cajetilla de cigarrillos*
page *página* (f.)
  yellow pages *páginas* (pl.) *amarillas*
  webpage *página web*
pain *dolor* (m.), *pena* (f.)
painter *pintor/pintora* (m./f.)
painting *pintura* (f.), *cuadro* (m.)
pajamas *pijama* (m.)
palace *palacio* (m.)
palm *palmo* (m.)
Panamanian *panameña/panameño* (m./f.)
pants *pantalones* (m. pl.)
papaya *papaya* (f.)
paper *papel* (m.)
  research paper *trabajo* (m.) *de investigación*
Paraguay *Paraguay* (m.)
Pardon me? *¿Cómo?*
parents *padres* (pl.)
Paris *París*
park *parque* (m.)
parking lot *parqueadero* (m.)
part *parte* (f.)
partial *parcial* (m./f.)
particular *particular* (m./f.)
part-time *a tiempo parcial*
party *fiesta* (f.)
pass (to) *aprobar, pasar*
  pass a course (to) *aprobar un curso*
  pass a test (to) *aprobar un examen*
passport *pasaporte* (m.)
past *pasado/pasada* (m./f.)
  at a half past five *a las cinco y media*
  at a quarter past six *a las seis y cuarto*
pastry *dulce* (m.)
path *camino* (m.)
patience *paciencia* (f.)
  be patient (to) *tener paciencia*
patterned, with a pattern *estampado/*

estampada (m./f.)
pay *sueldo* (m.)
pay (to) *pagar*
  pay cash (to) *pagar en efectivo*
payment *pago* (m.)
pear *pera* (f.)
pedestrian *peatón* (m.)
pediatrician *pediatra* (m./f.)
  regular pediatrician *pediatra* (m./f.) *de cabecera*
pediatrics *pediatría* (f.)
pen *bolígrafo* (m.), *pluma* (f.)
pencil *lápiz* (m.)
penicillin *penicilina* (f.)
pension *pensión* (f.)
people *gente* (f.)
people (impersonal pronoun) *se*
pepper *pimienta* (f.) (spice), *pimiento* (m.) (vegetable)
perceive (to) *percibir*
percent *por ciento*
perceptibly *sensiblemente*
perfect *perfecto/perfecta* (m./f.)
perfume *perfume* (m.)
perhaps *tal vez*
period *período* (m.)
period *término* (m.)
permanent *fijo/fija* (m./f.)
person *persona* (f.)
Peru *Perú* (m.)
Peruvian *peruano/peruana* (m./f.)
peso *peso* (m.)
pharmacist *farmacéutico/farmacéutico* (m./f.)
pharmacy *farmacia* (f.)
philosophy *filosofía* (f.)
phone book *guía* (f.) *telefónica*
phone call *llamada* (f.)
  make an international/local/national call (to) *hacer una llamada internacional/local/nacional*
photograph *foto* (f.)
photography *fotografía* (f.)
phrase *frase* (f.)
physics *física* (f.)
piano *piano* (m.)
pick up (to) *recoger, coger, buscar*
picture *foto* (f.), *cuadro* (m.)
  take a picture (to) *hacer una foto*

piece   *pieza* (f.)
  one-piece   *enterizo/enteriza* (m./f.)
  two-piece   *de dos piezas*
pig   *cerdo/cerda* (m./f.)
piglet   *chanchito/chanchita* (m./f.)
pill   *pastilla* (f.)
pink   *rosado/rosada* (m./f.)
pity   *lástima* (f.), *pena* (f.)
  It's a pity that …   *Es una lástima que …*
place   *lugar* (m.), *sitio* (m.)
  in place of   *por*
place (to)   *poner*
plaid   *a cuadros*
plan   *plan* (m.)
plant   *planta* (f.)
plastic   *plástico* (m.)
plate   *plato* (m.)
play (to)   *jugar, practicar (sports), tocar (instrument)*
  play sports (to)   *hacer deporte*
  play the piano (to)   *tocar el piano*
  play the guitar (to)   *tocar la guitarra*
play (theater)   *obra* (f.)
player   *jugador/jugadora* (m./f.)
plaza   *plaza* (f.)
pleasant   *agradable* (m./f.)
please (to)   *gustar*
  Pleased to meet you.   *Encantado./Encantada.* (said by a man/said by a woman)/*Gusto en conocerlo/la.*
Please.   *Por favor.*
pleasure   *placer* (m.), *gusto* (m.)
  It's a pleasure.   *Mucho gusto.*
plumber   *fontanero/fontanera* (m./f.)
plus (+)   *más*
p.m.   *de la tarde, de la noche*
  at four p.m.   *a las cuatro de la tarde*
  at seven p.m.   *a las siete de la noche*
pocket-knife   *navaja* (f.)
point   *punto* (m.), *término* (m.)
police officer   *policía* (m./f.)
  policewoman   *mujer* (f.) *policía*
polka-dot   *de lunares*
polyester   *poliéster* (m.)
pond   *estanque* (m.)
pool   *piscina* (f.)
poor, poor person   *pobre* (m./f.)
  poor (the)   *los pobres*

poorly   *mal*
pork   *cerdo* (m.), *carne* (f.) *de cerdo*
Portuguese   *portugués/portuguesa* (m./f.)
position (job)   *puesto* (m.)
possible   *posible* (m./f.)
  as soon as possible   *lo antes posible*
  It is possible that …   *Es posible que …*
post (job)   *puesto* (m.)
postage stamp   *estampilla* (f.)
post office   *correo* (m.)
postpone (to)   *retrasar*
potato   *papa* (f.), *patata* (f.)
pound   *libra* (f.)
  half pound   *media libra*
powder   *polvo* (m.)
  powdered milk   *leche* (f.) *en polvo*
practice (to)   *practicar*
prayer   *oración* (f.)
precisely   *precisamente*
prefer (to)   *preferir*
  prefer that … (to)   *preferir que …*
preferable   *preferible* (m./f.)
  It's preferable that …   *Es preferible que …*
pregnant   *embarazada* (f.)
prepared   *preparado/preparada* (m./f.)
presentation   *presentación* (f.)
president   *presidente/presidenta* (m./f.)
pressure   *presión* (f.)
  have high/low blood pressure (to)   *tener la tensión alta/baja*
prestigious   *prestigioso/prestigiosa* (m./f.)
pretty   *bonito/bonita* (m./f.)
prevent (to)   *impedir*
price   *precio* (m.)
  price tag   *etiqueta* (f.) *con el precio*
  reasonable price   *precio económico*
printer   *impresora* (f.)
prison   *cárcel* (f.)
prize   *premio* (m.)
probation   *prueba* (f.)
  probationary period   *período* (m.) *de prueba*
problem   *problema* (m.)
produce (to)   *producir*
product   *producto* (m.)
profession   *profesión* (f.)
professional   *profesional* (m./f.)
professionally   *profesionalmente*
professor   *profesor/profesora* (m./f.)

program *programa* (m.)
  television program *programa de televisión*
prohibit (to) *prohibir*
project *proyecto* (m.)
promise (to) *prometer*
proof *prueba* (f.)
protect (to) *proteger*
psychology *sicología* (f.)
punctual *puntual* (m./f.)
purchase *compra* (f.)
purple *morado/morada* (m./f.), *púrpura* (m./f.)
put (to) *poner*
  I'm putting you through. (on the phone) *Lo paso.*
  put on hold (to) *poner en espera*
  put something on (to) *ponerse*

Q

qualification *cualificación* (f.)
qualified *cualificado/cualificada* (m./f.)
quarter *cuarto* (m.)
  at a quarter past six *a las seis y cuarto*
  at a quarter to six *a las seis menos cuarto*
question *pregunta* (f.)
questionnaire *cuestionario* (m.)
quick *rápido/rápida* (m./f.)
quickly *rápidamente, rápido, aprisa*
quiet *tranquilo/tranquila* (m./f.)
quietly *silenciosamente*
quite, quite a lot *bastante*

R

radio *radio* (f.)
  on the radio *por la radio*
railroad *ferrocarril* (m.)
rain *lluvia* (f.)
rain (to) *llover*
  It's raining. *Está lloviendo.*
raincoat *gabardina* (f.)
raise (to) *levantar*
ramp *rampa* (f.)
rash *brote* (m.)
razor *navaja* (f.) *de afeitar*
read (to) *leer*
reader *lector* (m.)
reading *lectura* (f.)
ready *listo/lista* (m./f.), *preparado/preparada* (m./f.)

Ready? *¿Listos?/¿Preparados?*
realism *realismo* (m.)
realistic *realista* (m./f.)
Really? *No me digas.*
reason *razón* (f.)
reasonable price *precio* (m.) *económico*
receive (to) *recibir*
reception desk *recepción* (f.)
receptionist *recepcionista* (m./f.)
recess *receso* (m.)
recipe *receta* (f.)
recognize (to) *reconocer*
recommend (to) *recomendar*
  recommend that … (to) *recomendar que …*
record *registro* (m.), *historial* (m.), *disco* (m.)
record (to) *anotar*
recreation *recreo* (m.)
red *rojo/roja* (m./f.), *colorado/colorada* (m /f.)
  red wine *vino* (m.) *tinto*
reduce (to) *reducir*
reduced *rebajado/rebajada* (m./f.)
reference *referencia* (f.)
refrigerator *nevera* (f.)
regain strength (to) *coger fuerzas* (f. pl.)
regarding … *en cuanto a …*
region *región* (f.)
regional *regional* (m./f.)
register (to) *matricularse*
registration *matrícula* (f.)
regret that … (to) *sentir que …*
relationship *relación* (f.)
relative *pariente* (m./f.)
remain (to) *quedar*
remember (to) *recordar*
rent (to) *alquilar*
repayment *retribución* (f.)
repeat (to) *repetir*
  Repeat, please. *Repita, por favor*
reply to (to) *contestar*
report *informe* (m.)
  report card *calificaciones* (f. pl.)
representative *representante* (m.)
request (to) *solicitar*
  request that … (to) *pedir que …*
research *investigación* (f.)
  research paper *trabajo* (m.) *de investigación*
reservation *reserva* (f.), *reservación* (f.)
resolve (to) *resolver*

responsible *responsable* (m./f.)
rest *resto* (m.)
rest (to) *descansar*
restaurant *restaurante* (m.)
result *resultado* (m.)
résumé *historial* (m.) *de trabajo, currículum vítae, hoja* (f.) *de vida*
retain (to) *quedar*
retired, retired person *jubilado/jubilada* (m./f.)
return (to) *regresar, volver*
rice *arroz* (m.)
rich *rico/rica* (m./f.)
ride (to) *montar*
right *derecho* (m.), *ya*
　be right (to) *tener razón*
　right? *¿verdad?*
　on the right *a la derecha*
　on the right-hand side *a mano derecha*
　right now *en este momento, ahora mismo*
　right side *derecha* (f.)
　right-side *derecho/derecha* (m./f.)
　That's right. *Es verdad./Así es.*
　Turn right. *Gira a la derecha.*
ring *anillo* (m.)
ring (to) *sonar*
rise (to) *levantarse*
river *río* (m.)
robe *albornoz* (m.), *bata* (f.), *deshabillé* (m.)
rock *roca* (f.)
romance novel *novela* (f.) *rosa*
romantic *romántico/romántica* (m./f.)
　romantic films *películas* (f. pl.) *románticas*
room *alcoba* (f.), *cuarto* (m.), *habitación* (f.)
rose *rosa* (f.)
　wear rose-colored glasses (to) *ver todo color de rosa* (lit., *to see everything pink*)
rotten *podrido/podrida* (m./f.)
rough *agitado/agitada* (m./f.)
round *redondo/redonda* (m./f.)
route *recorrido* (m.)
run (to) *correr*
rural *rural* (m./f.)
Russian (language) *ruso* (m.)

S

sack *bolsa* (f.)
sad *triste* (m./f.)
　It's sad that … *Es triste que …*
sadly *tristemente*
safe *seguro/segura* (m./f.)
safety *seguridad* (f.)
salad *ensalada* (f.)
salary *salario* (m.)
sale *venta* (f.)
　buy on sale (to) *comprar en rebaja*
salesman/saleswoman *vendedor/vendedora* (m./f.)
salsa *salsa* (f.)
salt *sal* (f.)
salty *salado/salada* (m./f.)
same *mismo/misma* (m./f.)
　The same to you. *Igualmente.*
sand *arena* (f.)
sandals *sandalias* (f. pl.)
Saturday *sábado* (m.)
sauce *salsa* (f.)
save (to) *ahorrar, guardar*
say (to) *decir*
　How do you say " … " in … ? *¿Cómo se dice " … " en … ?*
　say good-bye (to) *despedirse*
scarf *bufanda* (f.)
scary *espantoso/espantosa* (m./f.)
schedule *horario* (m.)
scholarship *beca* (f.)
school *escuela* (f.), *academia* (f.)
　school subject *materia* (f.)
science *ciencia* (f.)
scoreboard *marcador* (m.)
scream *grito* (m.)
scream (to) *gritar*
screen *pantalla* (f.)
sculpture *escultura* (f.)
sea *mar* (m.)
season *estación* (f.)
seat *silla* (f.)
seat (to) *sentar*
　be seated (to) *estar sentado*
second *segundo/segunda* (m./f.)
　second year *segundo año*
secondary school *colegio* (m.)
secret *secreto* (m.)
secretary *secretaria* (m./f.)
section *sección* (f.)
security *seguridad* (f.)
see (to) *ver*

I'll see you later. *Hasta luego.*
Let's see… *Vamos…/A ver…*
See you. *Nos vemos. (lit., We see each other.)*
See you soon. *Hasta pronto.*
See you tomorrow. *Hasta mañana.*
seem (to) *parecer*
seldom *casi nunca*
sell (to) *vender*
semester *semestre* (m.)
send (to) *enviar*
sense *sentido* (m.)
sensibly *sensatamente*
September *septiembre* (m.)
series *serie* (f.)
serious *grave* (m./f.), *serio/seria* (m./f.)
serve (to) *servir, atender*
service *servicio* (m.)
  Is service included? *¿Está incluido el servicio?*
session *sesión* (f.)
set off (to) *partir*
seven *siete*
  at seven p.m. *a las siete de la noche*
  seven hundred *setecientos/setecientas* (m./f.)
  twenty-seven *veintisiete*
seventeen *diecisiete, diez y siete*
seventy *setenta*
several *varios/varias* (m./f.)
sewing *costura* (f.)
shake hands (to) *dar la mano*
shampoo *champú* (m.)
shave (to) *afeitar*
  shave (oneself) (to) *afeitarse*
shaving cream *crema de afeitar*
she *ella*
sheet (of paper) *hoja* (f.)
shelf *estante* (m.)
shirt *camisa* (f.)
shoes *zapatos* (m. pl.)
  shoe store *zapatería* (f.)
  tennis shoes *zapatillas* (f. pl.) *deportivas*
  What shoe size do you wear? *¿Qué número calza?*
shop (to) *comprar*
shopping mall *centro* (m.) *comercial*
short *bajo/baja* (m./f.), *corto/corta* (m./f.)
shoulder *hombro* (m.)
shout (to) *gritar*
show (to) *mostrar, dar*

shower *ducha* (f.)
shrimp *camarón* (m.), *gamba* (f.)
shy *tímido/tímida* (m./f.)
siblings *hermanos* (pl.)
sick *enfermo/enferma* (m./f.)
sickness *mareo* (m.), *náusea* (f.)
side *lado* (m.), *parte* (f.)
  on the left-hand side *a mano izquierda*
  on the right-hand side *a mano derecha*
sidewalk *andén* (m.), *acera* (f.)
  on the sidewalk *por el andén/la acera*
signal *señal* (f.)
signature *firma* (f.)
silk *seda* (f.)
silver (color) *plateado/plateada* (m./f.)
simply *simplemente*
since *desde, pues*
sing (to) *cantar*
singer *cantante* (m./f.)
single *único/única* (m./f.), *soltero/soltera* (m./f.)
sink *lavabo* (m.), *fregadero* (m.) *(kitchen)*
sister *hermana* (f.)
sister-in-law *cuñada* (f.)
sit down (to) *sentarse*
situation *situación* (f.)
six *seis*
  at a quarter past six *a las seis y cuarto*
  at a quarter to six *a las seis menos cuarto*
  six hundred *seiscientos/seiscientas* (m./f.)
  twenty-six *veintiséis*
sixteen *dieciséis, diez y seis*
sixty *sesenta*
size *talla* (f.), *tamaño* (m.)
  What shoe size do you wear? *¿Qué número calza?*
ski (to) *esquiar*
skill *destreza* (f.), *cualificación* (f.)
skimmed *descremado/descremada* (m./f.)
  skim milk *leche* (f.) *descremada*
skin *piel* (f.)
skip (to) *saltar*
skirt *falda* (f.)
sky *cielo* (m.)
  sky blue *celeste* (m./f.)
sleep *sueño* (m.)
  be sleepy (to) *tener sueño*
sleep (to) *dormir*
sleepiness *sueño* (m.)

slice *rebanada* (f.), *tajada* (f.)
slippers *chinelas* (f. pl.), *pantuflas* (f. pl.),
  zapatillas (f. pl.)
slow *lento/lenta* (m./f.), *retrasado/retrasada*
  (m./f.)
slowly *despacio, lentamente*
  Speak more slowly, please. *Hable más*
    despacio, por favor.
small *pequeño/pequeña* (m./f.)
  smaller *menor* (m./f.)
  smallest (the) *el/la/los/las* (m. sg./f. sg./m. pl./f.
    pl.) *menor*
smart *inteligente* (m./f.)
smell (to) *oler*
smile (to) *sonreír*
smog *niebla* (f.) *tóxica/con humo*
smoke (to) *fumar*
smoked *ahumado/ahumada* (m./f.)
snack time *merienda* (f.)
snake *serpiente* (f.)
sneakers *zapatillas* (f. pl.) *deportivas*
snow *nieve* (f.)
snow (to) *nevar*
  It's snowing. *Está nevando.*
so *así, pues*
  I hope so! *¡Yo espero que sí!*
  I think so. *Creo que sí.*
  so-so *más o menos*
  So… *Así que…*
  so to speak *por así decir*
so (very) *tan*
soap *jabón* (m.)
soccer *fútbol* (m.)
socks *calcetines* (m. pl.), *medias* (f. pl.)
soda *refresco* (m.)
sofa *sofá* (m.)
soft *suave* (m./f.)
soft drink *refresco* (m.)
sole *solo/sola* (m./f.)
solely *sólo*
solitude *soledad* (f.)
solution *solución* (f.)
some *unos/unas* (m. pl./f. pl.), *algún/alguno/*
  alguna (before m. sg. nouns/m. sg./f. sg.), *algunos/*
  algunas (m. pl./f. pl.)
somebody, someone *alguien*
  somebody else *alguien más*
something *algo, algún/alguno/alguna* (before

m. sg. nouns/m. sg./f. sg.), *algunos/algunas* (m.
  pl./f. pl.)
sometimes *a veces*
somewhat *algo*
son *hijo* (m.)
song *canción* (f.)
son-in-law *yerno* (m.)
soon *pronto*
  as soon as possible *lo antes posible*
  See you soon. *Hasta pronto.*
(I'm) sorry. *Lo siento.*
sound *sonido* (m.)
  sound system *sistema* (m.) *de sonido*
sound (to) *sonar*
soup *sopa* (f.)
sour *agrio/agria* (m./f.), *cortado/cortada* (m./f.),
  amargo/amarga (m./f.)
south *sur* (m.)
South America *Sudamérica*
space *espacio* (m.)
Spain *España* (f.)
Spanish *español/española* (m./f.)
Spanish (language) *español* (m.)
  I'm learning Spanish. *Estoy aprendiendo*
    español.
  I speak a little Spanish. *Hablo un poco de*
    español.
speak (to) *hablar*
  Do you speak English? (fml.) *¿Habla usted*
    inglés?
  Do you speak English? (infml.) *¿Hablas inglés?*
  I speak a little Spanish. *Hablo un poco de*
    español.
  I speak French fluently. *Domino el francés.*
  so to speak *por así decir*
  Speak more slowly, please. *Hable más*
    despacio, por favor.
  speak to … (to) *hablar con ….*
specialization *especialización* (f.)
specialize (to) *especializarse*
special of the day *plato del día*
specialty *especialidad* (f.)
spectator *espectador/espectadora* (m./f.)
speed *velocidad* (f.)
spend (to) *pasar*
  spend the day (to) *pasar el día*
spicy *condimentado/condimentada* (m./f.),
  picante (m./f.)

spinal column *columna* (f.) *vertebral*
spoiled *pasado/pasada* (m./f.)
spoon *cuchara* (f.)
sport *deporte* (m.)
  person who plays sports *deportista* (m./f.)
spot *pinta* (f.)
spring *primavera* (f.)
spy *espía* (m./f.)
square *cuadro* (m.), *plaza* (f.)
stadium *estadio* (m.)
staff *personal* (m.), *plantilla* (f.)
stairs *escaleras* (f. pl.)
stamp collecting *filatelia* (f.)
stand in line (to) *hacer una cola/fila*
star *estrella* (f.)
start (to) *comenzar*
  start ... (doing something) (to) *comenzar a ...*
  start from ... (to) *partir de ...*
state *estado* (m.)
station *estación* (f.)
  train station *estación de tren, estación de ferrocarril*
Stay in the right lane. *Siga por el carril de la derecha.*
steady job *trabajo* (m.) *fijo*
stepdaughter *hijastra* (f.)
stepfather *padrastro* (m.)
stepmother *madrastra* (f.)
stepson *hijastro* (m.)
stick *palo* (m.)
still *todavía*
stockings *pantymedias* (f. pl.), *medias* (f. pl.)
stomach *estómago* (m.)
  have an upset stomach (to) *tener mal de estómago*
stop *alto* (m.), *parada* (f.)
  Stop! *¡Alto!*
stop (to) *parar, cesar*
  stop ... (doing something) (to) *cesar de ...*
store *tienda* (f.)
  antique store *tienda de antigüedades*
  clothing store *tienda de ropa*
  convenience store *tienda* (f.)
  department store *tienda por departamentos*
  electronics store *tienda de electrodomésticos*
  store clerk *dependiente/dependienta* (m./f.)
storm *tormenta* (f.)

stove *cocina* (f.)
straight *recto, derecho*
  Continue straight. *Continúa recto.*
  Go straight. *Siga derecho.*
strange *extraño/extraña* (m./f.)
stranger *extranjero/extranjera* (m.)
street *calle* (f.)
streetlight *luz* (f.) *de la calle*
strength *fuerza* (f.)
  regain strength (to) *coger fuerzas* (f. pl.)
stressing, stressful *estresante* (m./f.)
stripe *raya* (f.)
striped *a rayas*
strong *fuerte* (m./f.)
student *estudiante/estudiante* (m./f.), *alumno/alumna* (m./f.)
study *estudio* (m.)
  studies *estudios* (pl.)
study (to) *estudiar*
stuffing *relleno* (m.)
style *estilo* (m.)
  in style *de moda*
subject *asignatura* (f.)
submit (to) *entregar*
subscriber *abonado/abonada* (m./f.)
suburban *suburbano/suburbana* (m./f.)
subway *subterráneo* (m.), *metro* (m.)
success *éxito* (m.)
such *tal*
suede *gamuza* (f.)
suffer (to) *sufrir*
sugar *azúcar* (m.)
suggest (to) *sugerir*
  suggest that ... (to) *sugerir que ...*
suit *traje* (m.)
suitcase *maleta* (f.)
summer *verano* (m.)
  summer job *trabajo* (m.) *de verano*
sun *sol* (m.)
  It's sunny. *Hace sol.*
Sunday *domingo* (m.)
sunglasses *gafas* (f. pl.) *de sol*
supermarket *supermercado* (m.)
supporter *hincha* (m./f.)
supposition *supuesto* (m.)
sure *seguro/segura* (m./f.)
  I'm sure. *Seguro/segura que sí.*
surprise *sorpresa* (f.)

be surprised (to) *sorprenderse*
be surprised that ... (to) *sorprenderse de que ...*
suspend (to) *suspender*
suspense *suspenso* (m.)
  suspense films *películas* (f. pl.) *de suspenso*
sweater *suéter* (m.), *jersey* (m.)
sweet (adjective) *dulce* (m./f.)
sweet (noun) *dulce* (m.)
swell (to) *hincharse*
swim (to) *nadar*
swimming *natación* (f.)
  swimming pool *piscina* (f.)
switchboard *centralita* (f.)
symptom *síntoma* (m.)
syndrome *síndrome* (m.)
  carpal tunnel syndrome *síndrome del túnel del carpio*
system *sistema* (m.)
  sound system *sistema de sonido*

T

table *mesa* (f.), *tabla* (f.)
tableware *vajilla* (f.)
tag *etiqueta* (f.)
  price tag *etiqueta con el precio*
tail *cola* (f.)
take (to) *tomar, traer, coger, usar, llevar*
  take a bath (to) *bañarse*
  take a blood test (to) *hacerse un examen de sangre*
  take a picture (to) *hacer una foto*
  take a shower (to) *ducharse*
  take a test (to) *hacer un examen, presentarse a un examen*
  Take care. *Que estés bien.*
  take care of (to) *atender*
  take into acount (to) *tener en cuenta*
  take medication (to) *tomar un medicamento*
  take out (to) *sacar*
  take the blood pressure (to) *tomar la tensión*
talented *dotado/dotada* (m./f.)
talk (to) *hablar*
talk show *programa* (m.) *de entrevistas*
tall *alto/alta* (m./f.)
taste *gusto* (m.)
taste (to) *saborear, probar, saber*
tax *impuesto* (m.)

tax return *planilla* (f.) *de impuestos*
taxi *taxi* (m.)
  taxi driver *taxista* (m./f.)
tea *té* (m.)
teacher *maestro/maestra* (m./f.)
teakettle *tetera* (f.)
team *equipo* (m.)
technology *tecnología* (f.)
teenager *adolescente* (m.)
telephone *teléfono* (m.)
  answer the phone (to) *contestar el teléfono*
  call ... on the phone (to) *llamar por teléfono a ...*
  dial a phone number (to) *marcar un número de teléfono*
  hang up the phone (to) *colgar el teléfono*
  make a phone call (to) *llamar por teléfono*
  on the phone *por teléfono*
  telephone booth *cabina* (f.) *telefónica*
  telephone number *número* (m.) *de teléfono*
telephonic *telefónico/telefónica* (m./f.)
television *televisión* (f.)
  television program *programa* (m.) *de televisión*
  television set *televisor* (m.)
  watch television (to) *mirar la televisón*
tell (to) *contar, decir*
  tell a dirty joke (to) *contar un chiste verde (lit., to tell a green joke)*
  tell time (to) *dar la hora*
temperature *temperatura* (f.)
temple *templo* (m.)
ten *diez*
  at eight ten (8:10) *a las ocho y diez*
  It's ten after one in the morning. *Es la una y diez de la madrugada.*
  ten thousand *diez mil*
tendon *tendón* (m.)
tennis *tenis* (m.)
  tennis shoes *zapatillas* (f. pl.) *deportivas*
tension *tensión* (f.)
term *término* (m.)
terrible *pésimo/pésima* (m./f.)
test *examen* (m.), *prueba* (f.)
  fail a test (to) *suspender un examen*
  pass a test (to) *aprobar un examen*
  take a blood test (to) *hacerse un examen de sangre*

take a test (to) *hacer un examen, presentarse a un examen*

text *texto* (m.)

textbook *libro* (m.) *de texto*

than *que*

less … than … *menos … que …*

more …/-er than … *más … que …*

thanks *gracias* (pl.)

be thankful (to) *agradecer*

give thanks (to) *dar (las) gracias*

Thanks a lot. *Muchas gracias.*

Thank you. *Gracias.*

Thank you for your help. *Le agradezco su ayuda.*

that (demonstrative) *ese/esa* (m. sg./f. sg.) (*near the listener*), *aquel/aquella* (m. sg./f. sg.) (*far from the speaker and the listener*)

that (one) *ése/ésa* (m. sg./f. sg.) (*near the listener*)

that (one) over there *aquél/aquélla* (m. sg./f. sg.) (*far from the speaker and the listener*)

that (one, thing) (neuter) *eso* (m.) (*near the listener*)

that (one, thing) over there (neuter) *aquello* (m.) (*far from the speaker and the listener*)

That's it. *Ya está.*

That's right. *Es verdad./Así es.*

That's too bad! *¡Qué pena!*

that (conjunction, relative pronoun) *que*

the *el/la/los/las* (m. sg./f. sg./m. pl./f. pl.)

of the (m.)**/from the** (m.)**/about the** (m.) *del* (*de + el*)

to the (m.)**/at the** (m.) *al (a + el)*

theater *teatro* (m.)

their *su/sus* (sg./pl.)

theirs (m./f.) *suyo/suya/suyos/suyas* (m. sg./f. sg./m. pl./f. pl.)

theirs (f. pl.) *el de ellas* (m. sg.), *la de ellas* (f. sg.)

theirs (m. pl./mixed group) *el de ellos* (m. sg.), *la de ellos* (f. sg.)

them (direct object pronoun) *los/las* (m./f.)

(to/for) them (indirect object pronoun) *les, se* (used in place of les when preceding lo/la/los/las)

themselves *se*

then *entonces, luego, pues*

Until then. *Hasta entonces.*

there *ahí, allí*

There is …/There are … *Hay …*

There's no … that/who … *No hay ningún … que …*

There's no one who/that … *No hay nadie que …*

There's nothing that … *No hay nada que …*

therefore *por lo tanto, pues*

these *estos/estas* (m. pl./f. pl.)

these (ones) *éstos/éstas* (m. pl./f. pl.)

they *ellos/ellas* (m. pl. & mixed group/f. pl.)

thick *espeso/espesa* (m./f.)

thief *ladrón* (m./f.)

thin *delgado/delgada* (m./f.), *ligero/ligera* (m./f.)

thing *cosa* (f.)

How are things? *¿Cómo van las cosas?*

think (to) *creer, pensar*

Don't you think? *¿No crees?*

I think so. *Creo que sí.*

not think that … (to) *no pensar que …*

What do you think of …? *¿Qué te parece …?*

third *tercero/tercer/tercera* (m. sg./m. sg. before a noun/f. sg.)

third year *tercer año*

thirst *sed* (f.)

be thirsty (to) *tener sed*

thirteen *trece*

thirty *treinta*

thirty-one *treinta y uno*

thirty percent off *treinta por ciento de descuento*

this *este/esta* (m. sg./f. sg.)

this (one) *éste/ésta* (m. sg./f. sg.)

this (one, thing)(neuter) *esto* (m.)

this afternoon *esta tarde*

this day *este día*

this evening *esta noche* (f.)

those *aquellos/aquellas* (m. pl./f. pl.) (*far from the speaker and the listener*)

those (ones) over there *aquéllos/aquéllas* (m. pl./f. pl.) (*far from the speaker and the listener*)

thousand *mil*

hundred thousand *cien mil*

ten thousand *diez mil*

twenty thousand *veinte mil*

three *tres*

It's three o'clock. *Son las tres.*

It's three o'clock sharp. *Son las tres en punto.*

one hundred and three dollars *ciento tres dólares*

three hundred *trescientos/trescientas* (m./f.)

twenty-three *veintitrés*

throat *garganta* (f.)

have a sore throat (to) *tener dolor de garganta*

through *por*

from ... through ... *de ... a ...*

go through a light (to) *saltarse el semáforo*

I'm putting you through. (on the phone) *Lo paso.*

thunder *trueno* (m.)

Thursday *jueves* (m.)

ticket *billete* (m.), *boleto* (m.), *pasaje* (m.), *tiquete* (m.), *entrada* (f.)

tie *corbata* (f.)

tie (to) *empatar*

tied *empatado/empatada* (m./f.)

be tied (to) *quedar empatados*

tight *ajustado/ajustada* (m./f.)

time *hora* (f.), *tiempo* (m.), *vez* (f.)

at the present time *actualmente*

At what time is it? *¿A qué hora es?*

Do you have time?/How are you doing for time? *¿Cómo estás de tiempo?*

full-time *a tiempo completo*

on time, in time *a tiempo*

overtime *horas* (f. pl.) *extras*

part-time *a tiempo parcial*

tell time (to) *dar la hora*

What time is it? *¿Qué hora es?/¿Qué horas son?*

What time do you have? *¿Qué hora tiene?*

tingling feeling *cosquilleo* (m.)

tip *propina* (f.), *punta* (f.)

tired *cansado/cansada* (m./f.)

be tired (to) *tener cansancio*

to *a, con*

in order to *para*

It's five to one. (12:55) *Es la una menos cinco.*

to the (m.) *al (a + el)*

toast *tostada* (f.)

today *hoy*

toe *dedo del pie*

together *junto/junta* (m./f.)

toilet *inodoro* (m.)

toilet paper *papel* (m.) *higiénico*

toll *peaje* (m.)

tomato *tomate* (m.)

tomorrow *mañana* (f.)

Until tomorrow./See you tomorrow. *Hasta mañana.*

tone *tono* (m.), *señal* (f.)

leave a message after the tone (to) *dejar un mensaje después de oír la señal*

tongue *lengua* (f.)

tonight *esta noche*

too *también*

too much, too many *demasiado/demasiada* (m./f.)

tooth *diente* (m.)

touch (to) *tocar*

tour bus trip *recorrido por autobús*

tourism *turismo* (m.)

tourist *turista* (m./f.)

toward(s) *hacia, para*

towel *toalla* (f.)

town *ciudad* (f.), *pueblo* (m.)

around town *por la ciudad*

toxic *tóxico/tóxica* (m./f.)

traffic *tráfico* (m.)

go through a traffic light (to) *saltarse el semáforo*

traffic jam *embotellamiento* (m.)

traffic light *semáforo* (m.)

train *tren* (m.), *ferrocarril* (m.)

train station *estación* (f.) *de tren, estación* (f.) *de ferrocarril*

transfer (to) *trasladar*

translate (to) *traducir*

travel *viaje* (m.)

travel (to) *viajar*

treat (to) *tratar*

How's life treating you? *¿Cómo te trata la vida?*

treatment *tratamiento* (m.)

tree *árbol* (m.)

trip *viaje* (m.)

go on a trip (to) *salir de viaje*

Have a good trip. *Buen viaje.*

true *cierto/cierta* (m./f.)

It is not true that ... *No es cierto que ...*

truth *verdad* (f.)

try (to) *tratar, probar*

try ... (to do something) (to) *tratar de ...*

try on (clothes) (to) *probarse*

T-shirt *camiseta* (f.)

Tuesday *martes* (m.)

tuition *derechos* (m. pl.) *de matrícula*
tuna *atún* (m.)
tunnel *túnel* (m.)
turn *vuelta* (f.)
turn (to) *doblar, girar, volver, ponerse*
  turn around (to) *dar la vuelta*
  Turn left. *Gira a la izquierda.*
  turn off (to) *apagar*
  turn off the lights (to) *apagar las luces*
  Turn right. *Gira a la derecha.*
twelve *doce*
  It's twelve noon. *Son las doce del mediodía.*
twenty *veinte*
  twenty-eight *veintiocho*
  twenty-five *veinticinco*
  twenty-four *veinticuatro*
  twenty-nine *veintinueve*
  twenty-one *veintiuno*
  twenty-seven *veintisiete*
  twenty-six *veintiséis*
  twenty-three *veintitrés*
  twenty-two *veintidós*
two *dos*
  twenty-two *veintidós*
  twice a week *dos veces por semana*
  two hundred *doscientos/doscientas* (m./f.)
  two-piece *de dos piezas*
type *tipo* (m.)
typical *típico/típica* (m./f.)

U

ugly *feo/fea* (m./f.)
umbrella *paraguas* (m.)
uncle *tío* (m.)
uncomfortable *incómodo/incómoda* (m./f.)
under *bajo*
undergarments (men's) *calzones* (m. pl.)
underneath *debajo*
  underneath … *debajo de …*
underpants (men's) *calzoncillos* (m. pl.)
undershirt *camisilla* (f.), *camiseta* (f.)
understand (to) *comprender, entender*
underwear (women's) *bombachas* (f. pl.), *bragas*
  (f. pl.), *calzoncitos* (m. pl.), *pantis* (m. pl.)
unemployed *parado/parada* (m./f.)
unfortunately *desafortunadamente, por*
  desgracia
unfriendly *antipático/antipática* (m./f.)

union *sindicato* (m.)
unique *único/única* (m./f.)
united *unido/unida* (m./f.)
United States (the) *los Estados Unidos*
university *universidad* (f.)
  university course *carrera* (f.)
unpleasant *desagradable* (m./f.)
until *hasta, para*
  Till then. *Hasta entonces.*
  Until later. *Hasta más tarde.*
  Until then. *Hasta entonces.*
  Until tomorrow. *Hasta mañana.*
urban *urbano/urbana* (m./f.)
urgently *urgentemente*
Uruguay *Uruguay* (m.)
Uruguayan *uruguayo/uruguaya* (m./f.)
us (direct object pronoun); (to/for) us (indirect
  object pronoun) *nos*
use (to) *usar*
  use for the first time (to) *estrenar*

V

vacation *vacaciones* (f. pl.)
  on vacation *de vacaciones*
variety *variedad* (f.)
vegetable *vegetal* (m.), *verdura* (f.)
Venezuela *Venezuela* (f.)
Venezuelan *venezolano/venezolana* (m./f.)
vertebral *vertebral* (m./f.)
very *muy, mucho*
veterinarian *veterinario/veterinaria* (m./f.)
view *vista* (f.)
village *aldea* (f.)
vinyl *vinilo* (m.)
  vinyl record *disco* (m.) *de vinilo*
violet (color) *violeta* (m./f.)
violin *violín* (m.)
visit (to) *visitar*
visitor *visitante* (m./f.)
voice *voz* (f.)
  voice mail *buzón* (m.) *de voz*
voucher *vale* (m.)

W

wage *paga* (f.), *jornal* (m.)
wait *espera* (f.)
wait (to) *esperar*
waiter *camarero* (m.), *mesero* (m.)

waitress *camarera* (f.), *mesera* (f.)
wake up (to) *despertarse*
walk (to) *andar, caminar, ir a pie/caminar*
wall *pared* (f.)
wallet *cartera* (f.)
want (to) *querer, desear*
  want that/to … (to) *querer que …*
wish (to) *desear*
  I wish … *Ojalá que …*
  wish that … (to) *desear que …*
wash (to) *lavar*
  hand wash (to) *lavar a mano*
  wash oneself (to) *lavarse*
wash basin *lavabo* (m.)
washing machine *lavadora* (f.)
watch *reloj* (m.)
watch (to) *mirar*
  watch television (to) *mirar la televisón*
water *agua* (f.)
  mineral water *agua mineral*
  water (the) *el agua*
  waters (the) *las aguas*
way *camino* (m.), *forma* (f.)
  one-way *de sentido* (m.) *único*
we *nosotros* (m. pl./mixed group), *nosotras* (f. pl.)
weak *débil* (m./f.)
wear (to) *llevar, calzar* (shoes)
  wear rose-colored glasses (to) *ver todo color de rosa* (lit., to see everything pink)
  What shoe size do you wear? *¿Qué número calza?*
weather *tiempo* (m.)
  The weather is good. *El tiempo es bueno.*
web (on the computer) *web* (f.)
  webpage *página* (f.) *web*
  website *sitio* (m.) *web*
Wednesday *miércoles* (m.)
week *semana* (f.)
  every week *todas las semanas*
  last week *semana pasada*
  next week *próxima semana, semana que viene*
  this week *esta semana*
  twice a week *dos días a la semana*
weekend *fin* (m.) *de semana*
  long weekend *puente* (m.)
weekly *semanal* (m./f.)
weigh (to) *pesar*
Welcome. *Bienvenido./Bienvenida.* (m./f.) (to a man/to a woman)
  You're welcome. *De nada.*
well *bien, pues*
  be not doing well (to) *estar mal*
  May you be well. *Que esté bien.*
  well-done *bien asada*
west *oeste* (m.), *occidente* (m.)
what *qué, cuál/cuáles* (sg./pl.)
  At what time is it? *¿A qué hora es?*
  What a coincidence! *¡Qué coincidencia!*
  What color is … ? *¿De qué color es … ?*
  What do you do for a living? *¿En qué trabaja?*
  What do you think of … ? *¿Qué te parece … ?*
  What does that mean? *¿Qué quiere decir eso?*
  What shoe size do you wear? *¿Qué número calza?*
  What time do you have? *¿Qué hora tiene?*
  What time is it? *¿Qué hora es?/¿Qué horas son?*
  What would you like? *¿Qué desea?*
  What?/Pardon me? *¿Cómo?*
  What's going on? *¿Qué hay?*
  What's happening? *¿Qué tal?*
  What's up?/What's going on? *¿Qué hay?*
  What's your name? *¿Cómo se llama usted?* (fml.)/*¿Cómo te llamas?* (infml.)
when *cuándo* (question), *cuando* (relative adverb)
where *dónde* (question), *donde* (relative adverb)
  Where are you from? *¿De dónde eres?*
which *cuál/cuáles* (sg./pl.) (question), *cual/cuales* (sg./pl.) (relative pronoun)
  of which (relative pronoun) *cuyo/cuya/cuyos/cuyas* (m. sg./f. sg./m. pl./f. pl.)
while *mientras*
white *blanco/blanca* (m./f.)
  white wine *vino* (m.) *blanco*
who *quién/quiénes* (sg./pl.) (question), *quien/quienes* (sg./pl.) (relative pronoun)
  Who knows? *¿Quién sabe?*
  Who's calling? *¿De parte de quién?/¿Quién lo llama?*
whole *entero/entera* (m./f.)
  whole milk *leche* (f.) *entera*
whom (question) *quién/quiénes* (sg./pl.)
  whom (relative pronoun) *quien/quienes* (sg./pl.)
whose (relative pronoun) *cuyo/cuya/cuyos/cuyas* (m. sg./f. sg./m. pl./f. pl.)
  Whose … ? *¿De quién … ?*

why *por qué*

wide *ancho/ancha* (m./f.)

wife *esposa* (f.), *mujer* (f.)

win (to) *ganar*

   I hope they win! *¡Ojalá que ganen!*

wind *viento* (m.)

   It's windy. *Hace viento.*

window *ventana* (f.)

   display window *escaparate* (m.)

wine *vino* (m.)

   red wine *vino tinto*

   white wine *vino blanco*

wineglass *copa* (f.)

   glass of wine *copa de vino*

winter *invierno* (m.)

wish *deseo* (m.)

with *con*

   with you *contigo*

without *sin*

woman *mujer* (f.), *tía* (f.)

   businesswoman *mujer de negocios*

   policewoman *mujer policía*

wonder *maravilla* (f.)

wonderful *estupendo/estupenda* (m./f.)

wood *madera* (f.)

wooden *de madera*

wool *lana* (f.)

word *palabra* (f.)

work *trabajo* (m.)

work (to) *trabajar, funcionar*

   What do you do for a living? *¿En qué trabaja?*

working day *jornada* (f.)

world *mundo* (m.)

   world championship *campeonato* (m.) *mundial*

worldly *mundial* (m./f.)

worldwide *mundial* (m./f.)

worry (to) *preocuparse*

   Don't worry. *No se preocupe.*

   worry that ... (to) *preocuparse de que ...*

worse *peor* (m./f.)

worst (the) *el/la/los/las* (m. sg./f. sg./m. pl./f. pl.) *peor*

wrist *muñeca* (f.)

write (to) *escribir*

   write down (to) *anotar*

writer *escritor/escritora* (m./f.)

wrong *equivocado/equivocada* (m./f.)

wrong number *número* (m.) *equivocado*

Y

year *año* (m.)

   be ... years old (to) *tener ... años*

   fifties (the) *los años cicuenta*

   last year *año pasado*

   next year *año que viene*

   second year *segundo año*

   third year *tercer año*

   this year *este año*

yellow *amarillo/amarilla* (m./f.)

   yellow pages *páginas* (f. pl.) *amarillas*

yes *sí*

yesterday *ayer*

yet *todavía*

you (after a proposition) *ti* (infml. sg.)

   you (direct object pronoun) *lo/la/te/los/las/ os* (m. sg. fml./f. sg. fml./sg. infml./m. pl./f. pl./pl. infml)

   you (impersonal pronoun) *se*

   (to/for) you (indirect object pronoun) *le/les* (fml. sg./pl.), *se* (fml. sg./pl.) (used in place of le/les when preceding lo/la/los/las), *te/os* (infml. sg./pl.)

   you (subject pronoun) *usted/tú/ustedes/ vosotros/vosotras* (sg. fml./sg. infml./pl./m. pl. & mixed group infml. used in Spain/f. pl. infml. used in Spain)

young *joven* (m./f.)

   young boy *niño* (m.)

   young child *párvulo/párvula* (m./f.)

   young girl *niña* (f.)

   younger *menor* (m./f.)

   youngest (the) *el/la/los/las* (m. sg./f. sg./m. pl./f. pl.) *menor*

your (pl. fml. & infml.) *su/sus* (sg./pl.)

   your (pl. infml.) *vuestro/vuestra/vuestros/ vuestras* (m. sg./f. sg./m. pl./f. pl.) (used in Spain)

   your (sg. fml.) *su/sus* (sg./pl.)

   your (sg. infml.) *tu/tus* (sg./pl.)

yours (pl. fml. & infml.) *suyo/suya/suyos/suyas* (m. sg./f. sg./m. pl./f. pl.), *el de ustedes* (m. sg.), *la de ustedes* (f. sg.)

   yours (pl. infml.) *vuestro/vuestra/vuestros/ vuestras* (m. sg./f. sg./m. pl./f. pl.) (used in Spain)

   yours (sg. fml.) *suyo/suya/suyos/suyas* (m. sg./f. sg./m. pl./f. pl.), *el de usted* (m. sg.), *la de usted* (f. sg.)

yours (sg. infml.) *tuyo/tuya/tuyos/tuyas*
(m. sg./f. sg./m. pl./f. pl.) (infml.)
yourself *se/te* (fml./infml.)
yourselves *se/os* (fml./infml.)
youth hostel *hostal* (m.)

Z

zero *cero*